CRASH COURSE IN

# CREATIVITY

CRASH COURSE IN

# CREATIVITY

**Brian Clegg**
**Paul Birch**

KOGAN PAGE

**First Indian Edition 2009**



**Kogan Page India Private Limited**
4737/23 Ansari Road,
Daryaganj
New Delhi 110 002

*This edition is for sale in the Indian subcontinent only. Not for export elsewhere.*

ISBN-10: 81-7554-430-9
ISBN-13: 978-81-7554-430-7

Published by Vinod Vasishtha for Kogan Page India Private Limited,
4737/23, Ansari Road, Daryaganj, New Delhi 110 002.

Printed and bound by Anand Sons, Delhi - 110 092.

# Contents

# Introduction

Over nearly a decade of working as creativity consultants we have pulled together a wide range of techniques for developing both group and personal creativity. Many of these have been published in the past in the Kogan Page *Instant* series. In this book we have taken the best of the techniques and assembled them into a structured course designed both to develop personal creativity and to enhance the ability to facilitate creativity in others.

Creativity is a business skill – or rather a life skill – that cannot be simply learnt. The only way to enhance your creativity is through practice. This puts activity-based learning at the core of the course. Creativity is also hugely important to both individuals and organizations – yet at the same time it's hard to put aside large chunks of time to work on personal development. For this reason, *Crash Course in Creativity* (along with its companion books *Crash Course in Personal Development* and *Crash Course in Managing People*) is oriented to getting up to speed as quickly of possible with manageable units of exercises and information.

The book comprises two main sections. In the 'getting the basics' chapter we lay the foundation of understanding on which the exercises and techniques are built. It is very important to have this understanding before engaging in an activity like creativity which can sometimes seem counter-intuitive. This chapter is short and can be read in a couple of hours.

After a progress checklist comes a programme of exercises and techniques – exercises to develop your personal skills and techniques you can bring to play when working with others. The programme is split into units, designed to be manageable in your spare time in a week, though if you want to take the crash course to its extreme, each unit can be fitted in within a day. Each unit also introduces one or two recommended books. Wider reading will always help with a subject like creativity, and though it is not essential to read all (or even any) of these other books, they have been selected to enhance the impact of the course.

At the back of the book you will find a review section to pull together what you have learnt, including a collected reading list (in case you decide not to go with the books at the time of working through the programme) and tables that support the techniques or can be used to pick and choose individual techniques for a specific requirement. You will also find Web links for further reading and to help with the exercises.

Be prepared to learn, but also be prepared to have fun – creativity should never be a chore.

# 1 Getting the basics

## WHY CREATIVITY?

### Creativity or bust

Depending on your point of view, the prospects for business are terrifying or elating. Once upon a time, business life was like being on a train, moving from station to station according to a timetable. Now it's a roller coaster that has lost its guard rails. There has never been more pressure. Competitive pressure, brought on as more new ideas, more new competitors hit the market. Cost pressure as customers demand more for less. Customer service pressure as those pesky customers expect good service on top of all the savings. Time pressure as blossoming technology compresses everything from communications to the manufacturing cycle into less and less time.

There's only one way out. Creativity. It's not fanciful to state that without creativity there are very few companies in existence today that will still be around in a few years' time. Change is the name of the game, and innovation is the essential requirement to stay above water as yet another wave of change hits the shore. Without creativity you are going to be wheeling out the same old solutions to problems. It's not enough any more to sit back and say 'if it ain't broke, don't fix it.' The problems are changing under your feet, and the opposition is getting better all the time. Meanwhile you'll be pushing the same old products and services. Products and services that are already out of date. Creativity isn't a nice-to-have, it's a survival factor.

## Can you catch it from a book?

It is all very well to acknowledge that every business needs creativity, but it's quite a different prospect to do something about it. A natural inclination might be to rush out and recruit some creative people. That may not be a bad idea. But the fact is that everyone has a lot more creativity in them than they generally use.

There are a number of reasons for this. It might the wrong time of day. Your participants may be tired, stressed or bored. And worst of all, everyone's natural potential for creativity has been suppressed. This comes from a combination of socialization – it is often advisable to lower creativity to enhance survival prospects – and education, which is generally more about getting to the required answer than coming up with a creative solution. There is nothing wrong with this, but it gets in the way when you need creativity.

This book can't inject a magic dose of creativity from a big syringe labelled 'innovation', but it can act as a catalyst to free up some of the natural creativity which is bottled up by habit, training and (lack of) energy. The course consists of a series of short exercises and techniques, designed to shatter constraints and get the participants thinking differently. These techniques aren't creative in themselves, any more than a typewriter or word processor actually produces novels. But they are effective tools to release our pent-up creativity.

# CREATIVITY PRIMER

## What is it?

It is possible to know that you really need something without being sure what it is – creativity is frustratingly like that. The problem with creativity is that it's a blanket term for several related things. There's artistic creativity, the production of a book or painting or piece of music that is in some way original. There's the creativity of discovery, whether it's Archimedes leaping out of his bath shouting 'Eureka!' or a new product concept. And there's the creativity of humour. There is something special about humour, because it involves seeing the world in a different way, and that is an essential for creativity.

It is true that much business creativity centres on the second of those types. We are looking for the solution to a business problem, or an idea to come up with a new product or service. Yet in reality, almost every act of creativity merges the three. To really be innovative, the chances are there will be elements of artistic creativity present – whether it's in the elegance of a business plan or the style of a design. And to be creative effectively usually demands the presence of humour. If this is a problem, ask yourself what you've got against people enjoying themselves, just because they're working. Does it really make sense?

## What stops it?

It is often easier to stop people being creative than to enhance their creativity. We do it all the time. We have already referred to the restraints of social and educational conditioning. It's not surprising that there are social restraints on creativity. Young children have a very creative view of the world. They aren't constrained by habit and teaching. But they are also at risk from hazards they aren't prepared for. Some of our creativity is pushed aside to keep us safe. Yet when using creativity to solve a business problem we are in a safe, cushioned environment. We can afford to take more virtual risks; in fact we need to if something new and wonderful is to emerge.

In education, creativity is frowned on, because it runs counter to the desired output of the system. Like it or not, our education processes are largely designed to get young people through exams. This means getting them to give the answers the examiners want. Not the most original answer, not the creative answer, but the single right answer that is on the answer sheet. Real life isn't like that. Any problem, any requirement is likely to have many right answers. When we need to get creative it is because the obvious answer isn't good enough. Someone else has already done it. It has already been tried. We need something new and different.

If being creative means taking risks, appearing silly (most great ideas sound crazy initially) and failing more frequently, we've another problem. These traits are not popular. As individuals, we don't like them. Corporate culture is generally very heavy on failure. 'You only get one chance to make a mistake here.' Even very constructive measures like total quality management (TQM) have their downside, because the implication is that failure is always bad. Yet there's only one way to be really original: to throw off restraint, and go for it. There will be lots of failure, but it shouldn't matter because failure is the best basis for learning – and it is only by sticking your neck out that you will also achieve real creativity. One of the best ways to improve creativity quickly is to prevent the fresh green shoots of new ideas from being trampled on by practicality. Until everyone is prepared to come up with something they think will sound silly, knowing it won't be laughed at or frowned on, you won't have a truly creative team.

As if that isn't enough, there is yet another danger: the expert syndrome. We are increasingly developing a culture of experts. Expertise is one of the prime commodities we have to sell. Yet expertise can be dangerous when it comes to creativity. Expertise depends on knowing a lot about how things have been before. While the best experts can then flexibly interpret a different situation, all too often expertise means tunnel vision when faced with the new – experts are great at knowing what is *not* possible. We should be looking for creative input beyond those who are very closely involved in a project or business if we want real innovation. Don't throw your experts away, but take your input more widely.

## The five-way course

Ever since the 1940s there has been serious effort put into the study of creativity and the ways it can be enhanced. Broadly, it seems, there are five ways that we can encourage and support creativity, whether as individuals or as organizations.

These five paths to creativity are culture, techniques, personal development, mental energy, and fun.

Taking culture into account is important because it is easy for a culture – whether that of society at large or of an organization we are part of – to shut down creativity. Culture will feature least in this course, as achieving cultural change is a wider issue than creativity and tends to be addressed separately.

Techniques are the mechanisms that have been developed to help us to tap into our creativity. They aren't a new concept. Leonardo da Vinci used a documented technique in order to dream new ideas (he would scribble on a sheet of paper with his eyes closed, then turn the scribbles into a picture that would inspire his idea). But the techniques that are now widely used in creativity largely date to the twentieth century, and act to free up our thinking and encourage the formation of new ideas.

Listing mental energy as one of the factors is not a psychiatric diagnosis, but rather a recognition that our surroundings and mood have an influence on how creative we feel and on how easily ideas will flow.

Personal development is important too. Creativity may not be something that can be learnt, but it is certainly something that can be practised and developed. Knowledge handling and memory skills can be used to build a wider idea pool from which to generate new concepts. And the mechanisms of the brain work in such a way that practice at forming new connections makes it easier to generate further different ideas in the future.

Finally there is fun. Fun is inextricably linked with creativity. It is almost impossible to be truly creative and not be having fun. And approaches to work that generate fun will almost always result in more creativity. This final consideration feeds back into the first, as it is often the case that culture in the workplace frowns on fun. 'Work is a serious business' seems to be the message. But creativity should mean being able to have fun and still produce serious results.

Before beginning the course proper, let's spend a couple of minutes on each of those five ways that combine to generate a course for creativity.

# CULTURE

## Give them the tools...

It's easy to think that it's enough to give individuals the tools to be creative, then to sit back and wait for the great ideas to come. In practice, though, the mechanisms of creativity are more complex. We've already seen that social conditioning actually works against innovation. Our social culture has partly evolved to help us stay safe in circumstances where being creative – trying out new ways of doing things – can be terminally dangerous. Overcoming this factor is part of the cultural aspect of supporting creativity, but in most organizations it is not the worst problem.

Instead, culture creates difficulties because of the strong linkage between creativity and failure. In order to be innovative, you have to be prepared to fail. That's not to say that you should intend to make mistakes, but there will always be a degree of risk about any creative venture, and however well that risk is controlled and mitigated there will be failure.

If the response to failure is to learn from the failure and move on swiftly, the result will be effective creativity. Richard Feynman, the great 20th-century physicist, said 'To develop working ideas efficiently, I try to fail as fast as I can.' All too often, though, business and organizational culture regards failure as a black mark. A more common quote would be 'fail once and you're in trouble, fail twice and you're out.'

This cultural reaction to the inevitable consequences of creativity is one that has a dire effect on innovation. No one is going to put their head over the parapet and propose a new idea if they are going to be shot at (metaphorically, I hope) if it fails. And inability to recognize this cultural devastation of the creative process is the single most common reason that an attempt to make an organization more creative fails.

## Start at the top

Making a cultural shift (and most organizations will have to) is practically impossible unless it is clearly and visibly supported from the top of the organization. As long as the directors and senior executives are seen to be taking the wrong attitude to failure, no one further down the organization is going to believe any fine words that are put about on the subject of 'blame-free culture' and 'supporting innovation'.

Visibility is a key in putting across a culture shift. The senior members of the organization need to be seen to be putting their time and effort behind the change. It is never possible to achieve culture change by lip-service alone – so unless you can get this support from the top there is little point in attempting to make an organization truly creative.

## A matter of trust and communication

The key factors in achieving a culture that supports creativity are trust and communication. Senior management need to trust their staff to take appropriate actions, to take appropriate risks. They need to support their staff in the actions they take. Similarly, the staff need to trust their management, otherwise they won't be creative, they'll play safe and not instigate change. An object lesson in supporting creativity is found in the US retailer Nordstrom, a company with a two-line policy and procedures manual. It reads:

> *Use your good judgement in all situations.*
> *There will be no additional rules.*

The implied trust in that statement makes creativity possible. At least, as long as this admirable commandment is what is really followed, rather than merely being awarded lip-service.

Communication is a less obvious factor in supporting creativity, but is equally important. The only way trust can be made to work in an organization is if there is good communication. It should be easy to pass an idea to the appropriate part of the organization to get something done. It should be easy to find out the potential cost of an action that is to be tried out. It should be possible to undertake research, say on the Web, to back up a new idea. Without trust, such free communication is frowned on. The staff are assumed to be wasting time 'playing with the Internet' or making unnecessary communications that aren't 'part of the job'.

## Personal space

One of the best ways of emphasizing how much an organization's culture has changed, and how much trust is real, is to give each employee a period of time – a good example would be 3M's traditional half a day a week – to work on a personal project. It can be whatever the employee likes, using company resources, provided the company has a stake in the final outcome. It may seem that giving up half a day a week's working time of a valuable employee is a terrible waste, yet in practice it has huge benefits.

Such a 'personal space' gives the individual time to really be creative, to take a step back from the everyday pressures that they are under. The benefits that the organization will reap long term far outweigh any short-term loss of time. And there's no better way to illustrate the reality of trust. Of course it will be easier for some than for others. Some employees will need help to make effective use of their time. But everyone from the chief executive to a cleaner can benefit from this approach – and can bring benefit to the organization too.

# TECHNIQUES

## Why techniques?

The main enemies of creativity are tunnel vision and lack of inspiration. Either we know too much about the past to do anything but continue trudging down the same path, or we haven't got the vision to see a new destination. The idea of a creativity technique is to push you away from that well-trodden path – to obtain a different viewpoint by forcing you to do something you wouldn't normally do. This can be uncomfortable, but it is the only way to make something happen.

This explains why something as mechanical and often irrelevant seeming as a technique can have such stunning results. Creativity techniques aren't creative; you are. What they are superb at, though, is pushing you to a different starting point, providing you with an opportunity to make new associations, helping you take a fresh view and come up with something completely different.

## Associations to ideas

Many of the techniques we describe require you to make associations with something and then relate these associations back to the problem or requirement. Rather than take up space within each of the techniques explaining this process we have tried to give an overview here that will serve for all of them.

In some ways this is the hardest part of the creativity process, although even this isn't as hard as some would have you believe. This is the point where you move from a mechanical technique to genuine creativity. This aspect of the process is highly dependent on experience. The more you do it, the easier it will become. It is because of this that we strongly advise regular practice using the exercises in this book, even if you don't have a specific problem to solve. This is particularly important when you are new to the field of creativity.

Let us assume that you are trying to develop a new confectionery product and that you have used a creativity technique that has generated the following associations:

Whiskers, collar, fur, fleas, paws, hunter, after dark, mice, killer, cuddly, fun, warm, friendly, aloof, independent, lazy, active, angry, spitting, hissing, claws, teeth.

In case it isn't obvious we have used a technique where a randomly selected word – in this case *cat* – is used to generate new starting points.

With product development more than with most problem solving or idea generation you have the option of inserting an intermediate phase into the translation process from the association to the idea. This is to describe your non-existent product in terms of the association. In this case we are looking for 'The <something> confectionery' or 'The confectionery with <something>'. For instance:

The cuddly confectionery
The killer confectionery
The furry confectionery
The confectionery with whiskers
The active confectionery

Sometimes on reading such a list, immediate ideas will pop into your mind as to what this phrase might mean. The second stage is to write a more detailed description of this. For instance, 'The confectionery with whiskers' rather oddly made us think of old-aged confectionery. This made us think of more mature confectionery. We saw this going in two directions, either confectionery for the more mature palette or confectionery that is matured for a fuller flavour.

On reading that through, you may have seen some ideas of your own. You may have thought that the ideas we have generated are not all that great. That doesn't really matter. What matters is that the process is clear. This two-stage process can be used wherever you can describe the problem in terms of a sentence in which you can insert a range of words.

Where this is not the case you must move more directly from the association words to ideas. To show an example of this, let's assume that we have the same words as above but that we are trying to solve the problem of poor attendance in a factory. This is harder to create sentences for so we must move more directly.

Looking at the list, killer made us think of killing off poor attendees. Not immediately practical but this could be developed as an idea where an attendance monitoring scheme is implemented that ultimately results in the dismissal of those with poor attendance records. Collar made us think of control and this led to the idea of high levels of follow-up and checking of attendance problems – talking to everyone after they have missed a day and finding out why, insisting on doctor's notes, etc. Fun made us think of making the workplace more fun so that people don't feel the need to stay away. Independent made us think of making small groups of staff responsible for their own results regardless of attendance. You can see how this works. These ideas are half-baked. This is always true at this stage of the process. Treat them like tender green shoots that need love and attention. If you trample on them too early in their lives (by evaluating them) you will kill them.

## Ideas aren't enough – the framework

One danger of using techniques is the assumption that all you need to be creative is to develop loads of new ideas – yet history is littered with great ideas that never got put into practice and so, arguably, were never creative. For this reason, it is essential to fit your techniques into a simple framework that will ensure that your ideas get implemented.

There are four essential stages in the development of any successful idea. The first is understand the problem. There is a real danger of trying to solve the wrong problem if you rush into generating ideas too soon. By spending a little time ensuring that you know what the real problem is, a lot of time and effort can be saved later on.

The second stage is generating the ideas. Although this is the most visible and 'glamorous' aspect of creativity, it can't be left in isolation.

The third stage is to select from the ideas you have generated and refine one or more of them. This refinement stage is essential as any idea, however great, will initially have some problems that need ironing out.

Finally, there is preparation for selling and implementing the idea. This need not be a huge effort, but will involve making sure that you know what the principal selling points of the idea are, how you will put them across, and what the main milestones will be in the implementation process. It is also worth establishing the resources you will employ and the means you have at your disposal for dealing with problems along the way. Such simple preparation is essential. It's all too easy to get fired up with your great idea and rush out to tell everyone about it without undertaking this preparation – and to find that your idea is shot down or dismissed.

The four-stage framework need not take long, nor does it have to be a rigorous process – it's more a mental checklist that you have taken the right actions to maximize the chances that your idea will flourish.

# PERSONAL DEVELOPMENT

The brain is our most important organ, yet we are given no instruction manual, and very little training in using it. One of the biggest holes in our education is how to use our brains – it just doesn't appear in the curriculum (at least in the UK and the US – there is more effort made in Australia). Everyone's brain has much more capability than is ever used. From memory techniques to knowledge acquisition, part of the aim of this course is to give your brain a chance to pump mental iron.

## Meet your brain

You don't need to know a lot about the brain itself to use it more effectively, but a little background helps put the rest into context. It's traditional to get rather excited about the brain, because the numbers involved are remarkable. A very basic model sees the brain as a set of simple switches – neurons – which, like a computer bit, can be in one of two states. However, given that the brain contains around 10 billion neurons, each capable of interacting with hundreds or thousands of others, the combinatorial explosion makes sure that simplicity doesn't enter into it. The numbers are dramatic. The dendrites that link the neurons amount to around 150,000 kilometres of wiring.

When you put the scale of the brain's capabilities against what it actually does, despite the immense complexity of the tasks it handles, there is no doubt that the brain is underworked. Estimates of the percentage usage vary from the conservative 10 per cent to as little as 0.1 per cent – whatever the true value, there is vast over-capacity.

It might seem reasonable that a particular part of the brain handles a particular function – in fact, this was the common understanding for many years – but sadly it isn't that simple. Even a basic brain function can result in action in many different areas. However, one way the brain is divided has value, even if it is only as a concept. For a long time it was argued that the left and right sides of the brain housed areas working in fundamentally different ways. The left was the cold, logical side. It was responsible for reasoning, language and maths. It handled tasks in a sequential, step-by-step manner. The right-hand side was the creative, arty side. It had a more parallel, holistic approach – hence was particularly appropriate for pattern recognition and visual imagery. The right-hand side was the creative side whereas the left-hand side was the practical, down-to-earth side.

This theory is now in considerable doubt, but it leaves behind a valuable legacy. It may not be the left/right split that means our brains have two distinct modes of operation, but there is no doubt at all that they do. It may be, in fact, that the distinction is instead between the conscious (left brain) mind and the unconscious (right brain) – but whatever the cause, we (especially in the West) work most often in what can conveniently be referred to as left brain mode. To be creative in an applied way requires a flip-flop between the two modes – or, even better, a mix of the two. Left brain to assess the position, right brain to generate new ideas, left brain to assess the ideas, right brain to fix any problems... with a similar progression through implementation. Not only do we need practice in using our brains more efficiently, we also need practice in this creative flip and mix.

## Education – brain stretching, or brain deadening?

Most of us spend between 11 and 17 years in full-time education. For some, learning goes on for the whole of their life. In fact, given the brain's immense capabilities, it is very sad when we don't continue to expand our knowledge and skills throughout our lifetime. However, it is easy to confuse learning and education. The formal education system has many worthy roles – but they aren't all about stretching the brain. In fact, while good education will improve your ability to gather and process knowledge, and will generally not influence your memory skills either way, there are few formal education systems that don't decrease an individual's creativity.

There are perfectly good reasons for this. As we have seen, creativity in dangerous situations puts survival at risk. Trying out different ways to leave a skyscraper may be creative, but flinging yourself from a 20th-floor window is not a life-enhancing move. Even when creativity is in theory safe, when dealing with the cushioned world of ideas, it can be threatening to education. Most educational regimes depend on getting through a set curriculum in a set time. Being too creative will disrupt this. A practical teacher is looking to get the answers that examiners want, not the most creative answer.

The result of this is that every individual suffers a reduction in creativity between starting school and leaving it. Worse still, peer pressure in schools often calls for conformity and hence more loss of creativity. If this sounds an indictment of schools, it isn't meant to be. Unless we wanted schools to do something completely different, some degree of conformity is essential. But this early training does mean that we have to go even further to give the brain a workout after school has finished with it.

## Knowledge, memory and making new connections

The brain has a vast array of functions and capabilities, but for the purposes of creativity there are three principal areas – knowledge, memory and making new connections. Each represents a particular aspect of what would generally be regarded as brainpower. How effective you are at building your store of knowledge and making use of it, how good your memory is and how easily you can generate ideas all contribute to the overall capabilities of your brain. After using some of these exercises you will have the opportunity to develop all three.

## Conscious and unconscious activity

As psychology professor Guy Claxton points out in *Hare Brain, Tortoise Mind* (see page 230), we are accustomed to give much weight to the conscious, step-by-step aspects of thought. Everything from scientific research to detective work places great emphasis on the objective, reasoned view (in fact even Claxton's book is full of scientific, reasoned argument). Yet we know that the unconscious mind is capable of remarkable things. We have all experienced the sudden realization that we have just undertaken a complex task like driving a car on automatic pilot. We have all been unable to remember something, no matter how hard we try, only to have the fact re-surface soon after apparently ceasing to think about it.

A number of these exercises seek to push some more of your thinking into the unconscious – to make use of the benefits available if you are prepared to give pressurized reasoning a break and allow your whole brain to address a need. Such exercises can seem a little waffly. It's easy to think 'what am I doing examining my navel, when I want to get on with something practical?' The fact is that these are practical exercises, but because they take an unusual direction, they may seem rather different.

It's not uncommon for proponents of delving into the unconscious to mention how much this follows a strong tradition of Eastern philosophy and mysticism. While this is true, it can be misleading. Although Western philosophy has often used a more deterministic approach, Western and Middle Eastern religions have just as strong a tradition of meditation and reflection as those of the Far East. There is no need whatsoever to stray into Zen or Buddhism if these conflict with your own beliefs – in fact, the Judeo–Christian–Moslem approach is more practical in that it combines both the conscious and unconscious modes, while Eastern practices tend to focus solely on the unconscious. If you have no religious beliefs at all, don't worry – the weight of scientific research supports the practical value of this approach, whatever the underlying regime.

## What is knowledge?

Despite sounding like one of those deep questions asked of mystics living in caves at the top of mountains (who then reply, enigmatically, 'a fish'), this is both a serious and tricky question. Knowledge stands at the top of the pyramid that begins with data, builds through information and climaxes with knowledge itself.

Data is a mass of facts, without any interpretation. The results of a series of races, or football matches, for example, are data. Information is a combination of data and analysis. The data is taken and something is done with it. The result might be data presented in a certain way to pull out a trend, or might be a commentary saying why the data is how it is – this is information. Knowledge, though, is something more. Knowledge is the combination of data and information with the active elements of a person's brain that enable that person to turn data into information. Knowledge pulls together experience and reasoning to deal with a new circumstance. Knowledge is the currency of the expert.

In the 21st-century world of frantic change and information overload, knowledge is the lifeline we all need. When things are consistent and calm, it's easy to manage with a set of rules. That's what most early 20th-century management was about – rules – and management by rule has carried on mostly by inertia to the present day. Unfortunately rules break down when everything is in flux. You can't depend on them – you need to have a set of principles and the knowledge to apply them appropriately to the new situation. That's why experts are so valued now, and why the ability to handle knowledge has become one of the principal skills for the individual.

## What about the Internet?

What indeed. In one sense there's nothing revolutionary about the Internet. It's just more of the same that we've always had to extend our personal knowledge library and network – communications and information retrieval. What is revolutionary is the scale and accessibility of the Internet. Here are near-instantaneous communications with other people from whom you may be able to extract knowledge and information. If you can find the information you want, here is a vast library to extend your personal information base, available at the desktop, 24 hours a day.

This book isn't the place to learn about using the Internet more effectively to expand your knowledge network. There are a couple of exercises touching on the Internet, but to find out more, see *The Professional's Guide to Mining the Internet*, also from Kogan Page (more information on page 230).

## Becoming better knowledge managers

Knowledge management is considered a science in its own right these days, but for the purposes of this book, we can be relatively simplistic and consider knowledge management to be the skills needed to find and process information, to categorize and structure it and to incorporate it into your personal knowledge base in order to enhance your creativity. This 'knowledge base' is the sum of what you hold in your memory, and what you know how to get hold of in your library. The library isn't just what is on your bookshelves, but CD ROMs, information on paper and on your computer, information on the Internet and at your local library. What turns this from information into knowledge is its integration into your expertise – your ability to find, call on and integrate the right information at the right time to carry out your purposes. (And I said it would be simplistic. If this sounded complicated, try reading a conventional book on knowledge management.)

## How memory works

You have two forms of memory – short-term and long-term (technically there's a third, medium-term memory that sits in between, but let's not complicate matters). Short-term memory is a working store, like the memory of a computer, which is lost when the computer is turned off. Your short-term memory is very small – in essence you can only cope with a handful of items, typically around seven – at a time in short-term memory. When you plug something else into the memory, it pushes an item out. You can see short-term memory in action between looking up a phone number in a book and dialling it. It might seem strange, if short-term memory is limited to around seven items, that you can cope with a 10-digit number. Luckily, human memory is more flexible than a computer. Where everything in the computer's memory is made up of simple bits – 0 or 1 – human memory can hold an image or a word as a single item. Familiar dialling codes, for instance, are only a single item, leaving space (just about) for the rest of the number.

Long-term memory is a whole different ball game. To all intents and purposes the capacity is unlimited. You have plenty of storage for everything you are ever likely to remember. Your long-term memory will house the concepts that will be juggled and interlinked by your creative processes to generate new ideas. But getting something into long-term memory is not as simple as short-term memory. Using short-term memory is an act of will that is implemented immediately – getting something into long-term memory requires work.

This is where the lack of training in using your brain becomes a real disadvantage. Unless you understand how the brain works, the actions needed to lock something into memory seem bizarre. However, once you understand that you hold images in a sort of map of what you are remembering, it becomes more obvious. To fix something in your memory it is best if you can see it in image form – hence the success of pictorial representations of information like mind maps – with the most vivid (in fact lurid) images you can imagine. To keep it there, you also need recaps. Ideally these should come straight after taking in the material, a few hours later and a few days later, with a top-up after a month and six months.

## Forgetting

Once we've got something into long-term memory, it's a reasonable question to ask why we ever forget it. After all, it would be very useful to be able to recall anything you've previously committed to memory. Forgetting isn't a simple process. When you have 'forgotten' something, it hasn't necessarily left your memory entirely. What is more likely is that it is partially lost, or that the pathways to reach it are not well trodden and have become overgrown. We've all forgotten something, only to have it pop up unexpectedly a few hours later. In such a circumstance it clearly wasn't erased from memory, but simply mislaid.

Although memories might sometimes go away because of the classic Freudian concept of repression (it was just too horrible to remember), generally it seems that we can't remember something either because we're in the wrong frame of mind to do so, or because other memories have confused and messed up the pathways to the particular thing you want to recall. It's not that you've run out of memory capacity – that isn't going to happen – but that the string of images and associations you use to recall a memory have become overlaid by other, similar images and associations. You might find it difficult to recall a beach holiday 10 years ago, because other beach holidays since have got in the way.

If this is the principal reason for forgetting, we can easily combat it by a combination of recaps and ensuring that the associated imagery is as strong and individual as is possible.

## Memory magic

We've already established that the brain has a pretty amazing capacity – so how come you can never remember where you left your keys? Memory can both deliver amazing feats with startling regularity and let us down on apparent basics.

Many people have trouble remembering names, and applying them to people, but we are all superbly well equipped to remember faces. Most of us remember thousands, from friends and family to actors on TV and casual acquaintances at work. Yet try to describe someone you know well in a way that will distinguish them from everyone else in your gallery of faces and you will have real trouble. The basic features don't vary all that much. In remembering a face, we pull together a whole complex set of shapes, patterns and colours. In fact, remembering a person also includes lots of clues from the rest of their body and their movements, which is why it's harder to recognize a photograph than a real person. About a year ago, I was on a tube station in London, waiting for a train. I happened to glance into the office on the platform. I recognized one of the two men in the office. This was despite the fact that he had nothing to do with London Underground, so I wouldn't expect to see him there, and that the glass was darkened, and that he had his back to me. I recognized him entirely from the way he moved.

Another example of memory failing is with telephone numbers. They just aren't easy to remember. I once spent a whole evening in a hotel room trying to remember my own home number. For some reason it had slipped my mind, and the more I tried to summon it back, the more it evaded capture. If such a well-known number can slip from your memory, it's not surprising that other telephone numbers are hard to keep hold of. In part it's because we aren't good at remembering more than six to eight items in a group, and despite the telephone companies' attempts to group numbers accordingly a telephone number is too long. But it's also because they are so impersonal and lacking in images. Unlike computer memory, human memory isn't about numbers or characters, it's about images. So despite the fuss TV presenters make about the complexity of e-mail addresses, it's an awful lot easier to remember the words (often with visual connotations) than it is to remember a telephone number.

So what do you do if you can't remember numbers or names? And how come some people who don't have eidetic memories (the rare capability to see a whole page of text and instantly commit it to memory) can do amazing feats like remembering the names of everyone in an audience or memorizing a phone book? Like most magic it's a trick. At least since the ancient Greeks it has been known that you can use little tricks to fix information in memory. These mnemonics (that's the Greeks for you) generally work by linking the item to be remembered to an image to make the memory more capable of handling it. We'll see a number of practical applications of these tricks in the exercises.

What often comes hardest is accepting that these tricks work for everyone. Okay, the memory man on the TV can do it, but perhaps he is especially skilled. Not at all – everyone is capable of these tricks. As a trivial example, when I first came across such memory techniques about 20 years ago, I went into a shop the same lunchtime and memorized the name of the first person I saw with a name badge. It was Mrs Anne Hibble. Without conscious effort, that once-sighted name has stayed with me for 20 years. There is a natural laziness that prevents people from using these techniques unless they are a regular habit. Like most skills, they need practising and keeping polished.

## The value of memory

Before leaving memory, it's worth establishing that there's some point to it. First let's deal with the problem some people have with memory tricks. 'We don't want to do tricks,' they say, 'we want to learn how to use proper memory better.' This is a misunderstanding. Mnemonics and the like are only tricks because they make something apparently difficult actually easy. What they are doing is converting the sort of item that your brain doesn't like handling into the sort of item it does. This is absolutely 'learning how to use proper memory better' – it just seems artificial.

But is there any reason for having a good memory these days, when everything can be calculated with ease, retrieved from a database or found on the Web? Absolutely. You have a huge wasted memory capacity which will serve you much more flexibly and quicker than resorting to a computer. By using a few memory tricks you can get huge personal advantage. For example, even if they know they are being manipulated, people react better if you call them by name – they just can't help it. If you can remember the names of everyone in a new team or group, you will be more effective at whatever it is you are trying to do with them. And in many other circumstances, memory can save you time and improve what you are trying to do. It's not a matter of being an information magpie and trying to remember everything about everything, but about capturing the information that will be of most value to you and having it readily to hand. Most importantly, though, as far as this course is concerned, a good memory will give your creative processes a richer source of starting points, associations and links.

## Born with it?

Quite separately from the effectiveness of our memory, it is widely recognized that some people are more creative than others – such people find it easier to make the new connections in the brain that result in generating an idea. Most of us are happy to bow to the creative genius of others, thinking that we're just down-to-earth people who might be reasonably good at picking up an idea and running with it, but we don't expect to be too creative. If your creativity were solely down to what you were born with, that would be the end of the story – but it's not that simple.

Just as channelling-like education that requires 'the right answer' to a question can reduce personal creativity, there are simple techniques and exercises that can increase personal creativity. This shouldn't be too surprising. In the end, creativity is all about being able to see outside the habitual tunnel of thought we all operate within. It shouldn't be too surprising that there are techniques that will move us out of the tunnel, opening up new prospects and possibilities. These techniques are not themselves creative, but act as a catalyst, releasing the potential creativity in all of us.

## The creativity workout

The ability to expand our abilities to make new connections is obviously highly desirable, but how is it to be achieved? Such personal creativity can't be learnt. Unlike creativity techniques, which are mechanistic processes that can reliably push an individual in a new direction, a general increase in the level of creativity is a much broader aim.

Much of the course consists of exercises for your personal creativity. It might be true that school shuts down much of our creativity, but at least it gave us some opportunity for practice. For many of us, the day we left school is the last time we attempted creative writing or art. For some people it's even the last time we read any fiction. That has to stop. If you want to enhance your personal creativity, you need to get some practice at these creative forms.

Note that this isn't an end in itself. It doesn't matter if you produce a story or picture then throw it away (once you've learnt something). The aim is not to turn you into a creative writer or an artist, but to increase the ease with which you take that creative step out of the tunnel – to make it just as natural as operating a spreadsheet or driving a car. If you have young children, you have a natural opportunity to expand your creativity workout. Young children are always asking you to draw something or to tell them a story. Your natural inclination may be to say 'I can't draw' or 'I'll read you a story' – but take the opportunity that is being offered you to stretch your own creativity with a low-risk audience.

Apart from the traditional creative elements, we will also be stretching our creative muscles using puzzles and by stimulating different types of thinking. Don't be put off if either of these don't come naturally to you. You don't actually have to enjoy puzzles (I don't) to get the benefit, any more than you need to enjoy running to get fit that way – though obviously it doesn't do any harm if you do enjoy them. Similarly, you may be sceptical of the value of techniques that explore your ways of thinking – perhaps it seems to be getting too close to the whole alternative therapy, touchy-feely business for you. Bear in mind that fuzzy alternative lifestyles and Eastern philosophies are not the basis for such exercises, but concrete research into the way the mind works.

# MENTAL ENERGY

## Considering the brain

Creativity is an activity of the brain, and seems particularly dependent on the mental energy. In part this is influenced by the physical environment, in part by energy levels and attitudes of those around you.

There are good physiological reasons for this. The brain has a tendency to use well-trodden pathways when under pressure. The ideal state to be in when looking for creativity is the relaxed state that can result in day dreaming. Too much pressure forces the brain to use the quick routes – the pathways that are already well developed. It's also true that under pressure, the body releases chemicals that can have a negative effect on creativity, forcing the brain to operate too quickly while dulling down responses.

This need to relax to be creative doesn't mean a need to be somnolent, however. Creativity, like any other mental activity, benefits from chunking, breaking the activity down into segments of no more than 45 minutes to an hour. Anything more and the concentration drops off, as do the effectiveness and creativity.

Apart from taking a simple break, three things can help in stimulating the brain into more creative action. Physical movement – getting energy into an individual or group, where things have become stagnant. Fun – producing humour and the associated mental activity. And forms of thinking that are particularly suited to the right hand side of the brain – spatial thinking, music and art, taking the overview. This is valuable as the process of sitting down and saying 'let's do some brainstorming' (or whatever) is very much focused on the left-hand side of the brain, and the ideal when being creative is to use the whole brain to make as many new connections as possible.

## Physical environment

Over the years, performing training in creativity, we have asked many people how and when they have ideas. They often say on a walk, while driving a car, in the bath, while sitting back and listening to music – and many other alternatives. But they hardly ever say while seated at their desk with the PC popping up e-mails, the phone ringing and the boss leaning over their shoulder asking for results.

Getting away from the ordinary working environment can be one of the best ways of helping the mental energy in terms of being creative. If you are intending to hold a creativity session, try doing it somewhere different – in a Jacuzzi, in someone's house, on a train, in the middle of a field. Think about the impact of the physical environment when trying to be creative.

## The impact of a team

Everyone knows that teams are great. Just try using 'teamwork' as an insult; it won't work. Every management text, every football game commentary, every corporate communication hammers in the message – the team is the ideal. Contrast 'team player' and 'loner' – which would you rather see on your performance report? Yet look at most real teams and you will see something less than perfect.

The theoretical benefit of a team can be summed up in one word – synergy. Synergy was originally a biological term, describing the way a combination of different parts of a body could provide more than simply the sum of the parts. More recently it has come to apply to a group of people in a similar way. Teamwork is supposed to combine the talents of the individuals to produce something more than is possible with each individual taken separately. We can all think of examples where this is true. But equally, it is possible to think of cases where the effect of pulling together a team has a negative effect. 'Teams' may have very positive overtones, but 'committees' (a camel is a horse designed by committee) and 'meetings' (not another meeting; all I do is go from one meeting to another) are very different.

All too often the result of pulling together a group of people is not to provide synergy but disruption. At best, the result is to bore everyone into minimal contribution. At worst, there will be active suppression of new ideas and blatant time wasting. Does this mean that all the hype about teams is mistaken? In certain circumstances, yes. There are some activities that simply work better when undertaken by an individual. But generally, and certainly in the business context, teams can bring real benefits. The trouble is, how can you get the team working together? It would help to know what is keeping it apart.

## The nature of the beast

A team is a collection of individuals. Always. This is one of those self-evident truths that it is very easy to ignore most of the time. It is terribly convenient to think of a team as a unit, as a single entity. It implies focus and control. But it's a convenient fiction; it just isn't true. The underlying individuality is essential. It's the reason you get synergy at all. If everyone thought and acted exactly the same way, you wouldn't get anything different (apart from increased physical contribution) out of ten people than out of one. Unfortunately, individuality is also a problem. It means that a new group will function poorly because other members seem strange. We treat them cautiously until they are familiar. There's a need to break down the barriers – not removing individuality, but increasing comfort with being together.

Groups of people are very good at picking up and amplifying mood. If there is a slight feeling of boredom, or of low energy, before long the whole team is drooping. Performance collapses. There's a need for a boost. Sometimes this can be physiological. Stimulants like coffee, sugar boosters like sweets and biscuits, can give a quick lift. But these are nowhere near as effective as finding a mechanism for increasing group energy.

Groups of people also get into ruts. That's the problem with brainstorming. It is very easy to get stuck in a particular line of thinking, to get tunnel vision. Despite synergy, groups can actually reinforce tunnel vision by suppressing anyone who comes up with a different idea. One dominant individual can also steamroller a group in a particular direction. Often there's a need to take a step back from the process, to be pushed for a moment into thinking in a different way. When the group returns to the problem, this activity should have moved them far enough away from their preconceptions to get moving again.

These three requirements: ice-breakers to break down barriers between people, warm-ups to increase energy and timeouts to change the direction of thinking feature in exercises and techniques throughout the course. They aren't miracle cures for a sick team, but they deliver the sort of boost that high energy drinks claim to give athletes.

## Silly games

There can be some resistance to using these exercises. They are seen as being silly games. It's not surprising – many of them are. Some would not be out of place at a children's party. But why is that a problem? If it is, it shows a lack of understanding of people. In engineering a change to the way a team works, we are acting at a low level. Although the team's tasks may be entirely cerebral, the interaction between team members is much more at the gut level. Similarly, the development of ideas may be very logical and thought-through, but the original creative spark is something deeper and darker. Is it really surprising, then, that the activities that are needed to improve teamwork operate at a similarly basic level? The fact is, cerebral activity tends to lower energy and interaction rather than increasing them. Like it or not, you need to get down to basics to improve teamworking.

You may appreciate this, but still have members of the group who don't; who refuse take part because 'it's silly' or 'it's not what I'm here for'. If this happens, it is important not to ignore them. Give everyone else a two-minute tea (or pee) break and take the individual to one side. Explain the scientific reasoning for working at a gut level. If this fails, appeal to their team spirit. They don't have to like it, but please just go along with it to humour everyone else. If you still fail (and it's rare), you may have to consider removing them from the group. Their actions could make their contribution so negative that the team will function more effectively without them.

## Ice-breakers

Whether you are dealing with a new team, a group of people from different parts of the company (or the world), or simply a new, unfamiliar situation, nervousness, shyness and inhibitions can all be barriers to effective creative teamwork. An ice-breaker can help.

One style of ice-breaker acts at the social level. Here we find out a little more about the other people in the group: their names, their interests, what they do in their spare time. This is an accelerated version of normal social interaction, moving the team members from strangers to part of your social grouping. Other ice-breakers are physical, putting people in close physical proximity and forcing them to interact. Because this is unacceptable with strangers, the other team members are automatically forced from being 'them' to being 'us'.

## Warm-ups

The whole purpose of a warm-up is to increase group energy. Whatever the purpose of the team, it will be more productive if the members have high energy levels. The two key mechanisms of a warm-up are physical activity and laughter. By their nature, business teams are largely sedentary, often working in over-heated offices with less than perfect air conditioning. The physical side of warm-ups helps counter the numbing effect of the environment. It is sometimes enough just to get people out of their seats, or out of the building, for a minute or two. But there is more to the physical aspect. Activity stimulates the body, and hence the brain, into more effective action, not just countering lethargy but positively increasing effectiveness.

The second factor, laughter, is easily disregarded. We are, after all, involved in a serious business. Yet laughter is a powerful force for building energy.

Many of the warm-up exercises will stimulate the team members to laugh: at their own ideas and actions, and at others' attempts. This laughter is a very positive force in overcoming lethargy and enhancing productivity.

### Timeouts

We have all been in situations where we are trying to work something out. There's just no way to do it. It's impossible. So you put the problem to one side for a little while and do something different. Somehow, when you come back to it, a new angle becomes visible. The problem isn't quite as intractable as you thought.

This approach has a more general application to creativity. It has been conclusively proved that a short distraction, dealing with something completely different, will improve an individual's or a group's creativity when dealing with a particular problem. It shouldn't be surprising. The distraction provides a new starting point, a new viewpoint, when returning to the problem.

This is the basis for the timeout. When the team has become bogged down, when it is lacking creativity, when it needs some inspiration, a timeout can help break out of the tunnel of habitual thought. It is sometimes hard to do. Team members may argue that you are breaking their concentration – they want to get on with the job. But when you are marching down a dead end, it's well worth the time taken to look in a totally different direction.

## FUN

### Can fun and work mix?

One of the hardest things about getting fun into the equation is the rather sour-faced work ethic that says (at least by implication) 'if they are enjoying themselves they clearly aren't working hard enough'. Particularly when times are hard – when there's recession, when backs are against the wall – it can be easy to see fun as inappropriate. There's also the danger of being regarded as unprofessional. A professional workplace, it is argued, has to be sober and free of fun to be taken seriously.

There is a grain of truth in this. There are times when we do want to get a serious response in the work environment. Few patients would be happy to have a doctor make jokes about a serious illness. But this shouldn't mean that workplaces can't be fun places to be. Consider what the American expert on fun in the workplace, Leslie Yerkes, has to say:

> Baby Boomers learned how to behave at work from their fathers. Bringing home the bacon was serious work; therefore, serious behaviour was called for. But that model, like many things in this hi-tech world, is changing. Today, we are learning how to behave at work from our children. Generation X, the driving force behind the dot-com craze, is making itself felt in many ways, including its attitude toward work. Gen-Xers expect that their work environments should have fewer rules and expansive boundaries. They don't want or need a dress code, and they expect something more – they expect that work should be fun!
>
> Before the days of Frederick Taylor, the developer of Scientific Management, work was fun. But with Taylor's emphasis on time-management and efficiency, we began to believe that fun was something that could only be earned by hard work. Fun happened after work, not during it. To have fun at work was to be unprofessional, not serious. And if work wasn't serious, it couldn't be profitable. A thorough study of today's successful companies tells a different story. The fusion of fun and work can be profitable. In addition to being good at their particular market segment, successful companies pay attention to the fundamentals (such as high quality, customer service, decisive leadership, long-term strategic planning) and are able to manage through the lows and highs of business better than their competitors who focus only on their core skill. In addition to the fundamentals, companies that incorporate the Principles of Fun/Work Fusion have the greatest success in attracting and retaining the most talented people available from a constantly shrinking labour pool.

You can see more from Leslie in her book *Fun Works* (see page 231 for details). Yerkes concentrates mostly on the benefits of fun in terms of keeping good staff, but it is equally valuable if you want your staff to make a creative contribution – or if you work alone to enhance your own creativity.

## The fun imperative

Fun works to support creativity for a number of reasons. If we are having fun we are less likely to be stressed, and as we have seen, stress is a major creativity killer. It's also true that humour and fun are all about seeing things differently, and this is an essential when becoming more creative. Without fun there is a very strong danger of limiting yourself to the obvious, to the safe and well tried. And failing entirely to innovate.

# GETTING STARTED

With fun fixed firmly in mind, let's move on to the course itself, a series of 30 units that can be undertaken on a weekly or daily basis – or however best suits you. The next chapter gives a brief introduction to the layout, and provides a checklist to record progress.

# 2 Work plan

## INTRODUCING THE COURSE

Each of the 30 units consists of a number of elements. There are five exercises or techniques. Exercises are designed to be performed immediately to help develop your creative skills. They will normally take between five and twenty minutes to undertake. Techniques are additions to your toolkit that can be brought into play as and when you have a need for a new idea or to solve a problem. It is sensible to read through the techniques, and note when you might next find the technique useful, but it will not usually be practical to undertake the technique straight away. Some items are marked exercise/technique – these form general techniques, but should also be undertaken immediately as an exercise.

How you organize the course is up to you. You could take a day over each unit, or a week – or however long you like. It's up to you how long you want the 30 units to take.

Each unit also contains one or more unit books. These are intended to help expand your knowledge and broaden your creative thinking. You aren't expected to read every book we recommend, but the more you can get in, the more effective the course will be. Most of our recommendations are available from public libraries, or you can build your own creativity library by buying them – there are links to online bookshops stocking them at our support Web site www.cul.co.uk/crashcourse.

Many of the units also have Web links, providing extra reading and information on the topic to help with your creativity. Remember also the support Web site, www.cul.co.uk/crashcourse, designed to extend your creativity knowledge base into the Web.

The next short section provides a checklist to monitor your progress. You may also find it useful to make some notes on the exercise and technique pages to help record your progress.

When you have completed all the units, there is a final section that provides an opportunity to recap and to revisit the unit books.

# CHECKLIST

## Unit 1: A taster

1.1 Surveying your mind ☐
1.2 Knots ☐
1.3 Random picture ☐
1.4 Life saver ☐
1.5 Ideas to get you fired ☐
Unit books ☐
Web links ☐

## Unit 2: Getting to know you – loosening up a new group

2.1 This is my friend ☐
2.2 Tower of Babel ☐
2.3 Twisters ☐
2.4 Follow my leader ☐
2.5 True and false ☐
Unit books ☐
Web links ☐

## Unit 3: Clarifying the problem – just what are you trying to do?

3.1 Compass ☐
3.2 Obstacle map ☐

- 3.3 Water into wine ☐
- 3.4 Destination ☐
- 3.5 Chunks and breaks ☐
- Unit books ☐
- Web links ☐

## Unit 4: Challenging assumptions – thinking differently about a problem to understand it better

- 4.1 Do nothing ☐
- 4.2 Up and down ☐
- 4.3 Round the world ☐
- 4.4 Time slices ☐
- 4.5 Questioning everything ☐
- Unit books ☐
- Web links ☐

## Unit 5: Good vibrations – positive thinking

- 5.1 Altered states ☐
- 5.2 Yes! ☐
- 5.3 Circle of energy ☐
- 5.4 Pub quiz ☐
- 5.5 Beam me up ☐
- Unit books ☐
- Web links ☐

## Unit 6: New 'how to's – getting different cuts at the problem

- 6.1 Excellence ☐
- 6.2 Restatement ☐
- 6.3 Versatile coat hangers ☐
- 6.4 Mud slinging ☐
- 6.5 Going down ☐
- Unit books ☐
- Web links ☐

## Unit 7: Incremental creativity – step change techniques

7.1 The level chain ☐
7.2 Car and goats ☐
7.3 Attributes ☐
7.4 Found story ☐
7.5 Technical creativity ☐
Unit books ☐
Web links ☐

## Unit 8: Distortion – idea generation techniques that modify the nature of the problem

8.1 Challenging assumptions ☐
8.2 Distortion ☐
8.3 Birthday bonanza ☐
8.4 Reversal ☐
8.5 Size matters ☐
Unit books ☐
Web links ☐

## Unit 9: Pure energy – injecting oomph

9.1 Spoon and string ☐
9.2 Piggyback plus ☐
9.3 Get another life ☐
9.4 Sit on my lap ☐
9.5 The paperclip race ☐
Unit books ☐
Web links ☐

## Unit 10: Seeking knowledge – building a personal knowledge base to feed creativity

10.1 Broken CD ☐
10.2 Sense and sensibility ☐
10.3 The little black book ☐

- 10.4 All that glisters ☐
- 10.5 Programmed thought ☐
- Unit books ☐
- Web links ☐

## Unit 11: Seeing it differently – looking at solutions through different eyes

- 11.1 Fantasy ☐
- 11.2 Someone else's view ☐
- 11.3 Get a laugh ☐
- 11.4 Metaphor ☐
- 11.5 No time to read ☐
- Unit books ☐
- Web links ☐

## Unit 12: A swift kick – random stimuli to generate a new starting point

- 12.1 Random word ☐
- 12.2 Cool site ☐
- 12.3 Found objects ☐
- 12.4 Quotations ☐
- 12.5 An excellent mistake ☐
- Unit books ☐
- Web links ☐

## Unit 13: Looking somewhere else – taking a look beyond the obvious

- 13.1 It's a steal ☐
- 13.2 Inside view ☐
- 13.3 Evil genius ☐
- 13.4 School daze ☐
- 13.5 Morphology ☐
- Unit books ☐

## Unit 14: Simple fun – laughter makers

14.1 Row of eyes ☐
14.2 I am and I know ☐
14.3 Makeover ☐
14.4 Steeplechase ☐
14.5 Giants, witches and dwarves ☐
Unit books ☐
Web links ☐

## Unit 15: Breakdown – techniques that break down a problem into components

15.1 Components ☐
15.2 Substitute ☐
15.3 Different views ☐
15.4 Been there before ☐
15.5 Long division ☐
Unit books ☐

## Unit 16: Touchy-feely – generating ideas using right-brain activities

16.1 Set it to music ☐
16.2 Da Vinci scribbles ☐
16.3 Touch me, feel me ☐
16.4 Draw it ☐
16.5 Squirrel box ☐
Unit books ☐
Web links ☐

## Unit 17: Natural input – using nature and science as tools to generate ideas

17.1 Frontiers ☐
17.2 Leaf mould ☐
17.3 Auntie gravity ☐

17.4 The thrill factor ☐
17.5 It's only natural ☐
Unit books ☐
Web links ☐

## Unit 18: Memories are made of this – memory techniques

18.1 Extremes ☐
18.2 Story chains ☐
18.3 Take a note ☐
18.4 Number rhymes ☐
18.5 Strengthening your ghosts ☐
Unit books ☐
Web links ☐

## Unit 19: Strange translations – generating ideas from misunderstanding

19.1 It's silly ☐
19.2 Cloak and dagger ☐
19.3 Lost in translation ☐
19.4 They're winning ☐
19.5 Spinning knowledge ☐
Unit books ☐
Web links ☐

## Unit 20: Creative comms – stimulating new approaches by forcing different modes of communication

20.1 In the dark ☐
20.2 Out for the count ☐
20.3 Buy me ☐
20.4 Blindfold birthday ☐
20.5 Lego™ construction ☐
Unit books ☐
Web links ☐

## Unit 21: Going green – environmental techniques to enhance creativity

21.1 Something completely different ☐
21.2 Unconscious creativity ☐
21.3 Go gallery ☐
21.4 Game theory ☐
21.5 Snapshots ☐
Unit books ☐
Web links ☐

## Unit 22: Spatial thinking – right-brain group sessions

22.1 The magic tunnel ☐
22.2 Handcuffs ☐
22.3 Quick on the draw ☐
22.4 Towering ☐
22.5 Plane sailing ☐
Unit books ☐
Web links ☐

## Unit 23: Selection techniques – which idea is best?

23.1 The £100 bid ☐
23.2 SWOT ☐
23.3 Material gains ☐
23.4 Basic option evaluation ☐
23.5 Sophisticated option evaluation ☐
Unit books ☐
Web links ☐

## Unit 24: Changing group dynamics – more energy and fun

24.1 You're an animal ☐
24.2 Bursting with energy ☐
24.3 On the square ☐
24.4 Magic carpet ☐
24.5 Peer groups ☐

Unit books ☐
Web links ☐

## Unit 25: Refinement techniques – polishing up your ideas

25.1 Signposts ☐
25.2 Hazard markers ☐
25.3 Horse whispers ☐
25.4 Second-best solution ☐
25.5 Stakeholders ☐
Unit books ☐
Web links ☐

## Unit 26: Knowledge expansion – more techniques to help personal knowledge management

26.1 On the box ☐
26.2 Category magic ☐
26.3 Doing and knowing ☐
26.4 Fact quest ☐
26.5 Binning paper ☐
Unit books ☐
Web links ☐

## Unit 27: Spock rules – logic exercises to challenge the brain

27.1 One spare square ☐
27.2 Contract fishing ☐
27.3 Ands ☐
27.4 Rules rule ☐
27.5 Racing demon ☐
Unit books ☐
Web links ☐

## Unit 28: Making it happen – techniques to expedite implementation

28.1 Planning for selling ☐
28.2 Planning for implementation ☐
28.3 Story time ☐
28.4 The top ten list ☐
28.5 Scribbling ☐
Unit books ☐
Web links ☐

## Unit 29: Right-brain teamwork – more exercises to encourage groups to engage the right brain

29.1 The wrong drawing ☐
29.2 Abstract drawing ☐
29.3 PR from Hell ☐
29.4 Passing the buck ☐
29.5 Fontastic ☐
Unit books ☐
Web links ☐

## Unit 30: Mental workout – personal creativity exercises

30.1 Metaphorically speaking ☐
30.2 Holistic awareness ☐
30.3 On the edge ☐
30.4 Muddled model ☐
30.5 Rapt concentration ☐
Unit books ☐
Web links ☐

# 3 The course

*Each unit comprises a mix of exercises – activities to undertake now as you read the book – and techniques that can be used later, whether working alone or with others. Sections marked as exercise/techniques can be used straight away as an exercise, but also provide a technique to use later on.*

# Unit 1: A taster

In this first unit we get a taste of things to come with a look at an exercise/technique that will help you to structure ideas (and also take more effective notes), a technique to inject energy into a group, an exercise that will generate lots of ideas, an exercise to help you think in a different way and a technique to encourage a team to approach a problem differently.

Do try out the exercises as you go. Put them off until later and you probably won't ever do them. Read through the techniques. Make notes about how and when you can use them. And make sure you give them a try in the next appropriate forum.

## Unit books

A book that can be read effectively alongside the course is *Imagination Engineering* (Brian Clegg and Paul Birch, FT Prentice Hall). It provides a framework for creativity and is a very tightly matched support to the course.

If you find the 'surveying your mind' exercise a useful way to give structure to your ideas, we recommend *The Mind Map Book* (Tony and Barry Buzan, BBC Books), which will help you develop your mind mapping further.

You can find more information on our unit books, or buy them, from our support site: www.cul.co.uk/crashcourse.

## Web links

Look out for links to sites giving an introduction to creativity, extra information on mind mapping and computer software than can be used to draw up mind maps on PCs and Macs at www.cul.co.uk/crashcourse.

# 1.1 Exercise/Technique: Surveying your mind

**Preparation** None.
**Running time** Ten minutes.
**Resources** Paper, flip chart or whiteboard and pens.
**Frequency** Regularly.

This technique is probably the best way to make notes or summarize content so that the brain can absorb it. There are many related techniques, generically called cognitive mapping. The best known variant, mind mapping, was developed by Tony Buzan, and is simple in concept. Start at the centre of a page or whiteboard and draw an image that represents the core of the issue. From this, radiate out branches that represent the major themes of the issue. From each of these, draw progressively lower and lower level themes.

On each branch write one or two keywords above the line to say what that issue is. For instance one branch might be profit, splitting into costs and revenues, with revenues splitting into direct sales and indirect, while costs splits into the major cost drivers.

Try to make the image organic. Start with larger, fatter branches at the centre moving to smaller ones and eventually twigs at the extremities. You might also use different colours for each major branch (with subsidiaries the same colour as the major branch).

**Feedback** Don't get hung up on the process of drawing the map. The objective is an image-based overview of the information, not a work of art. It's important you stick to keywords, which retain the maximum amount of information with the minimum number of words.

**Outcome** This technique is a must if you really want to make the most of your brain. Conventional note taking can't compete for flexibility or retentiveness.

**Variations** There are many different ways to draw mind maps. Adding colour and images, for example, can boost memory retention.

| | |
|---|---|
| Culture | ✪ |
| Techniques | ✪✪✪✪ |
| Personal development | ✪✪✪✪ |
| Mental energy | ✪✪ |
| Fun | ✪✪ |

# 1.2 Technique: Knots

**Preparation** None.
**Running time** Three minutes.
**Resources** Needs enough open space to get the team or teams standing in unimpeded circles.
**Frequency** As required.

Split the group into even numbered teams. If you have an odd number of participants, you will have to take part. The ideal number for a team is eight, but groups of six or ten are entirely practical. Arrange the team, or teams, into a rough circle, facing inwards. Each member reaches into the circle and hold right hands with the person opposite. They should then hold the left hand of a different person. The team is now in a knot. The aim of the exercise is to untie the knot, leaving the team in a circle. In doing this they can rotate grips, but should not break the chain of hands.

**Feedback** This exercise is trivial with four people, mildly challenging with six, a little more with eight, downright difficult with ten and verging on the impossible with twelve. After that the combinatorial explosion means that, while it's technically soluble, it's practically impossible to get untangled.

**Outcome** *Knots* is an excellent warm-up that combines movement with a degree of practical thinking and team interaction (usually plenty of laughing and shouting involved). There is an element of ice-breaking too from the physical contact, and assisting each other through contortions, but concentration on the task in hand means that it has limited value in getting to know other team members.

**Variations** If there is time, demonstrate with larger and smaller groups how much easier or harder it gets. It is often difficult to undertake this exercise in a meeting room. We have found it effective to move the groups into a public space. This gives more room to manoeuvre, and also increases the warm-up potential by throwing in some exposure. If the group is particularly sluggish, you might consider taking them outside to do this exercise, freshening them up and countering the effect of air-conditioning.

| | |
|---|---|
| Culture | ✪ |
| Techniques | ✪ |
| Personal development | ✪✪✪ |
| Mental energy | ✪✪✪✪ |
| Fun | ✪✪✪✪ |

# 1.3 Exercise/Technique: Random picture

**Preparation** None.
**Running time** Ten to fifteen minutes.
**Resources** A selection of pictures from which to select, or one picture chosen at random.
**Frequency** As required

*Random picture* involves selecting an image, then making any and every association that you can with that image and finally relating those associations back to your problem in the way that we examined in Chapter 2. How could the associations help with the problem? What types of solution do they make you think of? How could you change things to be like (or unlike) the associations?

Selecting suitable images requires a little thought. You should look for images that are not just a representation of a word. A photograph of a typewriter, for instance, will not give much more stimulation than the word typewriter. A picture of a typewriter with a bored secretary behind it, staring into space, would start off all sorts of stories in our minds.

The easiest source of random pictures for this technique is the Internet. Go to a search engine like Google (www.google.com) or AltaVista (www.altavista.com). Click on the images section. Enter a few randomly chosen words. Then pick an image that seems stimulating, interesting, rich in detail and not directly related to the problem.

**Feedback** This technique is one of the easiest to use when coming up with ideas, generating a rich set of associations.

**Outcome** The associations generated by this technique will tend to include some very off-the-wall ones. These should be forced into the idea development phase as the ideas that result will be more original.

**Variations** If working with a group, try splitting into teams and having a different image for each team. Printouts of the graphics help here. Alternatively, use a single image, get the group to think individually about associations, collect those on a flip chart or whiteboard and then get the whole group to work through the associations and suggest ideas that spring from them.

Alternatives to the picture are random selection from an encyclopaedia (preferably electronic), which gives a very rich source of stimulation, or from a catalogue.

| | |
|---|---|
| Culture | ✪ |
| Techniques | ✪✪✪✪ |
| Personal development | ✪✪✪ |
| Mental energy | ✪✪ |
| Fun | ✪✪✪ |

# 1.4 Exercise: Life saver

**Preparation** None.
**Running time** Five minutes.
**Resources** None.
**Frequency** Once.

A little problem to consider. You are locked in a cell. It has a circular floor, five metres in diameter, and smooth concrete walls four metres high. In the centre of the floor is a hole, 10 cm deep. At the bottom of the hole is a smooth wooden ball which drops easily into the hole, but is only a little smaller in diameter than the hole itself. You have been stripped and have nothing about your person. You are given three conventional wire paperclips. You will only be allowed out of the cell if you can get the ball out of the hole. What do you do?

**Feedback** If you haven't got a solution, keep trying for a little longer.

Last chance to try.

There's a natural tendency to assume that since you are only given one tool, there must be some way of using it. Unfortunately, this assumption is flawed. Just because you are given something, you don't have to use it. The paperclips aren't really very helpful. However, you do have a way of getting the ball out of the hole. After all, wooden balls float, so all you have to is get some liquid into the hole: the rest of the solution is left to your imagination.

**Outcome** Sometimes attempting to use everything that has been provided in coming up with a solution to a problem or in making a decision based on knowledge can be a positive block to a solution. This problem demonstrates how it is sometimes useful to drop some of the 'given' input to see what else is available.

**Variations** This doesn't say you need always ignore the tools you're given, but that giving some consideration to how things would work without them can be valuable. Try applying this thinking to various everyday problems and situations where tools are employed.

| | |
|---|---|
| Culture | ✪ |
| Techniques | ✪ |
| Personal development | ✪✪✪✪ |
| Mental energy | ✪✪ |
| Fun | ✪✪✪ |

# 1.5 Technique: Ideas to get you fired

**Preparation** Obtain flip chart/pad.
**Running time** Ten minutes.
**Resources** Flip chart or pad per team; room to split the group into a number of teams.
**Frequency** As required.

Split the group into teams, ideally three to five people each. Isolate the teams by using breakout rooms, or separating them as much as is possible in a single room. Each team spends five minutes brainstorming 'ideas to get you fired'. Encourage the teams to be wild and original. The teams should generate as many ideas as possible, each being a possible reason to lose your job. After generating ideas, the team should spend a minute choosing the idea they'd most like to put into action. Get the groups back together. Each team then has a minute to describe their favourite idea to the others. The other teams should come up with ways of making the idea practical.

**Feedback** When the teams come back together, forbid negative comment – only allow positive suggestions. This may involve modifying the idea, for example an idea involving killing someone (impractical) can be modified to finding a way to get them out of their job or into another job.

**Outcome** This exercise is about enhancing creativity. By looking at anti-establishment ideas, the participants will break the constraints limiting their innovation. The result will be lots of impossible ideas, but even if they remain such, the participants will be in a freer frame of mind, and it is quite possible that an effective idea will be generated. This isn't the objective, but it may be an outcome.

**Variations** You often get more originality by having each member of the team generate ideas individually, then pooling their thinking, however this requires an extra five minutes. You can choose five ideas rather than a single one to carry forward, but again this takes longer. If possible, get the flip charts from the sessions and put them around the area where the participants take a break. The more public the area, the better.

| | |
|---|---|
| Culture | ✪✪✪ |
| Techniques | ✪✪✪ |
| Personal development | ✪✪✪ |
| Mental energy | ✪✪✪✪ |
| Fun | ✪✪✪✪ |

# Unit 2:
# Getting to know you – loosening up a new group

The second unit focuses on the needs to get a newly formed group working together effectively for creativity. The group may literally be new – formed, perhaps, to deal with a particular project – or may be attempting creative problem solving for the first time. In such circumstances it is necessary to break down the barriers between individuals and inject energy into the group. The exercises and techniques in this section are particularly designed with that in mind. As most of the techniques cannot be carried out as you read through the course but will need others involved to try them out, the unit also includes an exercise purely intended to give you a mental creativity workout.

Do try out the exercises as you go. Put them off until later and you probably won't ever do them. Read through the techniques. Make notes about how and when you can use them. And make sure you give them a try in the next appropriate forum. Techniques like these, designed for ice-breaking and energizing, can be tried out whenever a group of people comes together – anything from a children's party to a board meeting.

## Unit books

This unit's book is Meredith Belbin's *Team Roles at Work*, which builds on this business guru's long-standing theories on management teams to investigate how individuals' different styles help and hinder team interaction.

You can find more information on our unit books, or buy them, from our support site: www.cul.co.uk/crashcourse.

## Web links

Our links provide information on the nature of teamwork at www.cul.co.uk/crashcourse.

# 2.1 Technique: This is my friend

**Preparation** None.
**Running time** One minute per team member.
**Resources** Standard room format, provided everyone can see the other people present. Circular or U-shaped tables are probably best.
**Frequency** As required.

Each member of the group takes a turn at introducing the person next to them. They have 60 seconds to tell the rest of the group about the other person. The subject's name should be accurate, but everything else should be made up. You might like to give the group a couple of minutes to generate ideas first, or the rest of the group will still be constructing their own introduction, rather than listening to their colleagues.

**Feedback** The more bizarre the association, the better the chance of remembering the person's name, especially if the name is repeated several times through the exercise. Be creative, but be aware of possible embarrassment.

**Outcome** This is a pure ice-breaker. It serves two purposes. The need to introduce someone by name will increase awareness of that name, particularly with the person doing the introducing – if the introduction is special enough, the name may well stick with many of the others too. The exercise also helps break down initial inhibitions by making the participants do something slightly silly, but very low risk.

**Variations** To increase the power of this exercise as an ice-breaker, and to add to the fun, you can set various limits. For example, there must be at least 10 statements about the individual and the whole thing can't take more than 60 seconds. The other participants can be issued with a weapon in case the person talking falters or goes over time: perhaps soft-balls or a water pistol. It will also happen occasionally that something true is said about a subject by accident – again this could be picked up on and used as an excuse to pelt or soak the participant.

| | |
|---|---|
| Culture | ✪✪ |
| Techniques | ✪ |
| Personal development | ✪✪ |
| Mental energy | ✪✪✪ |
| Fun | ✪✪✪✪ |

# 2.2 Technique: Tower of Babel

**Preparation** Obtain pads and markers.
**Running time** Five minutes.
**Resources** Two A4 (or letter) pads; two flip chart markers; enough open space for all participants to stand in. Chairs and tables would be appreciated.
**Frequency** As required.

Split the group into two teams of the same size (with a large group, it doesn't matter too much if one is bigger than the other). The exercise is a race against time. Each person in the two teams is to write the number of letters in their first name on a piece of paper. They then must arrange themselves in a group, in such a way that their heads are in descending order of name length – short names highest, long names lowest, same length same height. Each person should be holding the sheet of paper with their name length in their teeth. All sheets must be legible from the front. No feet or knees must be touching the floor or floor covering.

**Feedback** Be prepared to restart a team which hasn't complied fully with the rules. With a largish group there will be the need to use chairs and/or tables to gain height towards the back. Don't discourage this.

**Outcome** This activity could equally well be used to inject energy into a group or to get a new team working better together.

**Variations** With fewer than 10 people you could run this in a single team against some arbitrary time limit. Obviously this depends on the number of people – around one minute would work with nine people. Although it is not essential, this is an excellent activity to use an instant camera with. A photograph of each team makes an excellent talking point for coffee breaks, while scanned copies of the photographs (or electronic pictures) can be incorporated in post-event feedback to good effect.

| | |
|---|---|
| Culture | ✪✪ |
| Techniques | ✪ |
| Personal development | ✪✪✪ |
| Mental energy | ✪✪✪ |
| Fun | ✪✪✪✪ |

# 2.3 Exercise: Twisters

**Preparation** None.
**Running time** Five minutes.
**Resources** None.
**Frequency** Once.

As most of this unit consists of techniques, here's an exercise to ensure that you get a mental workout. Attempt an answer to each of these three short puzzles before moving onto the feedback section:

- What game (with four letters) starts with a T, originated in Scotland and is played outdoors?
- Pandas are endangered, but they have an aid to survival that is totally unique to their species. What is it?
- Why were so many great composers German?

**Feedback** Don't go any further until you've attempted some sort of answer to each. Last chance to consider your answer.

The answers are: golf (it starts with a tee); baby pandas; because they were born in Germany.

Each of these twisters depends on taking something about the information you are given and using it in a way that you don't expect. Once you've groaned at the answers (if you hadn't already guessed them), take a minute to examine what was happening.

**Outcome** Creativity is all about seeing the world in a different way, or coming at a problem from a different direction. These puzzles work in exactly the same way. By practising this sort of puzzle, you have a much better chance of coming up with creative ideas. In each case, you knew the answer – it was the question you didn't understand. It emphasizes the need for careful questioning when you are investigating the problem you are to work on.

**Variations** Get hold of a book of this sort of puzzle and practise the sort of thinking required. You may also find cryptic crossword puzzles give the same sort of exercise.

| | |
|---|---|
| Culture | ✪ |
| Techniques | ✪ |
| Personal development | ✪✪✪✪ |
| Mental energy | ✪✪ |
| Fun | ✪✪✪✪ |

# 2.4 Technique: Follow my leader

**Preparation** Two lists of participants' names, one in a random, non-alphabetic order, numbered from top to bottom, and the other divided into individual slips of paper, numbered in the same order as the random sheet.
**Running time** Five minutes plus.
**Resources** Paper; room for the participants to stand up.
**Frequency** As required.

Start by making sure your name lists match the participants, without giving away who is whom. During the exercise no one should wear a name badge, or use their own name. Give each member of the group a slip of paper with someone else's name on. They must not let go of this slip. The object of the exercise is for the team to end up standing in line in the order you have on your list (based on the numbering on the slips – your list is not on display). Reinforce the fact that no one must use their own name in any way.

**Feedback** There are two requirements here – to get the names into the right order and to match names to the individuals. Find out how the team decided what to do – was there any discussion, or did people just plunge in? Was there are a concerted tactic? How effective was it?

**Outcome** This exercise works best with large numbers. The less the group know each other, the more effective it is. It won't result in everyone knowing everyone else's name, but the names will be familiar, and they should know at least one very well. There is superb chaos as everyone shouts out the name on their slip.

**Variations** This works best as a group exercise, but it is possible to split into teams. This may be necessary if the group is extremely large. Bear in mind, though, that the exact attendees of any event on the day may be different from your list. Having several lists makes the initial administration more tricky. A minor variant is to finish with the group calling out their names in order – it reinforces the names and helps you to check they've succeeded.

| | |
|---|---|
| Culture | ✪✪ |
| Techniques | ✪ |
| Personal development | ✪✪ |
| Mental energy | ✪✪✪ |
| Fun | ✪✪✪✪ |

# 2.5 Technique: True and false

**Preparation** None.
**Running time** Ten minutes.
**Resources** Whatever room you are meeting in.
**Frequency** As required.

Each participant is given a couple of minutes to prepare. They need to have three 'facts' about themselves, two of which are false, one of which is true.

Go around the room allowing everyone to introduce themselves. They should say their name and then state the first fact. Then repeat their name and state the second fact. Finally, repeat their name and state the third fact. The rest of the team should decide for themselves which fact is true. Go round the room checking who believes what and then reveal the truth (a show of hands will do). Repeat this process for every participant. Each person should keep score of their hits and misses.

Finally, check the scores to see who is the most attuned to the group.

**Feedback** The repetition of name before each fact increases the memory of names far more than you would imagine. It is very easy to forget someone's name. It is hard to forget it when they tell you it three times in quick succession. We have found that stressing the need to make the true fact implausible increases the humour.

**Outcome** This introduction gives the names of the group to all of the members of the group in a way that increases the chance of remembering them. It also tags on a fact about that person.

**Variations** This can be run as a paired exercise with each member of the pair having to introduce their partner. If you do not introduce the true or false element at first, but ask them to find out a whole repertoire of surprising facts about their partner, then tell them to select the best and make up two lies; it increases the amount they know.

| | |
|---|---|
| Culture | ✪✪ |
| Techniques | ✪ |
| Personal development | ✪✪ |
| Mental energy | ✪✪✪ |
| Fun | ✪✪✪ |

# Unit 3: Clarifying the problem – just what are you trying to do?

When attempting to find a creative solution to a problem it is essential to first have a clear idea just what the problem is – otherwise there is a real danger of coming up with a solution to the wrong problem which simply won't help. Make sure when using techniques to clarify the problem that you don't slip into solutions – otherwise you have implicitly settled on what the problem is.

Do try out the exercises as you go. Put them off until later and you probably won't ever do them. Read through the techniques. Make notes about how and when you can use them. And make sure you give them a try in the next appropriate forum.

## Unit books

As one of the key points from the exercises in this unit concerns breaking up creative effort into manageable chunks, the Unit book is a collection of short stories. We've picked out the *Complete Short Stories* of H G Wells – despite being around a century old, these stories are still a challenging mix that can inspire new approaches to creative thinking.

Reading a little fiction, especially a genre like science fiction that challenges our normal way of looking at things, is a superb way to give your creativity a boost. Don't dismiss this suggestion because it's 'only fiction' – the value is immense. At our support site you will find extra recommendations for books of short stories.

You can find more information on our unit books, or buy them, from our support site: www.cul.co.uk/crashcourse.

## Web links

Links on H G Wells and on the creative impact of fiction can be found at www.cul.co.uk/crashcourse.

# 3.1 Exercise/Technique: Compass

**Preparation** A basic statement of your problem or requirement.
**Running time** Five minutes.
**Resources** None.
**Frequency** As required.

The *Compass* is a direction-setting technique that is used to find the real problems that underlie the problem statement as presented. In order to make it work you need to have developed a problem statement; ideally one that is owned by somebody within the group – try to put it in the form 'how to...' You then merely ask 'why' a great deal.

Given the initial problem statement ask 'why'. In other words, 'why is this a problem?' or 'why do you see it like that?' Whatever is the answer to this question, write it down and then probe the answer itself by asking 'why' again. Repeat this process on the next answer. This continues until you feel you have hit a dead end or until it all becomes terminally dull. For instance, if my problem is how to write this book faster. Why? Because I don't want to spend so much time on it. Why? Because I want to spend more time with my family. This can continue for some time from here.

You will find that each response to each question can be rephrased to form a 'how to' problem statement. Some of these will be much more fruitful areas of exploration than the original problem. Try out this technique now as an exercise on the problem of 'how to become more creative'.

**Feedback** It sounds simple and it is. That is not to say that it isn't useful. We've seen a problem entirely solved by merely rephrasing the problem statement, so don't underestimate the benefit of spending time doing this.

**Outcome** This is a very effective way of getting new questions and new directions from which to tackle a problem. You will find that the more you use this technique, the better you get at asking subtly different why questions that don't sound so repetitive.

**Variations** This activity can be run as a full group session or as a number of team sessions.

| | |
|---|---|
| Culture | ✪✪✪ |
| Techniques | ✪✪✪ |
| Personal development | ✪ |
| Mental energy | ✪✪ |
| Fun | ✪✪ |

## 3.2 Technique: Obstacle map

**Preparation** None.
**Running time** Five minutes.
**Resources** Flip charts (ideally three).
**Frequency** As required.

Line up three flip chart stands, or stick three sheets of flip chart paper on the wall. Start by outlining your objective. In pithy phrases, describe what you want to achieve and what things will be like when you succeed. If you are dealing with a product, this might be product characteristics or customer benefits. If you are dealing with a problem, it could be a world where the problem no longer exists. This output should be written on the far right flip chart.

Next, on the leftmost chart, describe the current state. Using the same factors as the description of your objective, where are you now? What is the world like?

In between, list the obstacles to achieving your outcome. Some obstacles may be reiterations or restatements of the starting position – this isn't a problem, your starting position often is an obstacle in its own right.

Most of the obstacles you have listed can now be rephrased as 'how to' statements. These form alternative problem statements, expanding your understanding of the question you are trying to answer.

**Feedback** Resist the temptation to jump straight to the obstacles. It is difficult to hold all the considerations in your head at once. Putting them on paper frees you to think of one thing at a time and improves the results significantly. Also, in a group some will have different views of where you are going or even where you are starting. It is important to capture these.

**Outcome** You are likely to find that you generate more 'how to' statements than you can use. Very often in the creative process you will generate more than you need and only use some of it. This is not a problem, it is the nature of the beast.

**Variations** The ways that you write up the obstacle map can be varied immensely. Try giving each group member sticky notes, or getting each group member to work independently first. However, don't be tempted to avoid writing all three parts down.

| | |
|---|---|
| Culture | ✪✪ |
| Techniques | ✪✪✪ |
| Personal development | ✪✪ |
| Mental energy | ✪✪ |
| Fun | ✪ |

# 3.3 Exercise: Water into wine

**Preparation** None.
**Running time** Five minutes.
**Resources** None.
**Frequency** Once.

In this little mind-stretching exercise, the clarification is not so much of the problem but of a fluid. I have two bottles, one containing water and the other containing wine. I pour one measure of wine into the water bottle. I then pour an equal measure from the water bottle back into the wine bottle. At the end, there is just as much water in the wine as there is wine in the water. Which of the following have to be true to make this possible (you can choose more than one):

- The bottles are the same size
- The water and wine are thoroughly mixed after the measure is poured into the water bottle
- The wine and water have to be thoroughly mixed after the measure is poured back into the wine bottle
- The wine has the same density as the water
- The water and wine are miscible

...or is it impossible to be certain that there is just as much water in the wine as there is wine in the water?

**Feedback** Don't go any further until you've attempted some sort of answer.
Last chance to consider your answer.

In fact, none of the conditions have to hold true – there will always be just as much wine in the water as water in the wine. Think of it like this: at the end of the process, the wine bottle holds exactly the same amount as it did initially, so it must have had exactly the same amount of water added to it as wine was removed.

**Outcome** Notice how the way that the question was phrased can distract you from the true facts. Even if you got the right answer, the chances are that the phrasing proved a distraction. You probably worried about partial mixing of water and wine, for example. Sometimes rephrasing the question is an essential for knowledge gathering and creativity.

**Variations** Look at few real-life problems you've dealt with and think how much you have assumed about the question that had to be answered.

| | |
|---|---|
| Culture | ✪ |
| Techniques | ✪ |
| Personal development | ✪✪✪✪ |
| Mental energy | ✪✪ |
| Fun | ✪✪✪ |

# 3.4 Technique: Destination

**Preparation** None.
**Running time** Five minutes.
**Resources** None.
**Frequency** As required.

The best representation of a problem (or requirement for an idea) is usually a statement beginning 'how to…' This statement is akin to a destination in a journey. It is your point B when travelling from A to B. Often the issue that you face is that you cannot see a way to get there but you are sure that B is where you want to get. This technique is an opportunity to question this position.

Really, technique is too strong a word. *Destination* is merely the act of questioning whether you really need to achieve your 'how to' or whether another destination would be as good or better.

Some of the techniques in this book produce different 'how to' statements. If you have time you can work on a selection of these. Whether you do this or not, consider any alternative formulations of the problem that spring to mind. There is always a temptation to hang on to your initial statement because that's the 'real' one.

Take a moment to display the range of 'how to' statements in front of you. Is there one statement that better encapsulates the whole problem than the one you started with? If so, switch to it. If not, stay with the original.

**Feedback** The reason that we have listed this as a technique is that it is a crucial stage in the creativity process and one that is too easily overlooked. The work that you invest in developing alternative views of your problem is devalued if you always regard your original statement as the real problem and the others as subsidiary.

**Outcome** In our experience you will decide to drop your original problem statement about half of the time.

**Variations** You can select an alternative statement by discussion, but there may still be argument. If it proves difficult, try using one of the selection techniques (see Unit 23).

| | |
|---|---|
| Culture | ✪ |
| Techniques | ✪✪✪ |
| Personal development | ✪✪ |
| Mental energy | ✪ |
| Fun | ✪ |

# 3.5 Exercise/Technique: Chunks and breaks

**Preparation** None.
**Running time** Five minutes.
**Resources** Notepad.
**Frequency** Once.

We've all been in the situation. You have to give a presentation/write an article/take an exam. Time is short and there is a huge amount of information that you need to digest and turn into knowledge. So you read long into the night, steaming open your eyelids with cups of coffee, hardly stopping at all.

Unfortunately, there is overwhelming evidence that this is not a great way to absorb information. The amount you retain drops off after time, but breaking the session into chunks with a series of short breaks means that more can be absorbed. There isn't a magic length for the chunks – experimenting may help – but it is usually between 15 minutes and an hour, with breaks of around 5 minutes to overcome the deterioration in retention.

In the few minutes allowed for this exercise, you aren't going to actually work through some information. Instead, take a task you have ahead (or invent one for the exercise) and rough out a schedule of chunks and breaks. Next time you actually do this kind of work, make sure you use your schedule.

**Feedback** It's tempting to carry on if everything is going excellently. This may be valid for pure productive work, but doesn't apply where your aim is to learn and absorb. However well it seems things are going, your ability to remember will benefit from breaks. The break should be something completely different, involving a different use of the mind. Getting out in the fresh air for a few minutes and unwinding is ideal.

**Outcome** Breaking things into chunks makes a lot of sense, but it's human nature to forge on and try to get through, especially under pressure. It often takes tight scheduling to get yourself breaking to begin with – but persevere for improved retention and enhanced knowledge.

**Variations** Try different chunkings to see which works best for you. The natural tendency is to try for the longest chunks as these seem more efficient. It isn't necessarily the case.

| | |
|---|---|
| Culture | ✪✪✪✪ |
| Techniques | ✪✪ |
| Personal development | ✪✪✪✪ |
| Mental energy | ✪✪✪ |
| Fun | ✪✪ |

# Unit 4: Challenging assumptions – thinking differently about a problem to understand it better

Assumptions are often one of the greatest blockages to creativity. We all make assumptions about the way things are, the way we do things, the way things have to be. Almost always some or all of those assumptions can be challenged – and this lies at the heart of creativity. In these techniques we challenge some assumptions to get a better understanding of a problem.

Do try out the exercises as you go. Put them off until later and you probably won't ever do them. Read through the techniques. Make notes about how and when you can use them. And make sure you give them a try in the next appropriate forum.

## Unit books

*A Kick in the Seat of the Pants* is one of Roger von Oech's classic books on creativity that constantly challenges assumptions. This Californian guru has none of the stuffy academic content you might find in some creativity books – it's all practical stuff.

You can find more information on our unit books, or buy them, from our support site: www.cul.co.uk/crashcourse.

## Web links

Links to Web sites that look more at the nature of assumptions can be found at www.cul.co.uk/crashcourse.

# 4.1 Exercise/Technique: Do nothing

**Preparation** None.
**Running time** Five minutes.
**Resources** None.
**Frequency** As required.

A fundamental assumption we tend to make when looking to solve a problem is that *something* has to be done. But what would happen if you did nothing?

The difficulty with taking this stance is that it is very easy to become wedded to the idea that we must do something, anything. This leads to us regarding the 'do nothing' option as completely unacceptable. This, in turn, leads to us creating exaggerated claims of the difficulties that we will face if we do nothing.

Stop and think for a while. If you are in a group, take a moment to discuss it. What would really happen if you were to do nothing?

Assuming that you decide that your problem still needs to be solved, this process leads to two outcomes. Firstly you will have a better idea of the benefits that will accrue from solving the problem. Secondly you will have generated some alternative problems to solve by discussing the difficulties that would arise as a result of doing nothing. For instance, let us assume that the problem was that a product line had to become more profitable next year than it had been in the past and the 'do nothing' discussion had highlighted the reason as being a tax break coming to an end. An alternative problem would be to extend or replace the tax break.

**Feedback** If you use none of the other techniques for questioning your 'how to' statement you should use this one. Try it now as an exercise. Take a high-profile problem in the news and spend a minute or two outlining just what would happen if the response was to do nothing.

**Outcome** You will end up with a better understanding of your 'how to' statement and you will possibly have generated some alternatives. You may even end up deciding to do nothing – this really does happen. This may generate a new problem – persuading the problem owner to give it up. *Do nothing* can also generate new solutions to problems – not doing nothing itself, but arising out of the consequences of doing nothing.

**Variations** As well as conducting this as an individual exercise or as a group discussion you could conduct a discussion by e-mail, fax or letter. Lay out for all interested parties your understanding of the problem and have them respond with their analysis of the result of doing nothing.

| | |
|---|---|
| Culture | ✪✪✪ |
| Techniques | ✪✪✪ |
| Personal development | ✪✪ |
| Mental energy | ✪✪ |
| Fun | ✪✪ |

# 4.2 Technique: Up and down

**Preparation** None.
**Running time** Ten minutes.
**Resources** None.
**Frequency** As required.

When formulating the problem, it is natural to take your own point of view. In this technique you will spend a few minutes looking up and down from your position. If you are at the very top of the company, try looking to the middle, then even further down to the bottom.

First look up. Put yourself in the position of the chief executive. What would he or she see as the underlying problem, the obstacle to success, or the new product direction? First try directly formulating the question from their viewpoint, then spend a minute thinking through the influences and requirements of this particular person, and try again.

Then look down. What would the lowliest worker in the company see as the problem? How would they see the problem affecting them and their world? Use these two insights to formulate different 'How to' statements.

**Feedback** Looking in these diverging directions can produce very different views of the problem. Try to think like real people, not caricatures. The top person isn't just concerned about company profitability (though this is important). The lowly worker isn't just worried about wage packets and working conditions. Take a broader view.

**Outcome** This technique can be used when looking for solutions, but it is particularly suited to finding the right questions, because these different views are just as important as your own when coming to a picture of the desired direction. The very different circumstances and needs underlying the viewpoints will combine to produce a much rounder, fuller picture of the problem.

**Variations** It is possible to talk to the real people involved, but the person at the top may not have time, and the person at the bottom may find it difficult to give you the required information. Try splitting a team in two. Each half takes one of the standpoints, spending a few minutes developing their ideas. Then let them share the ideas in a mock meeting, being prepared if necessary to stand up for their position and knock down anything that seems unreasonable.

| | |
|---|---|
| Culture | ✪✪✪ |
| Techniques | ✪✪✪ |
| Personal development | ✪✪ |
| Mental energy | ✪✪ |
| Fun | ✪✪ |

# 4.3 Exercise: Round the world

**Preparation** None.
**Running time** Five minutes.
**Resources** None.
**Frequency** Once.

This is an exercise in creative thinking. Don't skip it even if you don't like puzzles and logic problems. Exercise isn't always pleasant – it's the end result we are after, not the pleasure of getting there.

Imagine you had a very long rope with no stretch in it. This rope is just the right length to go round the equator of the world. Now imagine we added 3 metres to the length of the rope, and managed to lift it evenly off the surface of the planet to take up the slack.

Guess what size of gap would be formed between the rope and the surface of the earth. Don't try to work it out, just guess. Then take an extra couple of minutes to think about how you would work out exactly how far the rope would be from the earth.

**Feedback** If you haven't already done the two parts of the problem above, do them now. Don't read any further.

Last chance to consider your answer.

The guess is usually that the rope lifts a tiny distance off the surface – perhaps a millimetre or less – because those 3 metres have to be even up around about 40,000 kilometres of circumference. Unfortunately, circles don't work like that. The circumference is always $2\pi r$ – roughly six times the radius. So the radius was roughly C/6 where C is the circumference. Now the radius becomes (C+3)/6, – or C/6 + 3/6, – in other words, the radius has increased by roughly 3/6, about half a metre. Much bigger than you might expect.

**Outcome** Our instinctive reaction to a problem is based on feel. Sometimes this is very valuable. Complex or fuzzy problems are often not amenable to detailed analysis. However, it is important to be aware that common sense can lead you astray: be prepared to challenge it.

**Variations** Look out for other opportunities to test and understand your intuition.

| | |
|---|---|
| Culture | ✪ |
| Techniques | ✪ |
| Personal development | ✪✪✪✪ |
| Mental energy | ✪✪ |
| Fun | ✪✪✪ |

# 4.4 Technique: Time slices

**Preparation** None.
**Running time** Ten minutes.
**Resources** None.
**Frequency** As required.

Look at your problem area. Consider each of the following timescales: one minute, one day, one week, one month, one year. What is critical in each of these timescales? How will the problem change? What has to be considered in the different timings? What influences come into play? Would you state the problem differently if each of these timings was an imposed deadline (for completion of the entire requirement)? Would the 'how to' statement come out differently? If there isn't an imposed deadline, what considerations are likely to impact your problem on these timescales?

**Feedback** It is easy to make assumptions about timings which may not be valid, or at least may not be necessary. This technique forces you to examine your timing assumptions and how they impact the direction you are likely to take. The deadlines may not really be imposed, but trying out the assumptions of those deadlines can result in a considerable improvement in understanding. Often the significant 80 per cent solution is achieved in a fraction of the overall time, while the remaining time is spent on fining up the last details. Sometimes (for example, when looking at nuclear power plant safety) those details are critical – often they are irrelevant.

**Outcome** This technique will not produce solutions, or even precise 'how to' statements. Instead it produces a better broad understanding of just what the problem area is, which is essential (particularly with a complex problem) to coming to a sensible statement of the problem and a practical, creative solution.

**Variations** You may need to modify the timescales considered to fit a problem where there is already a reasonably clear end point in time, even if the destination is not clear. Make sure, though, that there are several, very different timescales involved. A group can split up and take one timescale per team – this reduces the monotony of repetition and makes a debate on the importance of different timescales a more effective contributor to the process.

| | |
|---|---|
| Culture | ✪✪ |
| Techniques | ✪✪✪ |
| Personal development | ✪✪ |
| Mental energy | ✪✪ |
| Fun | ✪✪ |

# 4.5 Exercise: Questioning everything

**Preparation** None.
**Running time** Five minutes.
**Resources** Trade magazine or technical book.
**Frequency** Once.

Take a copy of a trade journal or book that covers your own area of expertise. If you don't have anything appropriate, a factual newspaper story will do, but something in a specialist area of interest is best. Now spend five minutes assessing it. You aren't interested in the content directly. What you are looking for is assumptions – assumptions that the writer makes, assumptions that you would normally make in reading the piece (for a book, take the first few pages of the second chapter).

What would happen if these assumptions weren't true? Would anything be different? How do you know they are true?

**Feedback** This is an exercise to expose your own way of thinking. We all make assumptions all the time. These assumptions can sometimes block the development of knowledge, and can certainly prevent creativity. If we had stuck with the assumption that the sun (and everything else) rotated around the earth, we would have been unable to make many other deductions in disciplines as far ranging as astrophysics and theology. Our ability to think creatively is always being undermined by assumptions that don't necessarily hold true.

**Outcome** Once you can spot the assumptions you and others are making, it becomes easier to do something about them. This doesn't mean always ignoring them, but you can then act in the conscious awareness of the assumptions you are making.

**Variations** Assumption spotting can be an entertaining game when listening to speeches (especially political speeches) and reading almost anything factual. Try it now and then to keep your assumption awareness in trim (it's a particularly good way of getting through a boring speech).

| | |
|---|---|
| Culture | ✪✪✪✪ |
| Techniques | ✪✪ |
| Personal development | ✪✪✪✪ |
| Mental energy | ✪✪ |
| Fun | ✪✪ |

# Unit 5: Good vibrations – positive thinking

Frame of mind is vitally important when being creative. There is a lot of the self-fulfilling prophecy in creativity. If you believe that you are creative you will be. If you believe that you are not, you won't. This is because those who believe they aren't creative will suppress their own good ideas, not wishing to appear silly. After all, they know they aren't creative. Furthermore, a group with a negative attitude will tend to shoot down ideas, rather than encourage them and help them grow. Be careful, though. A technique like *Yes!* can take an already cynical group and make them even more negative.

Do try out the exercises as you go. Put them off until later and you probably won't ever do them. Read through the techniques. Make notes about how and when you can use them. And make sure you give them a try in the next appropriate forum.

## Unit books

There are few more inspirational writers (and speakers) than Tom Peters, and his *Circle of Innovation* is an excellent example of putting the positive thinking into creativity.

Another book well worth exploring is *Getting Everything You Can Out Of All You've Got* by Jay Abraham. Technically a marketing book, it's a wonderful guide to finding the right levers to get something across, whether you are selling a car or encouraging creativity.

You can find more information on our unit books, or buy them, from our support site: www.cul.co.uk/crashcourse.

## Web links

Look out for links to sites that will give you a buzz at www.cul.co.uk/crashcourse.

# 5.1 Exercise/Technique: Altered states

**Preparation** None.
**Running time** Ten minutes.
**Resources** None.
**Frequency** Once.

Sit in a comfortable chair. Close your eyes. Think of an occasion when you were engaged in a very successful activity, where everything went well, when you felt confident, relaxed and in control. As much as possible, imagine yourself into that memory. Take in as much as you can of your situation, any sights and sounds, smells and touches you experienced.

When you are feel comfortably part of the memory, choose a particular combination of senses and feelings which can act as a key to trigger the memory in as much detail as possible. If there were just one thing that could get you back to this memory as quickly as possible, what would it be?

Now get out of the chair, move around a little, then try the key to bring back the memory.

**Feedback** This technique is based on the approach that psychologist Mihaly Csikszentmihalyi calls flow. This is an approach that has been adopted by a number of successful athletes who need to maximize their performance at a particular time. The aspect we are dealing with is the way that recalling as completely as possible a previous state of mind will move your current state into a similar position. This is manipulating the brain at the most basic level.

**Outcome** By using the key memory to recall a state of mind where you were confident, in control and successful, you can bring yourself into a similar state in the present. The simple presence of such confidence gives you a better chance of success in an activity.

**Variations** When you have done the basic exercise, try using the key to bring back the memory in positions of greater and greater stress. To begin with it will be difficult to manage quickly enough and in the face of distraction, but you should be able to do it almost instantly with practice.

| | |
|---|---|
| Culture | ✪ |
| Techniques | ✪ |
| Personal development | ✪✪✪✪ |
| Mental energy | ✪✪✪ |
| Fun | ✪✪ |

# 5.2 Technique: Yes!

**Preparation** None.
**Running time** One minute.
**Resources** Enough open space for all participants to stand in a circle.
**Frequency** As required (but not too often).

Get everyone to stand in a circle holding hands. Ask them to crouch down. Explain that you are going to say 'yes', 'yes', 'yes' rhythmically, each time getting slightly louder and slightly higher until you end up with the group jumping into the air shouting 'YES!' Do it.

**Feedback** Explain that this probably makes them feel very silly – and that's not a bad thing. There are two reasons for this. One is that we often feel silly when coming up with new ideas and original thinking. As you want them to be original and innovative, they need to overcome this resistance to feeling silly. Practice helps – this is a primer in silliness. The second reason for undertaking the exercise is to put the group into a more positive frame of mind. Even if the participants feel absolutely ludicrous, they will get a warm glow and a feeling of shared purpose out of the totally positive nature of the content.

**Outcome** It's important that you give the feedback explaining the reasoning as some participants (particularly from feeling-suppressing cultures like the British) will feel negative about it otherwise, totally countering any benefit. Given that feedback, you should have introduced some energy, made them aware of a possible creativity killer and brought them closer together.

**Variations** It is a good move to repeat the exercise after the feedback. Now that the participants know the reasons behind what they are doing, they will feel more positive and get more out of the exercise. This variation is positively recommended, if time is available (this is, after all, a very quick exercise).

| | |
|---|---|
| Culture | ✪✪ |
| Techniques | ✪✪ |
| Personal development | ✪✪ |
| Mental energy | ✪✪✪✪ |
| Fun | ✪✪ |

# 5.3 Technique: Circle of energy

**Preparation** None.
**Running time** Five minutes.
**Resources** Space to arrange the group into a circle.
**Frequency** Once with any group.

Arrange the group into a circle. Explain that some people believe that everyone has energy flowing through their bodies; the Chinese call it *chi*, the Japanese call it *ka*. This circle is going to pass a ball of energy around.

Create an imaginary ball of energy in your hands and pass it on to the person on your left. Explain that anyone can add to or take from the energy as they see fit as they pass it around. When it has gone around the circle once, suggest that the next time you can get fancier by changing the shape or the consistency of the energy – it could be square, runny, sticky etc. You might even decide to start throwing rather than passing it.

Next go around the circle passing on a hand clap – ie clap and pass this on. Try to get faster and faster. Next, pass on the clap and shout (anything loud and short). Finish with everyone continuing to clap as it passes them.

**Feedback** This exercise doesn't work as well with small groups so try it with at least eight or ten people. If you have a smaller group that know one another already, they may be prepared to give it a go. As with the previous one, some care is needed to avoid cynical group members being turned off by a technique like this: use your judgement on whether or not it will work. Often it is better towards the end of a session, when participants are flagging but have already seen the benefits of creativity techniques.

**Outcome** Considering that the activity involves standing in a circle it is surprisingly energizing and involving. The outcome is both raised energy levels and pulling people together into a group.

**Variations** There are a few variations included above. This started life as a tai chi exercise, simply passing a ball of chi. The additions have grown. What you add is limited only by your imagination. If you, or members of the group, are uncomfortable with the elements of Eastern philosophy then just make it an imaginary ball. You can still change its shape and consistency.

| | |
|---|---|
| Culture | ✪✪ |
| Techniques | ✪✪ |
| Personal development | ✪✪ |
| Mental energy | ✪✪✪✪ |
| Fun | ✪✪ |

# 5.4 Exercise: Pub quiz

**Preparation** None.
**Running time** Five minutes.
**Resources** None.
**Frequency** Once.

This is a problem to give your brain skills a workout. Unlike some of the problems in this book, it is amenable to logic – but the solution isn't particularly obvious.

Every day I go down to the local tube station and stand between Eastbound and Westbound platforms. Both Eastbound and Westbound trains come every ten minutes. I catch whichever train comes first, travel one stop and get off. Then I go to the nearest pub for lunch. Somehow, though, I almost always go to the The Grapes (the pub near the Westbound station) rather than The Queen's Head (the pub near the Eastbound station). In fact, I've noticed that, on average, I only go the Queen's Head once a fortnight. Why?

**Feedback** If you haven't already got an answer, try to jot one down now. Don't read any further.

Last chance to consider your answer.

Both Eastbound and Westbound trains run every ten minutes. As it happens, the Westbound trains arrive at the station one minute before the Eastbound trains. Because of this, there is only one minute out of every ten when the next train is the Eastbound one. So I catch the Eastbound train, on average, once every ten tries, or once every two working weeks.

**Outcome** This is a problem that is totally obvious once it is explained. Much creativity and knowledge is like this. The exercise is a valuable lesson in the mechanics of knowledge building, and in the requirement to explore the problem area before plunging in with a solution.

**Variations** Look for simple solutions to problems as well as the complex.

| | |
|---|---|
| Culture | ✪ |
| Techniques | ✪ |
| Personal development | ✪✪✪✪ |
| Mental energy | ✪✪ |
| Fun | ✪✪✪ |

# 5.5 Technique: Beam me up

**Preparation** None.
**Running time** Five minutes.
**Resources** One chair per team of five and space to spread them.
**Frequency** Once with any group.

Divide the group into teams of exactly five people and ask them to select the largest member of the group to sit on the chair. The rest of the group stands around the chair, then each person entwines the fingers of both hands with the index fingers pointing straight out. They then place the index fingers under the knees and armpits of the person in the chair (one team member under one knee, one under the other, one under one armpit and one under the other). They should then attempt to lift the person using only these fingers. Most or all groups will fail.

Now, get the group to raise their hands over the head of the person and to wave them around 'to absorb the energy of the person to be lifted'. This needs to go on for quite a while so that the arms tire slightly. Now quickly repeat the lifting exercise. Many or all of the groups will find it easy.

We don't know how this works. It is probably something to do with adrenaline or getting used to lifting the arms or something. You may want to try this out sometime ahead of using it in earnest to convince yourself that it will work.

**Feedback** This feels like magic when it goes well. The group are collectively convinced that what they are about to do will fail and despite this it proves easy.

**Outcome** There is a lot of laughter and some amazement generated by this. You will undoubtedly be asked for an explanation. Since we can't give you one you could make it up, claim ignorance or confess that it is a secret handed down through generations of your family that you have sworn never to divulge.

**Variations** There are variations you could play on the story or the set-up of this technique but there's little you could do to alter the activity itself.

| | |
|---|---|
| Culture | ✪✪ |
| Techniques | ✪ |
| Personal development | ✪✪ |
| Mental energy | ✪✪✪✪ |
| Fun | ✪✪✪ |

# Unit 6: 'How to's – getting different cuts at the problem

One of the best things you can do when trying to get a better understanding of the problem and when trying to set yourself up for effective solutions is to find different ways of stating the problem. You might find a larger underlying problem, or just different aspects of the problem that could be attacked. If you have a large group working on the problem it can be very effective to give different 'how to' statements of the problem to each of several sub-groups, and that way develop a rich range of solutions. The techniques in this unit are useful in providing a range of problem statements.

Do try out the exercises as you go. Put them off until later and you probably won't ever do them. Read through the techniques. Make notes about how and when you can use them. And make sure you give them a try in the next appropriate forum.

## Unit books

*No Logo* by Naomi Klein is a remarkable analysis of what's wrong with globalization, examining the implications of the domination of branding and the global business ethic. If that sounds a turn-off, don't turn away – it is a fascinating book that could well change your views on business. It's particularly apt reading when looking at ways of seeing a problem differently as this is exactly what Klein does to the problem of making global business acceptable.

You can find more information on our unit books, or buy them, from our support site: www.cul.co.uk/crashcourse.

## Web links

Web sites that take a different look at business can be found at www.cul.co.uk/crashcourse.

# 6.1 Exercise/Technique: Excellence

**Preparation** Basic 'how to' statement.
**Running time** Five minutes.
**Resources** None.
**Frequency** As required.

Formulate a first shot 'how to' statement for your problem. Don't put a lot of effort into this – just let it flow. Most 'how to' statements are initially quite restrained. The object of this exercise is to push them into excellence.

Whatever the nature of your statement, make it more extreme. For example, if you said 'how to increase productivity', make it 'how to have the best productivity in our industry'. If you said 'increase sales', make it 'increase sales by 100 per cent'. Look for excellence in your statement. However high the aspirations of your rough 'how to' statement, make them even higher.

Now consider the implications. It may be enough to say that the extreme 'how to' should be your goal. Often excellence is both desirable and achievable. In some cases, though, you might have made a 'how to' statement which is either impractical or undesirable. For example, you might have gone from 'how to dominate our market' to 'how to dominate the world'. In such a case, consider how you might modify your original statement to make it more like the extreme – have more of the qualities of the extreme – without the negative or impossible aspects.

As an exercise, try out this technique on a current problem you have.

**Feedback** This is a technique that shouldn't be used too often. Most particularly, don't be thinking of using this technique when you originally come up with your rough 'how to' statement. If you have already decided to use it, make sure it isn't part of your original formulation. Don't be tempted to come up with an extreme statement initially. Start with an eminently practical statement, then push for excellence.

Over many years of running creativity sessions I am always surprised how difficult it is to push for excellence. I emphasize how important it is to be as crazy as you like and refine afterwards, as it's easy to inject practicality but not easy to add excitement and originality. And then out come a tentative set of problems. Reach for the stars.

**Outcome** A major reason for employing creativity techniques is to go beyond the ordinary, the everyday, to the extraordinary. This technique ensures that your goal is not too mundane, too easily achievable. It is very effective at tuning up a direction to your best advantage.

**Variations** There are no significant variations. If you aren't getting much result, try a second iteration – push your excellence statement to even greater extremes and consider the consequences.

| | |
|---|---|
| Culture | ✪✪✪ |
| Techniques | ✪✪✪ |
| Personal development | ✪✪✪ |
| Mental energy | ✪ |
| Fun | ✪✪ |

# 6.2 Technique: Restatement

**Preparation** Initial 'how to' statement.
**Running time** Five minutes.
**Resources** Flip charts.
**Frequency** As required.

This technique uses a specific approach to get the participants to recast the 'how to' statement that is used to initialize the process. As such, it only works as a second phase of question development rather than in generating an initial question.

Begin by asking the members of the group to produce at least one restatement each of the problem that uses none of the nouns, verbs or adjectives in the original and that, ideally, has a radically different slant on the problem.

These restatements can be collected by asking for them and listing them on the flip chart, or by giving flip chart paper to the group and ask them to write up their own, with four or five people sharing a sheet. The first works best with small groups and has the advantage of everyone hearing everyone else's restatement. The second is more efficient when the group is large but it does require you to allow time for perusal of the results.

**Feedback** This is a very simple technique and may seem like a statement of the obvious when you start. It is worth emphasizing the requirement for a radically different slant and stressing the strength that this will add to the final outcome.

**Outcome** Despite being very basic, this works remarkably well as a way of broadening the range of questions being attacked. You will find a high degree of overlap in the 'how to' statements generated and you may want to remove duplications. If you do, be sure to get group buy-in to this as they may see subtle differences between statements that look identical to you.

**Variations** You can obviously vary how long you spend and how you collect the output but the basic technique doesn't lend itself to significant change.

| | |
|---|---|
| Culture | ✪✪ |
| Techniques | ✪✪✪ |
| Personal development | ✪ |
| Mental energy | ✪✪ |
| Fun | ✪✪ |

# 6.3 Exercise/Technique: Versatile coat hangers

**Preparation** None.
**Running time** Five minutes.
**Resources** Notepad.
**Frequency** Once.

Spend two minutes jotting down everything you can do with a coat hanger. Don't go into detail, just a set of bullet-point headings.

Now spend another two minutes noting everything you can't do with a coat hanger.

Look at the two lists. It's usually easier to come up with more things you can't do than things you can. This isn't surprising when you consider what a very small part of 'everything' a coat hanger occupies.

Finally, pick a couple of your 'can't' entries and turn them around. Assume that you can do absolutely anything with a coat hanger. How can you make this use possible? You might not succeed, but you will be surprised how often it is possible.

**Feedback** I often use this exercise in creativity seminars, and usually manage to defeat most attempts at finding an impossible use. In finding things you can't do, you are limited by your own assumptions. For example, it was never stated that the coat hanger was a wire one, or that you couldn't process it in some way. So for instance, if the challenge is to drink it, the coat hanger could be made of ice – just melt it and drink it. Another popular one is to have sex with it: luckily, people make excellent coat hangers. About the only use I normally concede defeat on is using it as an effective car aerial.

**Outcome** The more you practise overcoming your personal restraints on creativity, the better you will be at developing creative solutions.

**Variations** Use this exercise as a technique to help groups think more creatively. If you had trouble disproving your negative arguments, try again now you realize that the coat hanger can be made of anything, processed in any way, human, animal, vegetable, mineral – the choice is yours.

| | |
|---|---|
| Culture | ✪✪✪✪ |
| Techniques | ✪✪ |
| Personal development | ✪✪✪✪ |
| Mental energy | ✪✪✪ |
| Fun | ✪✪✪ |

# 6.4 Technique: Mud slinging

**Preparation** None.
**Running time** Five to ten minutes.
**Resources** None.
**Frequency** As required.

This technique is particularly applicable to defining appropriate 'how to' statements in product and service development. All that is needed is to agree on the company's most successful product or service and to throw mud at it. In other words, to generate areas in which this star product is actually useless.

Having slung mud at this product you then have available to you a whole list of areas of development that would make the product better. All you need to do is to rephrase them as 'how to' statements.

You may find that with many of the criticisms generated you are not actually talking about enhancements to the existing product that was your starting point, but that an entirely new product would be needed to address the requirement. This is a good thing in that it broadens your areas of questioning.

**Feedback** This is a fun and high-energy exercise. It is extremely good at generating new areas of investigation when developing a product. It is pretty well useless at tackling other sorts of problems.

**Outcome** The problem you are most likely to face in using this technique is volume. You will generate a huge number of alternative questions and approaches and you will need to line up a selection process of some sort to whittle these down. See Unit 23 for some useful techniques.

**Variations** Remember that product and service can be very broad terms. If you don't produce anything physical or if you are an internal service department within an organization then you will be able to adapt the definitions to suit you. If you really can't think of anything you produce or any service you provide then you should be thinking of whether you really have a role to fulfil or not.

| | |
|---|---|
| Culture | ✪✪✪✪ |
| Techniques | ✪✪✪ |
| Personal development | ✪✪✪ |
| Mental energy | ✪✪✪ |
| Fun | ✪✪✪ |

# 6.5 Exercise: Going down

**Preparation** None.
**Running time** Five minutes.
**Resources** None.
**Frequency** Once.

You may have heard this problem before. Don't stop reading; we are going beyond the usual conclusion. Every morning a man gets into the lift (elevator) on the floor of the high rise block he lives in and rides down to ground level. Every evening he comes home, gets in the lift, rides up to the tenth floor (four below his own), gets out and walks the rest of the way. Why?

If you haven't heard it before, think about it for a while before reading on.

Now an extra piece of information. The man was easily tall enough to reach every button in the lift. Think about the problem some more.

**Feedback** Last chance to think.

There are many solutions. The man could want a little exercise, but four floors of stairs are enough. He might suspect his wife of adultery and want to surprise her. He could stop off at a friend's four floors below for a drink each evening. And so on. But what if he actually *has to* get out rather than wants to – surely the conventional solution is now the only one? No. The higher lift buttons could be broken. The owners of the building could charge for each floor you ride up. He only has a ten-floor ticket, so he has to walk the rest. Or there is building work going on in the afternoon which restricts the travel of the lift. Feel like arguing with these solutions? The traditional solution is equally frail – whenever there is someone else in the lift he can get to the right floor.

**Outcome** There are two issues here. The first is that a late-arriving piece of information can totally change our knowledge base – and it's difficult to give up an established position. The second is to observe just how many solutions there are – and how conditions can be used to question any idea, however valid.

**Variations** Whenever you come across puzzles like this, look for alternative solutions.

| | |
|---|---|
| Culture | ✪✪✪ |
| Techniques | ✪✪ |
| Personal development | ✪✪✪✪ |
| Mental energy | ✪✪ |
| Fun | ✪✪✪ |

# Unit 7: Incremental creativity – step change techniques

It's easy to be misled into thinking that creativity is all about ground-breaking changes, after which the world will never be the same again. It's certainly true that this is one aspect of creativity, and tends to hit the headlines, but it's certainly not the only opportunity for innovation. The techniques in this unit will usually result in smaller step changes, incremental enhancement – but are no less important because of that.

Do try out the exercises as you go. Put them off until later and you probably won't ever do them. Read through the techniques. Make notes about how and when you can use them. And make sure you give them a try in the next appropriate forum.

## Unit books

One of the greatest business books ever written, Ricardo Semler's *Maverick!*, details how a Latin American engineering firm was turned around by transforming it from a place of distrust and doubt to one where the open flow of information and genuine trust made it possible for everyone in the company to make a transformed contribution. Trust is a fundamental requirement for change, as Semler found (initially to his cost), whether dealing with incremental step change or huge leaps.

You can find more information on our unit books, or buy them, from our support site: www.cul.co.uk/crashcourse.

## Web links

Further Web references on the subjects of trust and managing change can be found at www.cul.co.uk/crashcourse.

# 7.1 Exercise/Technique: The level chain

**Preparation** None.
**Running time** Five minutes.
**Resources** None.
**Frequency** As required.

*The level chain* works by taking a random chain of items, products, concepts – whatever fits the requirement – and using it generate fresh ideas. Start with something to do with the area you are looking for a new idea in – or something completely different. Then generate a chain of objects or concepts which are either more general (at a higher level) or more specific (at a lower level). Whenever your chain makes you think of an idea, stop and note it down. For example, a chain looking for a new telecoms product, starting at phone, might go (up to) communicator (down to) politician (down to) bench (up to) seating. Now an idea strikes. Why not have an armchair with a built-in phone, so you can chat comfortably?

It is important that the participants don't analyse during *The level chain*. Let the chain flow in free association, stopping whenever something attracts your attention. Chains should be quick – in five minutes it should be possible to generate five to ten chains. Try out the level chain now to develop a new product for your business (or, if that's not possible, for, say, a paint manufacturer).

**Feedback** *The level chain* is very easy to pick up once it has been demonstrated, but it is essential to have an example. If pulling together the output from a number of individuals, it is best to get some verbal feedback on where their chains went, but only note down the outcomes.

**Outcome** This is a superb vehicle for generating new ideas, products and services. It almost invariably comes up with a good range of original possibilities, and is a good exercise to persuade participants of the value of creativity techniques.

**Variations** *The level chain* is essentially individual, but can be stretched in various ways. Used in a group, it is best if each person conducts their own chains, then shares the outcome. An alternative approach, which works particularly well using e-mail, is for one individual to start a chain, then send it around a distribution list, with each recipient adding one item to the chain.

| | |
|---|---|
| Culture | ✪ |
| Techniques | ✪✪✪✪ |
| Personal development | ✪✪ |
| Mental energy | ✪✪ |
| Fun | ✪✪✪ |

# 7.2 Exercise/Technique: Car and goats

**Preparation** None.
**Running time** Ten minutes.
**Resources** None.
**Frequency** Once.

Here's a problem to tax your creative thinking. You are a game show contestant and reach the final round. The game is simple. The host shows you three doors. Behind one is a sports car. Behind the other two are goats. You choose a door, and win whatever is behind it.

You choose a door. Before you open it, the host (who knows what is behind every door) opens one of the other doors and shows you a goat. She now gives you the chance to stick with the door you first chose, or to change your choice. What should you do? Stick, change – or does it not matter what you do?

**Feedback** If you haven't already got an answer, jot one down now.

When I perform this exercise with a group, I conduct a survey at this point. Most say it doesn't matter, some say stick, a few say move. Only the few are correct. You double your chances of winning by changing. This does not seem logical. After all, of the remaining doors one is a car and one is a goat. Surely there's a 50:50 chance?

The reasoning is this. Initially you have a one in three chance of guessing the correct door, so there's a two in three chance that the car is behind one of the others. The host shows you one of the other doors it isn't behind, but there's still a two in three chance you guessed wrong. If that doesn't make sense, read it a few more times. Don't worry if it still seems crazy – when this puzzle was first published there were angry letters from professors denying the truth of it. But you can prove it with a computer – changing is the right thing to do.

**Outcome** Here's a situation where common sense is outraged: it shows how intuition should be treated carefully and so can make a great group technique when dealing with the assumptions we all make. Don't use it with others unless you are totally confident about its working yourself.

**Variations** If you can't accept the result, let it simmer for a few days, then look at it again.

| | |
|---|---|
| Culture | ✪✪✪ |
| Techniques | ✪ |
| Personal development | ✪✪✪✪ |
| Mental energy | ✪✪✪ |
| Fun | ✪✪✪ |

# 7.3 Technique: Attributes

**Preparation** Getting hold of catalogues.
**Running time** Ten minutes.
**Resources** A selection of catalogues with a wide range of products in them.
**Frequency** As required.

This technique makes use of the fact that your problem is actually made up of a series of sub-elements. Even if you are dealing with product development rather than idea generation or problem solving you still have a series of attributes attached to the product.

Take a selection of catalogues and find a way of randomly selecting products. Letting the catalogue fall open in your hands will suffice. Take a few products (three to six) and select a single attribute from each. Attributes could be the colour, the texture, the power, the functions or anything else about them that takes your fancy.

Now combine those attributes into the solution to your problem. If you are dealing with new product development this is relatively easy to do. If you are solving a problem it seems harder, but isn't. You simply need to build those attributes into your solution in the way that we have used associations elsewhere (see Chapter 1, page 10 for more information). Think how your solution could have these attributes. Think what other things you know (not just the items in the catalogues) have these attributes. Make use of your experience.

**Feedback** Whilst ideally suited to product development, this technique works well for more general problem solving. It often proves fun, particularly if you are not altogether random in your product selection and engineer some odd combinations. Be prepared to re-select if the combination is too tame.

**Outcome** You will find some new avenues of thought with this technique and have a laugh or two on the way.

**Variations** *Attributes* works well with teams or individuals. If using with teams, one spin that you could put on it is to compete to see how many attributes can be built into one solution. With more time, an intermediate phase, especially effective with groups, can be to construct a picture of something (anything) which embodies all these attributes and use this to spark off your thinking.

| | |
|---|---|
| Culture | ✪ |
| Techniques | ✪✪✪✪ |
| Personal development | ✪✪ |
| Mental energy | ✪✪ |
| Fun | ✪✪ |

# 7.4 Exercise/Technique: Found story

**Preparation** None.
**Running time** Ten minutes.
**Resources** Notepad.
**Frequency** Once.

Spend a couple of minutes taking a walk outside (or around a building if outside isn't practical). Find an object you can take back to a quiet place. It can be anything – just something portable that catches your eye.

Now take a minute to think of a context for this object. It should be something totally incongruous. Think of the object in a sensationalist newspaper headline. For example, it might be 'the nutcrackers from outer space', or 'the wallet that ate my hamster' or 'my personal organizer is having a baby'.

Finally take five minutes to write a short story on this theme. It should take the context entirely seriously. It can be in the form of a newspaper article or a narrative. Don't spend ages thinking about it – force yourself to write, whatever drivel you produce.

**Feedback** Despite appearances, this isn't about creative writing – it's the thought process that's important, not the writing. Creativity is all about generating new ideas and concepts which somehow don't quite fit with current thinking. At a later date they will be absorbed into the mainstream, but initially they will often seem odd. Often, before you can make the mental leaps prompted by a technique, you need the ability to detach yourself from a conventional train of thought. Exercises like this are designed to do just that.

**Outcome** By chipping away at your normal, blinkered view of the world, this technique improves your capability to be creative.

**Variations** There are almost an infinite number of contexts in which you can put any object. These can range from the mundane ('the stone that wasn't there yesterday') to the unusual ('the stone that got a degree from Cambridge'). It's a good idea to keep the context unusual, because that helps force a creative viewpoint.

| | |
|---|---|
| Culture | ✪✪✪ |
| Techniques | ✪✪ |
| Personal development | ✪✪✪ |
| Mental energy | ✪✪ |
| Fun | ✪✪✪ |

# 7.5 Exercise/Technique: Technical creativity

**Preparation** A problem statement.
**Running time** Ten minutes.
**Resources** Notepad
**Frequency** Once.

For this exercise we need a problem statement or idea requirement. It needn't be a real problem, but it doesn't do any harm if it is. State the problem in a single sentence beginning 'how to'. For instance, 'how to increase throughput of the production line.'

Turn a piece of paper on its side and write the problem statement across the middle of the page. Ring the key words in the sentence. In this case they would be 'increase', 'throughput', and 'production line'. From each of these ringed words or phrases, draw lines with alternatives, opposites, or just things they make you think of. For instance, 'increase' could generate 'decrease', 'throughput' could generate 'cat flap' and 'production line' could generate 'chorus line'. Each ringed word will normally generate several alternatives.

Finally, try using different words in the problem statement. What might you do to decrease the catflap of the production line, or increase the throughput of the chorus line? Don't worry if the result sounds nonsensical – think of the possibilities. What does it imply for your problem? Some catflaps, for example, are one-way doors. Are there one-way parts of the production line which could be reversed to increase productivity?

**Feedback** Like many of the idea generation techniques that will feature in the following units, this technique is equally valuable as an exercise to develop your personal creativity and a technique to use to solve a real problem. Try it out as an exercise now, but then make sure it's part of your mental toolkit for future use.

**Outcome** When used as a technique, the benefit is to generate a new idea or to solve a problem. As an exercise it has value in encouraging a different way of looking at the world, and hence a more creative frame of mind.

**Variations** None.

| | |
|---|---|
| Culture | ✪ |
| Techniques | ✪✪✪✪ |
| Personal development | ✪✪ |
| Mental energy | ✪✪ |
| Fun | ✪✪ |

# Unit 8: Distortion – idea generation techniques that modify the nature of the problem

We have already seen how the assumptions we make about a problem can be fundamental in limiting the solutions we can generate. The set of techniques in this unit, many of them classics developed by the father of the theory of creativity Alex Osborn, change or distort the nature of the problem to make it possible to develop startling new solutions.

Do try out the exercises as you go. Put them off until later and you probably won't ever do them. Read through the techniques. Make notes about how and when you can use them. And make sure you give them a try in the next appropriate forum.

## Unit books

Much of the focus of this course is on the use of techniques to enable new ideas to be generated, but sometimes it is necessary to distort not just the problem but the culture in which we are attempting to be creative. Unless there is an organizational culture that supports creativity, it doesn't matter how good the ideas, they won't be successfully implemented. *Creativity and Innovation for Managers* by Brian Clegg concentrates on the cultural and organizational aspects of enhancing creativity.

You can find more information on our unit books, or buy them, from our support site: www.cul.co.uk/crashcourse.

## Web links

Links providing more information on Alex Osborn and the development of creativity techniques can be found at www.cul.co.uk/crashcourse.

# 8.1 Technique: Challenging assumptions

**Preparation** None.
**Running time** Fifteen minutes.
**Resources** None.
**Frequency** As required.

Creativity is all about breaking unwarranted assumptions. This technique, one of the oldest in the creativity armoury, does so directly. Consider your problem or requirement. What is the prime assumption in it? What is absolutely essential, absolutely key to the requirement? Now, consider what would happen if this assumption weren't true. For example, if you were trying to improve the profitability of an accountancy firm, how would you do it if the company didn't employ any accountants? If you were trying to come up with a new wall covering, what would you do if you weren't allowed to use any colours? Or attach them to walls?

Once you have assessed the implications of your switch of assumption, feed the results back into your problem. Okay, you can actually have colours in your wall coverings, but what did you discover by looking at the possibilities without colouring? How could you apply these possibilities (with or without colours)? How could you modify them to fit your market?

**Feedback** Like many techniques, the hardest part here is the leap back from the implications of the broken assumption to the real problem. This gets much easier with practice – in fact, we recommend that you practise these techniques whether or not you have a specific problem, just to make the associations easier. See page 10 in Chapter 1 for more detail on making associations.

**Outcome** It isn't always possible to identify a key assumption, but it is amazing how often the result of relaxing one is to totally open up the problem, making solutions plentiful.

**Variations** Only work on one assumption at a time, but if after a couple of minutes you are hitting a brick wall with a particular assumption, try another one. Most problems will actually have several key assumptions. Try to make the assumptions specific rather than woolly and generalized. With a larger team, consider splitting into two or three subgroups, each using a different assumption.

| | |
|---|---|
| Culture | ✪✪✪✪ |
| Techniques | ✪✪✪✪ |
| Personal development | ✪✪✪ |
| Mental energy | ✪✪ |
| Fun | ✪✪ |

# 8.2 Exercise/Technique: Distortion

**Preparation** None.
**Running time** Fifteen minutes.
**Resources** None.
**Frequency** As required.

Most problems have clear dimensions. They might be spatial, numerical or time oriented. For example, if we wanted to improve a supermarket's checkouts, dimensions might include number of counters, number of staff, number of customers, size of checkout and time the checkout was open.

In this exercise, you will take a key dimension of your problem and distort it. Make it much bigger, or much smaller than it currently is. In the checkout example you might look at the implications of having one checkout or 1,000. Having one customer or a million. Having checkouts the size of a matchbox or the size of a warehouse. Opening a checkout for one second or one year at a time. Don't try to cover everything – choose one dimension and stick with it. As an exercise, try this out right now on the supermarket example.

When you have noted down the implications of the distortion, look back at the real world. For example, if you had chosen a matchbox checkout, you could use a direct output from the distortion – smaller checkouts just for baskets, making more space. Or you can look at an implication like having tiny staff. In the real world, tiny staff would mean lots of room behind the checkout. Is the space given to the employee getting in the way of giving good service? Could a change in space or layout improve things? And so on.

**Feedback** With some problems, usually the very people-oriented, it is difficult to find an appropriate dimension. If so, try another technique. It is also possible that the dimension chosen doesn't work very well. Choose another, but make sure you have really examined the possibilities first – don't skip around just because the distortion seems uncomfortable; it is supposed to.

**Outcome** When this technique works well, it works very well, because the dimension selected was a major restraint in your thinking.

**Variations** Resist the inclination to handle multiple distortions in a single group, but with multiple teams it is well worth parcelling out the distortions to get a wider range of suggestions.

| | |
|---|---|
| Culture | ✪✪ |
| Techniques | ✪✪✪✪ |
| Personal development | ✪✪ |
| Mental energy | ✪✪ |
| Fun | ✪✪ |

# 8.3 Exercise: Birthday bonanza

**Preparation** None.
**Running time** Five minutes.
**Resources** None.
**Frequency** Once.

Spend a few moments thinking about this.

There are 365 days in a year (forgetting leap years for the moment). If you were offered a straight bet on whether or not there will be at least two people in a group of 30 with the same birthday (date, but not year), should you accept it?

What would you say was the break-even number of people you would need in a group so there was a 50:50 chance of having two people with the same birthday?

**Feedback** If you haven't already got an answer, try to jot one down now. Don't read any further.

Last chance to consider your answer.

Remarkably, the number is quite low. With 30 people there is a roughly 2 in 3 chance of a match – the break-even number is around 23. This doesn't seem right, because the numbers involved are so large. Think of it like this. With two people, there is a 364/365th chance of not being a match. With three people, there is a 363/365th chance of the new person not having the same as the other two, but we then multiply the two together to get the chance of having no matches at all. As each extra person is added, another fraction is added to the multiplication, resulting in a surprisingly quick reduction in odds. If you don't believe it, try it in practice.

**Outcome** Probability is often counter-intuitive. It requires just the same approach of coming at a problem from a different direction. For example, in probability, we normally calculate the chances of something happening by multiplying together the chances of the component parts not happening and subtracting from one – a sort of backward logic.

**Variations** Look for other opportunities to apply backward logic when presented with problems.

| | |
|---|---|
| Culture | ✪✪✪ |
| Techniques | ✪ |
| Personal development | ✪✪✪✪ |
| Mental energy | ✪✪ |
| Fun | ✪✪✪ |

# 8.4 Technique: Reversal

**Preparation** None.
**Running time** Fifteen minutes.
**Resources** None.
**Frequency** As required.

*Reversal* is the extreme case of *Distortion*. Here, instead of taking an aspect of the problem and distorting it, we turn the problem inside out to actually reverse what we are trying to do. For example, if the requirement were to improve the company's position in a published league table, reversal would be to think 'what could we do to make our position in the league table worse?'.

Spend five minutes brainstorming ideas to actively negate your 'how to' statement. Then look at the implications of the idea you have generated. Worryingly often, these will be practices that are actually undertaken in your company. A classic example is the problem 'how to improve communications within our company'. Many of the suggestions for 'how to make communications fail in our company' seem already to be under way in many large companies. One outcome, therefore, is to modify or stop these existing practices. Other deductions will be more indirect, looking at the implications of the negative suggestions. For example, fitting a muzzle (to stop communications) may make you think of someone holding a mobile phone to their face.

**Feedback** Make sure that you are prepared to go beyond the obvious, both in the negative suggestions and how these are applied back to the real problem. It's easy simply to list the obvious positive ideas in reverse, then turn them around again. But you are looking for something more than the obvious when using creativity techniques.

**Outback** This is not a good technique for new product development, but it is great for overcoming obstacles and other aspects of dealing with general problems.

**Variations** With a group you can split the team into 'bad guys', looking to make the proposition fail, and 'good guys' looking to reverse the bad guys' ideas and convert them into something useful. This can be made into a challenge – try to find something so negative that the 'good guys' can't use it.

| | |
|---|---|
| Culture | ✪✪ |
| Techniques | ✪✪✪✪ |
| Personal development | ✪✪ |
| Mental energy | ✪✪ |
| Fun | ✪✪✪ |

# 8.5 Technique: Size matters

**Preparation** None.
**Running time** Ten minutes.
**Resources** Flip chart.
**Frequency** As required.

Many of the restrictions in your thinking about your company originate from its size. This technique overcomes that by changing your image of your company.

Once you have a clear problem statement, move on to discussing it in the context of the size of your company. If you were much bigger than all of your competitors and you dominated the industry, what solutions would then be available to you that are not now? What changes would have to occur in the company to allow such an industry domination? Is it these changes that would bring about the solution or merely size?

An alternative, particularly for large organizations, is to consider this: if you created a small start-up company to handle this problem, what solutions would be available to them that are not available to your current organization? What gets in the way that a start-up doesn't face? What would they be doing and how would they go about doing it?

Having discussed this aspect of size and having generated some solutions, try to bring them back to reality. What aspects of these solutions could your existing company put into place? If being small/large is such an advantage, what techniques could you use to achieve some of these benefits?

**Feedback** This technique attacks one aspect of the assumptions that we make about our organizations. Make sure that the participants think themselves as much as possible into a small/large company mentality.

**Outcome** One interesting possibility is that the solution actually is to create a start-up, either as a wholly independent company or a subsidiary. This catch-all solution is increasingly being employed to overcome otherwise insoluble problems.

**Variations** Naturally size is only one limiting factor and you could substitute any other for it. Be aware that there is a great deal that comes with company size and that many of the other aspects that you might substitute for it could be encompassed within this dimension.

| | |
|---|---|
| Culture | ✪✪✪ |
| Techniques | ✪✪✪✪ |
| Personal development | ✪✪ |
| Mental energy | ✪✪ |
| Fun | ✪✪ |

# Unit 9: Pure energy – injecting oomph

Energy is an essential for creativity. Trying to be creative when you are lacking energy (we all have times of day when this is true), or trying to get a group to be creative when it is low in energy is simply asking for trouble. These techniques are designed to inject energy into a group and get them into a more creative state.

Do try out the exercises as you go. Put them off until later and you probably won't ever do them. Read through the techniques. Make notes about how and when you can use them. And make sure you give them a try in the next appropriate forum.

## Unit books

Energy is crucial to creativity – but there is one dangerous trap awaiting those who equate creativity with frantic activity. Too much haste can result in the collapse of creativity. When the brain operates under pressure it resorts to well-trodden paths. Explore *Hare Brain, Tortoise Mind* by Guy Claxton to get a better understanding of the difference between energy and haste.

You can find more information on our unit books, or buy them, from our support site: www.cul.co.uk/crashcourse.

## Web links

One of the best ways to inject energy into yourself is to do something completely different. Try going for a short walk – or explore some of the Web links we suggest for livening up the mind at www.cul.co.uk/crashcourse.

# 9.1 Technique: Spoon and string

**Preparation** For each team, a dessert spoon firmly attached to a long length of string (2 metres per team member).
**Running time** Five minutes.
**Resources** Spoons, string, enough room for the participants all to stand up in the same space.
**Frequency** Once for any group.

Give each team a spoon and string. In a race against time, the winning team is the first one to have the spoon tied to the other end of the string (putting the team in a bundle), with the string passing up and down alternate sets of clothes of the team members. The string must pass through at least one upper body garment and at least one lower body garment to comply. Warn the participants of the dangers of friction burns if the string is pulled through too fast.

**Feedback** Have small prizes for each team which manages to compete the exercise, with slightly less interesting prizes each time, so there is an incentive to keep going when the first team has finished. Feel free to comment both during and after the exercise on any interesting positions, use of garments, strange comments made by the participants and so forth. As it is much easier to get the spoon down than up, ask how the team decided who would pass it up their garments.

**Outcome** This is a high energy exercise, but qualifies as an ice-breaker because it brings the participants into very close physical contact, and also because the need to think about just where the string is passing inevitably breaks down some of the coldness and barriers which may be present initially. The ice-breaking effect continues as the string is removed. At one time a popular party ice-breaker, this is just as effective with business groups.

**Variations** Particularly sadistic operatives of this exercise might like to keep the spoons in a refrigerator until shortly before starting, maximizing discomfort. It is probably advisable not to use a freezer.

| | |
|---|---|
| Culture | ✪✪ |
| Techniques | ✪ |
| Personal development | ✪✪ |
| Mental energy | ✪✪✪✪ |
| Fun | ✪✪✪✪ |

# 9.2 Technique: Piggyback plus

**Preparation** Setting up obstacle course.
**Running time** Five minutes.
**Resources** One blindfold per team; room to set up an obstacle course that one person from each team can go round simultaneously.
**Frequency** Once with any group.

The exercise is a relay piggyback race. The group is split into even-numbered teams (if odd, one person goes twice). Each person either carries one other member of the team on their back, or is carried, around an obstacle course. When they return to the start, the next pair from their team leaves. The person doing the carrying is blindfolded, leaving the rider to direct them. The blindfold is the baton – the second pair can't leave until the first is back and the second mount has been blindfolded. The obstacle course can be anything from a complex course to simply negotiating the tables and chairs in a meeting room. It doesn't matter if space is tight in places, provided all the teams can race at the same time, and there are places where they can pass each other.

**Feedback** Encourage teams to shout for their riders, building up the atmosphere and making it harder for rider and mount to communicate. A small prize for the winning team will be appreciated. Find out from the successful team how the riders and mounts communicated. Get some feedback from the whole group as to how the exercise felt.

**Outcome** There's lots of movement and noise in this exercise, all conducive to increased energy when later contributing to the session. There is ice-breaking on two levels as well, pulling together the team but also specifically the rider and mount.

**Variations** The easiest variation is the degree of communication between rider and mount. Try the exercise with no speaking allowed. In the basic form, everyone is either a rider or a mount: you could require each person to take both roles. Make sure with this approach that you don't have a heavy team with one very light person in it. You must also make it clear that anyone is free to sit out. For instance, it would be unwise to insist that a pregnant woman took part.

| | |
|---|---|
| Culture | ✪✪ |
| Techniques | ✪ |
| Personal development | ✪✪ |
| Mental energy | ✪✪✪✪ |
| Fun | ✪✪✪✪ |

# 9.3 Exercise: Get another life

**Preparation** Get hold of a business biography book.
**Running time** Fifteen minutes.
**Resources** Book.
**Frequency** Several times a year.

As most of this unit focuses on techniques you can't undertake alone, this exercise is a different style of unit book. A particularly effective inspiration for business creativity is the business biography. The combination of the development of extraordinary businesses with some very strange personalities makes for an exploration of a very different view on life. The aim here isn't to turn you into another Bill Gates, but rather to help see the business world in a different way. Spend around quarter of an hour reading a section from one of these books. Try to do this on a regular basis – you may well find you need to finish the book once you've started: don't fight it.

**Feedback** Reading in the workplace is frowned on, even when the subject is serious business texts, so doing this in working hours may not be a good move. It ought to be – after all, this is probably more educational than many of the courses you may have attended, but the fact is that it is not an acceptable thing to do. That being the case, take the pragmatic view and read it in your lunchtime, or out of business hours.

**Outcome** Business biographies are a particularly effective aid to business creativity because they are readable (being dull is simply a turn-off for creativity) and they push you into a different way of thinking – often incorporating a new sort of energy that just isn't present in your own business life. Recommended.

**Variations** For specifics on finding business biographies, see www.cul.co.uk/books/bcdc1.htm.

| | |
|---|---|
| Culture | ✪✪✪ |
| Techniques | ✪ |
| Personal development | ✪✪✪✪ |
| Mental energy | ✪ |
| Fun | ✪✪✪✪ |

# 9.4 Technique: Sit on my lap

**Preparation** None.
**Running time** Two minutes.
**Resources** Enough space for all the participants to stand in a tight circle.
**Frequency** Once with any group.

Get the whole team standing in a circle, each facing the back of the person beside them (in front of them). Then the whole team simultaneously lowers themselves into a sitting position and sits on the knees of the person behind them. Talk them through this, with a countdown and specific time to sit. Emphasize that it doesn't matter if they've done it before, it still has value.

**Feedback** Many people have seen or done this exercise before. For those that haven't it seems absurd that the group can all be sitting on its own laps and not collapse. For those that have it is still pretty amazing but they will tend to be fairly blasé about it.

**Outcome** This gets people up and about and is also a quick and effective demonstration of trust and interdependence. This exercise simply cannot work if even one person in the group doesn't trust themselves or the group enough to commit to it. If the initial result is to collapse in a heap, have a number of retries – don't give up straight away.

**Variations** A more advanced version of this activity is to have the whole group lean back on themselves. In fact, we've been told that it is possible to have everyone fall back into each other's arms but we haven't tried that because our public liability insurance isn't high enough. After a first go has proved it is possible, the exercise can be extended by putting everyone into the centre of the space, then asking them to repeat the exercise without any speech. If they are finding it difficult or impossible, point out that this does not mean no sound. If it is still failing, give them a minute to talk to each other first, then try without speech. This extension pushes up the creativity factor, making this a good all-round exercise.

| | |
|---|---|
| Culture | ✪✪ |
| Techniques | ✪ |
| Personal development | ✪✪ |
| Mental energy | ✪✪✪✪ |
| Fun | ✪✪✪✪ |

# 9.5 Technique: The paperclip race

**Preparation** Obtain paperclips.
**Running time** Five minutes.
**Resources** Twice as many paperclips as people in the group; enough space for all the participants to stand in two lines.
**Frequency** Once with any group.

Split the group into two. Get them to stand in two rows and give each person two paperclips. The object of the race is to make a chain with the paperclips as quickly as possible. The first person starts the chain, then passes it on to the next. As soon as the chain is completed it must be passed hand-to-hand back to the start of the row. At this point the whole team is to shout 'paperclip' as loudly as possible.

**Feedback** Be careful not to specify whether or not people can join their two paperclips together before they receive the chain. If anyone asks, say you have explained all the rules. Make sure it's clear afterwards that anyone who thought that they had to wait for the chain to reach them before joining their two links was making a personal assumption – these are often a blockage to innovative thought.

**Outcome** The racing aspect gives this exercise considerable excitement. Help the teams to shout encouragement along the way. Standing up, moving around the room, engaging in physical dexterity are all helping to boost energy levels. Give the winning team a bag of sweets to share if you have one.

**Variations** Lots of possibilities here. Give each person more than two paperclips. Once the chain is complete, it is passed back, being unclipped again as it goes. Instead of allocating paperclips to individuals, give the team a big pile of clips and the task of matching in length (exactly) a chain you have made earlier and fixed on the wall. Perhaps most enjoyably, set the teams the task of making a long enough chain to entirely surround their team, with the chain joined to make a circle.

| | |
|---|---|
| Culture | ✪✪ |
| Techniques | ✪ |
| Personal development | ✪✪ |
| Mental energy | ✪✪✪✪ |
| Fun | ✪✪✪ |

# Unit 10: Seeking knowledge – building a personal knowledge base to feed creativity

Developing new ideas is a matter of making new links, new connections, starting from new directions. The ability to make links, to devise new directions is greatly enhanced by having a wide, rich personal knowledge base on which to base your creative thought. You don't have to be an expert in the problem area – in fact, when trying to be creative experts often suffer from a hang-up of knowing what isn't possible, and so limiting their own ideas – but it does help to have as broad and diverse a knowledge base as possible. This exercise-loaded unit will help you out.

Do try out the exercises as you go. Put them off until later and you probably won't ever do them. Read through the techniques. Make notes about how and when you can use them. And make sure you give them a try in the next appropriate forum.

## Unit books

The best way to support your ever-broadening knowledge base is to read very widely. Don't confine yourself to business books. A good mix of fiction and non-fiction is extremely valuable. Even if they aren't your natural taste, science fiction and popular science both provide very effective stimulators to help build your knowledge base.

Recommendations to stretch into these fields are *Surely You're Joking, Mr Feynman* – anecdotes from one the 20th century's top scientists who managed to combine working on the atomic bomb programme with attempting to break into safes – and the fascinating science fiction work *Donnerjack* by Roger Zelazny and Jane Linskold.

You can find more information on our unit books, or buy them, from our support site: www.cul.co.uk/crashcourse.

## Web links

Links to Web sites that can help feed your personal knowledge base can be found at www.cul.co.uk/crashcourse.

# 10.1 Technique: Broken CD

**Preparation** Invent scenario.
**Running time** Five minutes.
**Resources** A stooge.
**Frequency** Once.

Imagine a situation in which you have to complain about something. Persuade a colleague to act as a stooge in trying out this scenario. They are to counter your request. For example, you could be taking back a broken product and demanding a replacement, or asking for a refund in a restaurant. This is a variation on the classic *Broken record* technique. Think of at least half a dozen different ways of asking the same thing. They should be as different as possible without actually varying the outcome. Instead of repeatedly asking the same thing, run round your different phrasing. Probe the other person for aspects of the question that they don't understand.

**Feedback** Sometimes when you are trying to gain knowledge you will be resisted. This could be for three reasons – because the person doesn't know, because he or she simply doesn't want to tell you, or because he or she doesn't understand your question. This exercise gives some practice in dealing with the third possibility, with elements of the second thrown in for good measure. Make sure that you keep your repeated requests low key and friendly. Nod, agree, say 'Yes, I see,' to the other person's reasons for not coming up with the goods – then ask a different way. This technique is best used face-to-face; it's too easy for the other person just to put the phone down. If you find it very difficult, practise some more – it becomes relatively easy and even enjoyable.

**Outcome** It is surprising how often this technique will whittle away resistance and get a result, and it can be less irritating than the pure broken record technique.

**Variations** If there is a genuine circumstance in which you can practise the technique, so much the better. This could be either in the sort of scenario used here (complaint) or when you are trying to get information from reluctant source.

| | |
|---|---|
| Culture | ✪✪✪ |
| Techniques | ✪✪ |
| Personal development | ✪✪✪ |
| Mental energy | ✪✪ |
| Fun | ✪✪✪ |

# 10.2 Exercise: Sense and sensibility

**Preparation** None.
**Running time** Ten minutes.
**Resources** Magazine, notepad.
**Frequency** Once.

How we handle information and transform it into knowledge is very much influenced by our senses. Experts in the knowledge management field, never willing to use a simple word where a complex one will do, refer to these sensory views of the world as modalities.

Get hold of a magazine with reasonably long features (or take one of your own pieces of prose if you regularly write articles). Look through one article. Don't worry about the content of the piece – instead note how it makes use of the modalities: sight, hearing, touch (and motion), taste and smell. See if the writer has a particular bias. Does this give the piece a specific flavour? Could it have an effect on how you react to the article?

**Feedback** It's very difficult to deal with the world without using modalities. Notice how in the previous section, modalities were described as 'sensory views of the world'. The use of the term 'view' is itself a modality. No one actually viewed anything. Similarly, the term 'flavour' was used later on without anything being tasted. You may have to read the article a couple of times, as it is very easy to skip over modalities – they are such a natural part of the language, and often appear as stock phrases (like 'that rings a bell' or 'this needs hands-on management').

**Outcome** The main aim here is to understand how these sensory terms are used to fit information into our understanding. If you can be more aware of the process that is under way you can help to improve your own knowledge management.

**Variations** With a little more time, even if you haven't got a piece of your own prose, write a page or two describing one of your more complex pieces of knowledge in a way that a lay person could understand it. See how you make use of this sensory imagery.

| | |
|---|---|
| Culture | ✪✪✪ |
| Techniques | ✪ |
| Personal development | ✪✪✪✪ |
| Mental energy | ✪✪ |
| Fun | ✪✪ |

# 10.3 Exercise/Technique: The little black book

**Preparation** None.
**Running time** Five minutes.
**Resources** Address book.
**Frequency** Weekly.

Once a week, spend five minutes keeping your address book up to date. Add new business cards. Note any contacts you have made. Try to put in keyword information about the contact, not just bare name and address. Get an e-mail address if possible. Prune out a few people who aren't needed any more. To do this, you need an address book in the first place. The best type is an electronic one on a PC, as you can have as many entries as you like (usually), you can add and delete at will, letting the system sort out the alphabetical order, you can search on anything in the book and you can use categories to lump people together. Don't wait to do this – start the technique now by having a first stab at it.

**Feedback** Remember the hackneyed saying 'it's not what you know, but who you know'. If knowledge is the art of knowing, it's not surprising that managing who you know is valuable to your personal knowledge management. Of course the saying implies that it doesn't matter how clever you are, you can still be overcome by influence and corruption. But there's also a positive side to it. If you accept that you can't know everything (a wise step), you will sometimes need to look to others for help, support and advice. With an up-to-date little black book, containing enough keywords to pull out the right people, you have an instant knowledge support network.

**Outcome** Address books naturally grow out of date. By allocating a small amount of time on a regular basis (best to put it in your diary), you can ensure that this valuable knowledge resource remains current.

**Variations** The essentials for knowledge support are a telephone and e-mail, because there is often an immediacy that can't wait for the post. A specific variant is your little black book of Web sites. If the Web is to be as significant knowledge resource you will need to keep track of important sites.

| | |
|---|---|
| Culture | ✪✪✪✪ |
| Techniques | ✪✪ |
| Personal development | ✪✪✪✪ |
| Mental energy | ✪ |
| Fun | ✪ |

# 10.4 Exercise: All that glisters

**Preparation** None.
**Running time** Five minutes.
**Resources** Notepad.
**Frequency** Once.

Spend a minute jotting down all the regular sources of information you access to keep up to date in your areas of expertise. Include all sorts of media – magazines and journals, TV, radio, newspapers, the Internet, etc. Against each source estimate how much time a week you spend with it.

Do you feel you are totally on top of your subject(s), or are there not enough hours in the day to keep up to date?

If you feel you are being left behind, try this approach. Select a subset of your regular sources which you feel will give a good background. Instead of trying to absorb everything, limit yourself to this background information, but know how to pull in extra information at a moment's notice. See Unit 26 for further techniques and books to help with this.

**Feedback** There has never been such an age of information overload. It's hard enough keeping up with your specialities without having to chase down all the general information needed to make you a well-rounded person. An essential to managing your own state of knowledge is being aware that it is impossible to take in everything. There comes a point where being an information magpie and trying to pick up every little snippet on every possibly relevant topic simply gets in the way. There are some special cases here – it probably is a good thing to be a magpie when it comes to your contacts (see *The little black book* above), but not when you are trying to absorb information.

**Outcome** By understanding that you can't possibly take in everything, finding routes to get enough general background, and establishing the ability to pull in detailed information as and when required without storing it up, you can stay on top of information overload.

**Variations** Consider different ways of getting your information, both background and in-depth. Perhaps there are industry summaries or news summaries that will give you the basics without needing to search through many sources.

| | |
|---|---|
| Culture | ✪✪✪ |
| Techniques | ✪✪ |
| Personal development | ✪✪✪✪ |
| Mental energy | ✪ |
| Fun | ✪✪ |

# 10.5 *Exercise: Programmed thought*

**Preparation** Get a video recorder manual.
**Running time** Ten minutes.
**Resources** Notepad.
**Frequency** Once.

Find the part of a video recorder manual that tells you how to set the timer and phrase the instructions as a set of rules. Limit yourself to these instructions:

```
IF (something is true) THEN
(do something)
END of IF
WHILE (something is true) THEN
(do something)
END of WHILE
```

Put in the END line, so you can see where you have finished. You might like to use a programmer's trick of indenting. Move everything in the 'do something' section to the right, so it's obvious where it begins and ends. Feel free to include 'AND', 'BUT' and 'NOT' in your instructions. You can also extend IF with an alternative statement like OTHERWISE. So part of the result might be:

```
IF the video recorder is switched on THEN
   Press the button to set a new record time
   [Other instructions for setting a new start time]
   IF there is a tape in the recorder AND it is blank THEN
   Press the Timer button
   OTHERWISE
   [etc.]
   END of IF
OTHERWISE
   Switch it on
   Start again
END of IF
```

**Feedback** Either ask someone else to check your rules, or leave them for a while then check them yourself. Have you taken into account every possibility (like putting in a blank tape)? Turning a task into rules shows how complex even a simple action can be – and why computer programs with millions of lines of code often include mistakes.

**Outcome** This is a good way of tackling a badly documented or complex procedure. It can help identify holes in the procedure, but needs several reviews to ensure that there is a good correspondence with reality.

**Variations** Try this approach on any procedure or piece of knowledge involving action (even mental action like decision making). It is best applied to a non-trivial but well-contained area.

| | |
|---|---|
| Culture | ✪✪ |
| Techniques | ✪✪✪ |
| Personal development | ✪✪✪✪ |
| Mental energy | ✪ |
| Fun | ✪✪ |

# Unit 11: Seeing it differently – looking at solutions through different eyes

Bearing in mind how experts can be the last people to be creative (because they know what isn't possible, or at least they think they do), it's not entirely surprising that one of the best ways to generate new ideas is to develop solutions by seeing the problem through fresh eyes. You can do this literally – bring in someone who isn't involved, or virtually by putting yourself into another viewpoint so that you see the problem differently.

Do try out the exercises as you go. Put them off until later and you probably won't ever do them. Read through the techniques. Make notes about how and when you can use them. And make sure you give them a try in the next appropriate forum.

## Unit books

Two very different books on seeing things differently. In the science fiction classic, *Flowers for Algernon*, writer Daniel Keyes sees the world through the eyes of a man with learning difficulties who is treated chemically to reach super intelligence, but then becomes aware that he is reverting to his original state. James Gleick's book *Chaos* provides a fascinating insight into the theory that turns the whole way we look at the world on its head.

You can find more information on our unit books, or buy them, from our support site: www.cul.co.uk/crashcourse.

## Web links

Humour always involves looking at the world in different ways, and the links at www.cul.co.uk/crashcourse provide different insights to humour on the Web.

# 11.1 Technique: Fantasy

**Preparation** None.
**Running time** Ten minutes.
**Resources** None.
**Frequency** As required.

The fantasy technique is the practical application of the daydream. Sit back and say 'wouldn't it be wonderful if...' Imagine that there were no obstacles, no limits to your abilities. What would you do? What would the solution look like? One of the real problems with coming up with a creative solution to a problem is the left brain/right brain split. Whether or not this alleged phenomenon is true, we do seem to separate logical, sequential activity and 'artistic', holistic activity. Creativity often requires a step into the fuzzier right brain – if you can move out of problem solving mode, usually a left-brain activity, and into daydreaming you have a much better chance of reaching a creative solution.

As usual, when you have some results you may need to modify them to make them more practical, or just use them as a stepping-off point which makes you think of a different, but associated, practical solution which still remains creative.

**Feedback** It is absolutely essential to get out of left-brain, problem-solving mode before this technique will work. You may find it helpful to have a two-minute distraction from the problem – glance at the newspaper, go outside, do anything to get off track.

**Outcome** This technique will often not generate a refined solution. Instead it is good at providing a broad sweep of solution space which can then be modified to a final result. Many will find it difficult to lose logicality in a business context. For them, one of the other techniques which more explicitly forces you out of your conventional pattern will be more appropriate.

**Variations** As an alternative approach, try drawing a picture of a solution to your problem. If you've got problems with drawing, or want to make this more a group activity, collect a set of appealing images (catalogues and Sunday supplements are usually a good source), cut them out and make a collage of a solution.

| | |
|---|---|
| Culture | ✪✪ |
| Techniques | ✪✪✪✪ |
| Personal development | ✪✪✪ |
| Mental energy | ✪✪ |
| Fun | ✪✪ |

# 11.2 Technique: Someone else's view

**Preparation** None.
**Running time** Fifteen minutes.
**Resources** List of 'other people'.
**Frequency** As required.

As a big blockage to creativity is tunnel vision, this technique uses another person's opinion to provide a different solution. Pick another person – historical, fictional, topical or just a role (like 'plumber' or 'brain surgeon'). It doesn't matter who, as long as they're a long way from you in experience and outlook. To make it easier, we've provided a list in the appendices (page 234), but feel free to pick someone yourself. You needn't know a lot about this person – just enough to have a caricature of who they are or were.

Now imagine that you are this person. Get under their skin. Spend a few moments getting the feel of being them. Then address your problem. How would your adopted persona deal with the problem? How would they understand (and misunderstand) what it was all about? Get together a good list of ideas from this person's point of view.

Finally, pull the suggestions back to the real world. Are they practical? Could they be modified? What do they make you think of?

**Feedback** It is common for participants to reject a persona because they don't feel comfortable with it, or they feel it's unsuitable, or they have no idea who the person is. Only the last argument is valid. As long as the participant has a vague idea who they are meant to be, the persona will be valuable – and the less 'suitable' for the problem the better.

**Outcome** Provided the participants throw themselves into this technique, it is reliable. Without inhibitions, it is very effective.

**Variations** In a team, each member could take the same person, but it is better if each takes a different one. Team members should think of their ideas separately, then pool them. At a large event with more time, this technique can be enhanced by giving participants the opportunity to dress up, maintaining their persona for a considerable period of time. As a variant, imagine phoning up an old friend with whom you've lost touch and asking for their views.

| | |
|---|---|
| Culture | ✪✪✪ |
| Techniques | ✪✪✪✪ |
| Personal development | ✪✪✪ |
| Mental energy | ✪✪✪ |
| Fun | ✪✪✪ |

# 11.3 Exercise: Get a laugh

**Preparation** Get hold of a business humour book.
**Running time** Fifteen minutes.
**Resources** Book.
**Frequency** Several times a year.

Humour is one of the vital components of creativity. Almost all humour involves taking the familiar and looking at it in a different way – the core of creative inspiration. One of the best ways to enhance your creativity around a business theme is to indulge in some business humour. Get hold of a humorous business book – Scott Adams' *Dilbert* books or Robert Townsend's *Up The Organization* series are a good start. On a regular basis, make sure that you read a chunk of one of these books. It may well be, once you are started, that you find you want to read the whole book. If so, don't fight it. See our support site: www.cul.co.uk/crashcourse for many more business humour books.

**Feedback** Reading in the workplace is frowned on, even when the subject is serious business texts, so having a funny book on your desk in working hours may not be a good move for your career prospects. It ought to be – after all, this is probably more educational than a course that wastes much more of your time – but company culture is unlikely to support it. That being the case, take the pragmatic view and read it in your lunchtime, or out of business hours.

**Outcome** The great thing about a business humour book is that you win on several counts. It is entertaining in its own right. It exposes you to a creative view of the business world, enhancing your own potential creativity, and it points out very specific flaws in business practice that you can learn from. Not bad for one book.

**Variations** For some recommended business humour titles see www.cul.co.uk/books/bcec1.htm.

| | |
|---|---|
| Culture | ✪✪✪ |
| Techniques | ✪ |
| Personal development | ✪✪✪✪ |
| Mental energy | ✪ |
| Fun | ✪✪✪✪ |

# 11.4 Technique: Metaphor

**Preparation** None.
**Running time** Ten to fifteen minutes.
**Resources** None.
**Frequency** As required.

At the heart of all of creativity techniques is the notion that you need to be taken away from your problem to generate creative solutions. Otherwise, you could do so from a standing start without the aid of techniques. Metaphor is powerful because it can be the basis of a whole range of ways of tackling your issues, and because we all use metaphors in our understanding of the world.

At its simplest all you need to do is to generate a metaphor or an analogy for your problem and then work on it. Say the problem is 'how to overtake our main competitor in sales', an obvious metaphor might be 'our problem is like a Grand Prix race'. You could then look at why this was the case, deriving associations from the metaphor. Equally you could use a more obscure metaphor – 'our problem is like a bowl of porridge'. Now the initial task is constructing a set of justifications as to why the metaphor is valid. These can (and should) be as wild and tenuous as you like. Then use these justifications and the metaphor itself to generate associations.

**Feedback** It is often tough to find a metaphor that really represents a problem. This shouldn't be an issue. If an obvious metaphor occurs to you and it is sufficiently different from your problem that it will take you away from it, use it. If one does not occur, use any metaphor and force-fit a relationship. We have often used a list of topics (the random word list in the Appendices, for example) and selected one at random.

**Outcome** Metaphor is at the heart of the creative process. We have frequently run entire sessions based around a single metaphor. These sessions can then use additional techniques within the overall session but the theme remains intact.

**Variations** If working with a group you can split into teams and challenge teams to find metaphors that other teams will be unable to use to generate ideas and then get them to do just that. This is one way of ensuring genuinely creative solutions.

| | |
|---|---|
| Culture | ✪ |
| Techniques | ✪✪✪✪ |
| Personal development | ✪✪✪ |
| Mental energy | ✪✪ |
| Fun | ✪✪ |

# 11.5 Exercise: No time to read

**Preparation** None.
**Running time** Five minutes.
**Resources** Diary.
**Frequency** Once.

Are you one of these people who has 'no time to read'? Whether or not this is the case, try out this exercise. Spend a minute jotting down the amount of reading you do in a month. Don't worry about detail, just go for ballpark guesses. For the purpose of this exercise, we'll just consider books: break them down into novels, business books and other non-fiction. Just estimate the number of books in each category you get through in a month.

Reading books is fundamental to creativity and knowledge enhancement, yet few of us give it enough time. Consider the balance you have. Should you take on another business book a month? Should you double your fiction intake? Check in your diary for opportunities to do a little more reading – and stick to it. A good starting point would be to make sure you take on the unit books for this Crash Course.

**Feedback** Everyone could read more, and 'I just haven't got time' simply isn't an acceptable excuse. All that says is you've got bad time management. Everyone should be able to make time for at least one book in each category a month – most of us many more. Consider time when you could sensibly read: on trains and planes; in your lunchtime; in the evening instead of watching TV; in bed. It might be that you read plenty, but you never read fiction. In that case, you are in danger of having an unbalanced diet. Fiction, especially speculative fiction, is a great way of stretching your imagination. Don't ignore it. Similarly, don't stick to your specialist areas of non-fiction. Explore chaos theory or music to get new insights.

**Outcome** Reading a little more is one of simplest ways of contributing to your knowledge and creativity. Much creativity comes from spotting something in a totally different field that is relevant to your requirement: reading a wide range of topics is the best way to achieve this. Everyone can manage it.

**Variations** None.

| | |
|---|---|
| Culture | ✪✪✪✪ |
| Techniques | ✪ |
| Personal development | ✪✪✪✪ |
| Mental energy | ✪ |
| Fun | ✪✪✪✪ |

# Unit 12:
# A swift kick – random stimuli to generate a new starting point

Our ability to be creative is fenced in by habit and assumptions. When thinking about a particular problem we usually work our way down well-trodden paths, and not surprisingly can find it difficult to come up with totally new ideas. One of the most powerful types of creativity technique uses a random stimulus to jolt our thoughts into a whole new path. Instead of starting from our usual experience, we come at the problem from a different direction.

Because these techniques are so effective, there is a tendency to think they're all you need – but it is easy to become stale when being creative. These techniques are a very valuable part of your toolkit, but should be used in a mix with other techniques.

Do try out the exercises as you go. Put them off until later and you probably won't ever do them. Read through the techniques. Make notes about how and when you can use them. And make sure you give them a try in the next appropriate forum.

## Unit books

The name Edward de Bono is synonymous with creativity in the UK and Australia. The best de Bono book to get a wide picture of his input to the creative process is *Serious Creativity*, which pulls together the contents of many of his other books.

You can find more information on our unit books, or buy them, from our support site: www.cul.co.uk/crashcourse.

## Web links

The Imagination Engineering software supports the main stages of the creative process – clarifying the problem, idea generation, refinement and planning for implementation. A full version of the software (Windows only) is available from our support site. Look also for Web sites that can be used to provide a random stimulus at www.cul.co.uk/crashcourse.

# 12.1 Technique: Random word

**Preparation** None.
**Running time** Ten to fifteen minutes.
**Resources** Word list.
**Frequency** As required.

*Random word* involves choosing a word at random, making as many associations with that word as you are able and then relating those back to your problem. The word that you choose will usually be a noun, but need not be. It will usually be emotive, but need not be. It will certainly bring to mind a range of images and associations.

To choose the word you can use a book or a dictionary and allow it to fall open at random. We prefer using a pre-selected list of suitable words and choosing at random from that. To get you started, there is a list in the appendices (page 232).

**Feedback** *Random word* and other random stimulus approaches are often favourite techniques for good reason. They work and they work well. It is easy to explain the techniques to others and we would almost always use one of them as an early demonstrator of a creativity technique (probably *Random picture* in Unit 1 is best of all for this). Some people want to choose a word that is relevant to their problem. Don't do this. Use a random word – it will turn out to be appropriate.

**Outcome** You will find that alone or in groups you have no trouble engaging with this technique. It will produce results.

**Variations** If working with a group you can make a show of the randomness by getting someone else to choose the word or call out a number to select from the list in the appendices. An alternative source of a random word is to input word-like nonsense into a PC spell checker, then see what emerges.

| | |
|---|---|
| Culture | ✪ |
| Techniques | ✪✪✪✪ |
| Personal development | ✪✪ |
| Mental energy | ✪✪ |
| Fun | ✪✪ |

# 12.2 Exercise/Technique: Cool site

**Preparation** None.
**Running time** Ten minutes.
**Resources** Access to the World Wide Web (ideally visible to all participants).
**Frequency** As required.

Many Internet pages list a 'cool site' – a regularly changing recommendation of something interesting, challenging or just weird. The ever-changing nature of these sites means that they are a useful source of random stimulation. They also provide a whole mix of words, images and even sounds to generate association and stimulation.

As with any reference to the World Wide Web, some of these addresses will be out of date by the time you read this book. You will find up-to-date listings at our support site www.cul.co.uk/crashcourse

Useful sites at the time of printing were:

www.coolsiteoftheday.com
www.coolcentral.com/moment

Or look on Yahoo (www.yahoo.com or www.yahoo.co.uk), click on 'What's New' and look for 'Yahoo Picks', 'Picks of the Week' or 'Cool Links'.

Once you have a site, use it like *Random picture* (Unit 1) to generate associations, then link them back to the problem. Try this one out now as an exercise. Use it on a problem you may have, or try it on 'how to make money out of the Internet'.

**Feedback** To use this process with a group it is advisable to download the site before displaying it. This has three advantages: firstly you know it is suitable, secondly you know it will work and thirdly you know it will be faster. Most modern browsers have the facility to store pages locally.

**Outcome** The nature of the Web means that you are likely to hit on some extremely effective stimulation. Careful editing in advance can enhance this further. As with all forms of random stimulation, don't be tempted to find a site that is relevant to the problem, as this will decrease the effectiveness of the exercise. The aim of editing is to provide more stimulation, not relevance to the problem.

**Variations** If working with a group you can either display a site for everyone to work on or you can use individual PCs for people to find their own stimulation. We have also worked with printouts of Web sites in the past, but these are less fun.

| | |
|---|---|
| Culture | ✪✪ |
| Techniques | ✪✪✪✪ |
| Personal development | ✪✪✪ |
| Mental energy | ✪✪ |
| Fun | ✪✪✪ |

# 12.3 Technique: Found objects

**Preparation** None.
**Running time** Twenty to thirty minutes.
**Resources** None.
**Frequency** As required.

If you are spending anything more than an hour generating ideas, you will find that you hit a lull in focus and energy. You will need frequent breaks to avoid this but another approach is to use a creativity technique that energizes. *Found objects* is an excellent technique for injecting energy and fun into a session and has the advantage that it is great at generating ideas too.

To use it, simply get the group to leave the room and come back with something that they have individually found somewhere else. It could be something as mundane as a cigarette end. We have run sessions where participants have unplugged telephones, stolen a cleaner's trolley, taken pictures off walls and turned up with a whole tree in a pot.

They then need to be able to talk to the rest of their team about the object with emotion and passion. Why is this object important and why does it hold the answer to the problem? This level of passion can be quite funny when the object is a discarded sweet wrapper or a sheet of toilet paper.

As each individual speaks, the rest of the group should be making links back to the problem out of what they hear. They then share these links and build on them to produce solutions.

**Feedback** This technique is most successful when you include in your set-up an implied challenge to find a bizarre or surprising object. It generates a lot of laughter and the energy from this pushes through to the idea session.

**Outcome** The two key outcomes of this technique are a change in the energy level and a collection of original ideas.

**Variations** The technique works best as a small team exercise, but can be used with larger groups split into teams or even by yourself. In practice, though, the whole business feels very artificial when working alone. If you have to do so, you still should express your passion and emotion as most of the associations result from this stage, not from the object itself.

| | |
|---|---|
| Culture | ✪✪ |
| Techniques | ✪✪✪✪ |
| Personal development | ✪✪ |
| Mental energy | ✪✪✪✪ |
| Fun | ✪✪✪✪ |

# 12.4 Technique: Quotations

**Preparation** None.
**Running time** Ten minutes.
**Resources** Dictionary of quotations, paper and pens.
**Frequency** As required.

Look for key words in the problem statement. Use a dictionary of quotations to come up with some choice quotes that involve these key words. There should be at least three and not more than seven. If you can't find the exact key words, consider variants of them. Write the quotations down, ideally on flip chart paper. Put them somewhere anyone involved in the exercise can see them.

Check our support site www.cul.co.uk/crashcourse for online dictionaries of quotations. At the time of writing, www.quoteland.com and www.quoteworld.org were worth a try.

Now look at the quotations. Consider them as advice on solving your problem. Look for suggestions of an idea in what they refer to. Is there something about their words or context that makes you think of a solution?

**Feedback** While belonging to the family of techniques which use a random stimulation, this approach is interesting because it uses key words related to the problem, but the quotations, out of context, will push those original key words in totally different directions. The use of quotations helps creative thinking because there is often humour, ambiguity or simple interest in the remark, all of which will help the creative process.

**Outcome** *Quotations* is a good technique to use with participants who are uncomfortable with creativity techniques, because there is a sense of consulting the wisdom of others, however spurious this may be. The results, however, are certainly not restricted to mundane ideas, as many of the quotations will be derived from a totally different world to that in which the problem exists.

**Variations** Instead of selecting by subject, select by person – think of someone whose opinion you'd like to consult. If the topic is known in advance, the quotations can be pre-written on flip charts to avoid wasting time looking them up. Note that many people are not familiar with dictionaries of quotations and may need some guidance. Online dictionaries of quotations are even better, as a full word search can be used. Rather than selecting the most provocative quotes, an alternative is to choose one at random (second in the list, say), use that one, then choose another.

| | |
|---|---|
| Culture | ✪✪ |
| Techniques | ✪✪✪✪ |
| Personal development | ✪✪✪ |
| Mental energy | ✪ |
| Fun | ✪✪✪ |

# 12.5 *Exercise: An excellent mistake*

**Preparation** Nonc.
**Running time** Ten minutes.
**Resources** Notepad.
**Frequency** Once.

Think back over the last few weeks. Work backwards until you hit something that really went wrong. Having your diary might help spot where it happened. Spend a couple of minutes thinking about what happened. What led up to the error? What was happening around it? What could you learn from it for the future?

**Feedback** Learning from mistakes is a crucial part of building knowledge and gaining creativity. If you are going to be creative, you will make mistakes. If you want to foster expertise, you will get things wrong along the way. Unfortunately, our culture (and especially our business culture) is not very positive about mistakes. Everything from Total Quality Management to the culture of taking the blame suggests that mistakes are wholly bad. But to keep developing, we need to be able accept mistakes, drop everything and start again in a different direction without feeling negative, learning from the experience.

**Outcome** By making learning from your mistakes a natural course, you can build your expertise and make more effective use of your creativity.

**Variations** Consider having a horror log, where you record things that go wrong, and enter some simple lessons for each mistake. This doesn't have to be a full-blown post-mortem; you can do it in a few minutes. Where there's a significant cock-up and you manage to turn things round quickly and effectively, consider a celebration of the disaster. Celebrating failures that you have learnt from can be beneficial.

| | |
|---|---|
| Culture | ✪✪✪✪ |
| Techniques | ✪✪ |
| Personal development | ✪✪✪✪ |
| Mental energy | ✪ |
| Fun | ✪✪ |

# Unit 13:
## Looking somewhere else – taking a good look beyond the obvious

It shouldn't be any surprise by now that it can be very valuable when trying to solve a problem to look elsewhere. Instead of looking directly at your problem, looking away from it can be a great way to generate new ideas, whether you are going to see how others have dealt with a similar problem or even look outward from the problem's own viewpoint.

Do try out the exercises as you go. Put them off until later and you probably won't ever do them. Read through the techniques. Make notes about how and when you can use them. And make sure you give them a try in the next appropriate forum.

## Unit books

American writer Gene Wolfe has an unparalleled ability to write books in which the story-line takes a look beyond the obvious. Any book by Gene Wolfe will demonstrate this, but try *Castleview* as a powerful example. The support site includes other Gene Wolfe options.

You can find more information on our unit books, or buy them, from our support site: www.cul.co.uk/crashcourse.

# 13.1 Technique: It's a steal

**Preparation** May require mobility.
**Running time** Thirty minutes.
**Resources** Competitor information, World Wide Web access.
**Frequency** Once for any group.

In an attempt to maintain company morale, it is not uncommon to give the impression that there is nothing to learn from your competitors, that 'we' are simply the best at everything. This is a serious mistake. For the first five minutes of the exercise, list who your competitors are. Consider general competitors of your company, and specific competitors around the problem area. Consider unconnected companies who could be competitors, but don't happen to do that sort of business right now.

With your competitor portfolio in mind, spend a while on research. Check out any information you have on the competitor and anything there may be about them on the World Wide Web. If your business makes it practical to visit a competitor's premises, and you have the time, do so. Always be looking with your specific problem in mind. What have they done? What can you steal (ideas, not products)? What can you improve on? Is there anything they have done in a different field that is applicable to your problem?

**Feedback** The aim here is not to copy, but to come up with something different, inspired by a combination of your problem and your competitors' actions. It is fine to reuse a concept or a feature that you feel you ought to have, but always be looking for that something extra that the opposition suggests, rather than duplication.

**Outcome** Sometimes this technique will result in incremental improvements rather than major enhancements, but this is by no means always the case.

**Variations** Try looking at totally different companies. Look for inspiration in the way they have handled a similar problem area. For example, a software company looking to package its products differently so they stand out on the shelf might want to look at a travel company, a manufacturer of washing powder and a car showroom.

| | |
|---|---|
| Culture | ✪✪✪✪ |
| Techniques | ✪✪✪ |
| Personal development | ✪✪✪ |
| Mental energy | ✪✪ |
| Fun | ✪ |

# 13.2 *Exercise/Technique: Inside view*

**Preparation** None.
**Running time** Ten minutes.
**Resources** None.
**Frequency** As required.

In this technique you will be getting into the heart of the problem – in fact, imagining you are part of the problem itself. For example, if you wanted to come up with a new hand-held electronic device, think 'what would it feel like to be one of these products? What would I like? What would irritate me?' Build a psychological profile of your target. Similarly, if you are looking to solve a problem, get into the 'mind' of the obstacle (if you know what it is). If not, pick something that typifies the problem itself and think your way into it.

Use the insights you gain from this insider's view to come up with new ways of developing a solution to your requirements. Try this as an exercise by imagining what it would be like to be a mobile phone and see if you can develop a new mobile phone product. It might be helpful to see the *Feedback* section below first.

**Feedback** There can be some resistance to this technique initially, because it involves thinking like an inanimate (or at least, inhuman) object. At its extreme, you might even be required to think like something insubstantial – sunlight, or a bad odour. This isn't as hard as it sounds. In *Imagination Engineering* (see unit books in Unit 1) we include an example of a story written from the point of view of a nasturtium. This is definitely one where practice helps.

**Outcome** The inside view can be very illuminating, because we always see situations from our own viewpoint. By looking from the inside out, the problem will appear very different – and hence this can be an extremely powerful technique.

**Variations** With a group you can usually split the internal viewpoint to give several approaches. For example, if you were looking to design a new air freshener, you could do it from the point of view of the freshener itself, the bad smell, the air molecules, any fabrics in the room and so on.

| | |
|---|---|
| Culture | ✪ |
| Techniques | ✪✪✪✪ |
| Personal development | ✪✪ |
| Mental energy | ✪✪ |
| Fun | ✪✪✪✪ |

# 13.3 *Technique: Evil genius*

**Preparation** None.
**Running time** Five minutes.
**Resources** None.
**Frequency** As required.

There's a natural human tendency to blame problems on 'them' or imagine conspiracies where there aren't any. This technique makes use of this tendency. Whatever your problem, let's assume that there is an evil genius behind it, that your desired outcome would be true today, if it weren't for this malevolent monster getting in the way. To make this possible you probably have to think about your problem in a slightly different way. If you wanted to cut costs, the evil genius could be both pushing up costs and thwarting any existing cost-cutting measures. If you want to come up with a fresh idea (though this is more a problem-solving technique) the evil genius could be making sure your competitors are one step ahead, and putting blockages in the way of making a new idea possible.

Think about the motivation of your nemesis. Why does he want things this way? Is there any way to satisfy him and still solve your problem? Is there any way of distracting him? Can you somehow trick him into solving the problem for you? Give it a try.

**Feedback** This technique picks up on a long folk-story tradition of people thwarting giants or the devil in their attempts to make things unpleasant. By personifying the obstacles that cause your problem you can see them in a different light, taking you towards a different solution.

**Outcome** While there is no role play involved, this technique works best with people who are good at throwing themselves into character, as they have to imagine the machinations of the evil genius. It is surprising how often an intractable problem can be made more approachable by adding the human touch.

**Variations** If using *Evil genius* in a group, you may like to have someone play the Devil's Advocate, putting the case for the EG. If so, this person should be good at improvising and acting. You can ring the changes by using a number of possible flavours of EG – the criminal mastermind, the mad scientist, the evil alien invader and so forth.

| | |
|---|---|
| Culture | ✪✪ |
| Techniques | ✪✪✪✪ |
| Personal development | ✪✪ |
| Mental energy | ✪✪ |
| Fun | ✪✪✪ |

# 13.4 Exercise: School daze

**Preparation** None.
**Running time** Five minutes.
**Resources** None.
**Frequency** Once.

Another problem to challenge your thinking skills that involves looking beyond the obvious.

I normally drive over to pick up my daughter from school at 4 pm. One day, she is let out of school one hour early and decides to walk back, meeting me on the way. We get back home ten minutes earlier than normal. If I always drive at the same speed, and left home at just the right time to pick her up at four, which of the following pieces of information would you need to determine how long she had been walking (you can choose more than one): her walking speed, my driving speed, the distance from home to school?

**Feedback** If you haven't already got an answer, try to jot one down now. Don't read any further.

Last chance to consider your answer.

There was an element of sleight of hand here. The answer is none of them: you already have enough information. As we got back ten minutes earlier than normal, I met her five minutes earlier than normal (trimming five minutes off outbound and inbound journeys), so she spent 55 minutes walking.

**Outcome** Often you will have too much information. Trimming out the unnecessary, or the search for the unnecessary, is a vital part of knowledge management.

**Variations** Consider occasions when you have chased unnecessary information. Are there ways of making information gathering 'just in time' so that it doesn't take unnecessary effort and conceal the knowledge?

| | |
|---|---|
| Culture | ✪✪ |
| Techniques | ✪ |
| Personal development | ✪✪✪ |
| Mental energy | ✪✪✪ |
| Fun | ✪✪✪ |

# 13.5 Technique: Morphology

**Preparation** None.
**Running time** Fifteen minutes.
**Resources** Flip chart and pen.
**Frequency** As required.

This technique uses the brain's ability to take something that doesn't fit in a particular place and force a connection. It is particularly useful for product development. We have used it for service development and we are sure that it could be used for idea generation and problem solving but we haven't tried to adapt it to work there.

Define the product or service area you are trying to develop, write it up on a flip chart and then forget it. Next, take a completely dissimilar product or service and list all of the attributes of it that you can. What shape is it? What colour is it? What benefits does it offer the user? What controls does it have? How heavy is it? How portable is it? List anything and everything that you can use to describe it.

Now take each of those characteristics in turn and relate them back to the product or service you are trying to develop. For each of these characteristics find customer benefits and start to think through how they could be made to happen.

**Feedback** The toughest stage of this process is convincing a sceptical group that their canned soup product has anything to learn from a pocket camera. The only way to overcome this is to persuade them to trust you and to demonstrate that it works. You might want to try this one on your own beforehand just to convince yourself of this.

**Outcome** Given the right mix of dissimilar products this technique will generate some truly original approaches. Make sure that they are not filtered out when you select ideas. It is too easy to stay within comfort zones at the selection and development phase.

**Variations** You could pre-select the product to be force fit or you could allow the group to select. With a little more time, you could use two very different products and combine their attributes.

| | |
|---|---|
| Culture | ✪ |
| Techniques | ✪✪✪✪ |
| Personal development | ✪✪ |
| Mental energy | ✪✪ |
| Fun | ✪✪✪ |

# Unit 14: Simple fun – laughter makers

When Arthur Koestler explored the nature of creativity he came up with three creative roles – the artist, the sage and the jester. Humour's relationship with creativity is very strong. While some experts on creativity rightly point out that being creative isn't just about having fun (see, for instance, de Bono's *Serious Creativity*, the unit book in Unit 12), it's certainly true that by making sure your group is having fun – or that you are enjoying your work – you are much more likely to be creative. Fun and creativity should go together. This unit focuses on simple exercises to create an atmosphere of fun. You will need other people to try these out – use a meeting or even a party to get the practical experience of using the techniques.

Do try out the exercises as you go. Put them off until later and you probably won't ever do them. Read through the techniques. Make notes about how and when you can use them. And make sure you give them a try in the next appropriate forum.

## Unit books

Fun and work are often seen as uncomfortable bedfellows. Try Leslie Yerkes' *Fun Works* for some insights into why this is the case and how we can bring work and fun together.

For a more direct injection of fun, see Scott Adams' classic illustration of everything that can go wrong in business, *The Dilbert Principle*.

You can find more information on our unit books, or buy them, from our support site: www.cul.co.uk/crashcourse.

## Web links

Links on fun at work can be found at www.cul.co.uk/crashcourse.

# 14.1 Technique: Row of eyes

**Preparation** None.
**Running time** Five minutes.
**Resources** Space to arrange the group into two rows.
**Frequency** Once per group.

Arrange the group into two rows, facing each other. Ask them to make eye contact with the person opposite. If there is an odd number of people, pick a person out at random to hold back in each round. The object of the exercise is to hear what the person opposite is saying without using words. It is important that the main focus is the eyes, but general body language is useful too. Messages could range from 'What the Hell am I doing here?' to 'What are you doing afterwards?' Tell participants to concentrate on hearing what the person opposite is saying to them – and not to forget to smile.

After 30 to 40 seconds rotate both groups in opposite directions for a count of five. Stop them facing a different person and repeat the exercise. Do this four or five times.

**Feedback** This is different to most ice-breakers in that it doesn't involve finding out facts. Instead, it works well at breaking down barriers. It is difficult to retain the initial barriers we erect around ourselves when really looking deeply into someone else's eyes. Tell the group this, after the exercise is complete.

**Outcome** As well as breaking down barriers, the exercise acts as a spur to people talking to one another. It works particularly well if you allow time for introductions immediately afterwards.

**Variations** To create pairs rather than a full team you could restrict the exercise to a single pairing. This could be followed by a more traditional 'getting to know you' exercise. With or without rotation, consider having brief verbal communication at the end of the non-verbal listening, in case curiosity makes participants frustrated. If the aim is general teambuilding, it is possible to undertake this exercise with the whole group in a circle, picking someone opposite to communicate with, but people may be left out. To maximize the team spirit aspect, participants can put arms around their neighbours' shoulders, but this reduces the body language options.

| | |
|---|---|
| Culture | ✪✪✪ |
| Techniques | ✪ |
| Personal development | ✪✪✪ |
| Mental energy | ✪✪✪ |
| Fun | ✪✪ |

# 14.2 *Technique: I am and I know*

**Preparation** Obtain ball.
**Running time** Ten minutes.
**Resources** A ball (tennis ball, or similar size); room to stand in a circle.
**Frequency** Once with any group.

Start with the ball and say, 'I am <your name> and I know <the name of a famous person>'. Throw the ball to someone else in the circle and they must say, 'I am <their name> and I know…' but this time the famous person's first name must start with the last letter of the famous person's name that you used. For instance, 'I am Paul Birch and I know Margaret Thatcher' – throw the ball – 'I am Brian Clegg and I know Ronald McDonald'.

If you cannot think of a name quickly enough to satisfy the group, you step out of the circle, passing the ball to your left. The next participant takes up where you failed. The last person in wins.

**Feedback** Bear in mind that those who are good at the exercise will have their names remembered more than those who are bad at it.

**Outcome** In general people take away a few names from this, but it is played as much for fun as effectiveness.

**Variations** When someone drops out and the ball is passed on, you can allow the person who picks up the ball to start from scratch with any name. This gives the opportunity for them to create some really tough challenges. If you are dealing with a group who already know one another you can use the exercise without the 'I am...' part. The linking letter can be also from first letter of surname to first letter of first name – eg from Michelle Pfeiffer to Paul Newman. A small variant if the exercise is proving too easy is that if someone gives a person with the first and last name starting with the same letter, the next player throws the ball back to them, rather than throwing it on to someone else. You can specify limits like real people or fictional characters.

| | |
|---|---|
| Culture | ✪✪ |
| Techniques | ✪ |
| Personal development | ✪✪ |
| Mental energy | ✪✪✪✪ |
| Fun | ✪✪✪ |

# 14.3 Technique: Makeover

**Preparation** Obtain props.
**Running time** Fifteen minutes.
**Resources** A selection of makeup, props, jewellery and costume items. Ideally a separate area for each team, otherwise space to spread.
**Frequency** Once with any group.

Divide the group into teams. You need at least three teams and at least three people per team. Otherwise only your resources limit numbers. Ask the teams to select a victim within the team that they will make up. To set the scene you can choose particularly overblown celebrities to make up in the style of, or you can leave it to the teams. The winning team is the one that has produced the most outrageous result in the time available.

**Feedback** This is a great warm-up for light-hearted or barrier-breaking events. You must make sure that the set-up is entirely humorous and that it is clearly a joke that all team members are taking part in, or else you might find that you have a real victim in the group. You might also be prepared, as once happened to us, for the teams to rebel and use the facilitators as models.

**Outcome** There is a real element of competition but the subject matter makes it extremely light hearted. The 'victim' is usually a volunteer and perversely, the more extreme the embarrassment factor, the more respected they become for volunteering. In fact, when building a team, making over the new team leader can be very positive.

**Variations** You can run this warm-up with no preparation and force the teams to rely on their own creativity to get hold of props, and use everyday items like paperclips. The results are usually less outrageous but more challenging. If you are taking this approach, allow five minutes' foraging time at the start, when team members can venture away from the meeting room to find items to use. There are circumstances, for example a residential course with many teams working simultaneously, where this exercise will benefit from having a camera to record the results, but only with the victims' permission, for a specific use.

| | |
|---|---|
| Culture | ✪✪✪ |
| Techniques | ✪ |
| Personal development | ✪✪ |
| Mental energy | ✪✪✪ |
| Fun | ✪✪✪✪ |

# 14.4 Technique: Steeplechase

**Preparation** A planned ride (see below).
**Running time** Five minutes.
**Resources** Space to arrange the group standing or crouching in a circle around the organizer.
**Frequency** Once with any group.

Put the group in a circle around you and explain that you are going on a steeplechase. You might also say that what you are about to do is extremely silly, but for a very serious reason. As you race around the course you will pass certain obstacles; their job is to imitate your actions.

Get everyone crouching like a racing jockey in the saddle and start them patting their thighs to make the sound of a galloping horse. Then take them around a course. Eg:

- A low branch – duck down and swish a hand over your head.
- Hedge – jump over it, so sit up in the saddle and stop the hoof noises.
- Left turn – lean in the saddle and pull the reigns over.
- Right turn – lean in the saddle and pull the reigns over.
- Trees to the left/right – swish a hand to the left/right of your head.
- 'Oh look, there's an old man' – stop galloping, stroke an imaginary beard and 'Hmmm' with disapproval at the horses (this comic interlude only works once).
- Race for the finish line – spur the horses faster and faster until you pass the line.

**Feedback** The success of this warm-up depends largely on your chutzpah. Make sure the group understands the benefits of the energy it will inject – and that silliness is a positive part of it, but don't be overly defensive. In the unlikely event that it is not working after a minute or so, kill it and do something completely different.

**Outcome** This is a great warm-up for getting people up on their feet, involved in physical activity and laughing. It is difficult for anyone to stand aloof once the group as a whole gets going.

**Variations** The actions above are a small sample of possible steeplechase obstacles. Throw in any you can think of, but do plan the course in advance – you must not be hesitant.

| | |
|---|---|
| Culture | ✪ |
| Techniques | ✪ |
| Personal development | ✪ |
| Mental energy | ✪✪✪✪ |
| Fun | ✪✪✪✪ |

# 14.5 Technique: Giants, witches and dwarves

**Preparation** None.
**Running time** Five to ten minutes.
**Resources** Space enough for the group to stand in two lines (possibly space enough to run around as well).
**Frequency** As required.

Divide the group into two teams, in lines facing each other. Explain the rules. *Giants, witches and dwarves* is a team version of paper, scissors and stones. Giants defeat witches by beating them on the head. Witches defeat dwarves by casting spells on them. Dwarves defeat giants by beating the knees out from beneath them. If a team decide to be giants they must all wave their fists above their heads and roar at the tops of their voices. If the team decide to be witches they must throw spells and cackle in a really loud voice. If the team decide to be dwarves they must drop to their knees and beat the knees out from under the giants whilst shouting 'Ni, ni, ni, ni'. Demonstrate these moves with over-the-top acting.

Give the team time to decide how they will all do the same thing at the same time. Any team with more than one type loses. Play the best of three or five. Between rounds everyone remains in earshot of the other team, so tactics can't be discussed explicitly.

**Feedback** There are messages about planning and communication that can be extracted. We have never used this activity without one of the teams either deciding that they need not plan, they'll play it by ear or going for an over-elaborate method of cueing the next round.

**Outcome** This is a high-energy game which changes the mood of a group swiftly.

**Variations** You can change the rules and have the winning team chase and capture one (or more) of the losing team. This is much more active but is also riskier. You will need to ensure that the room makes this practical without participants damaging it, its contents or each other.

| | |
|---|---|
| Culture | ✪✪ |
| Techniques | ✪ |
| Personal development | ✪ |
| Mental energy | ✪✪✪✪ |
| Fun | ✪✪✪✪ |

# Unit 15: Breakdown – techniques that break down a problem into components

The techniques in this unit tend to appeal particularly to people with a scientific or analytical background as there is there seems to be more systematic structure because the problem is being broken down in some way. This appearance is actually misleading – the way that the broken-down elements are used will inevitably move away from simple left-brain analysis – but it can make it easier to use some of these techniques with groups that resist more obviously off-the-wall creativity.

Do try out the exercises as you go. Put them off until later and you probably won't ever do them. Read through the techniques. Make notes about how and when you can use them. And make sure you give them a try in the next appropriate forum.

## Unit books

Taking a component approach is popular in business books. Even if you aren't interested in customer service per se, you may find *Capturing Customers' Hearts* by Brian Clegg interesting both for this component-led structure and the creative leap from customer service to charisma.

You can find more information on our unit books, or buy them, from our support site: www.cul.co.uk/crashcourse.

# 15.1 Technique: Components

**Preparation** None.
**Running time** Ten to fifteen minutes.
**Resources** None.
**Frequency** As required.

Every problem you face has components that contribute to it and make it more or less soluble. These components get ignored because they are part of a bigger issue.

This technique involves breaking the problem down into its component parts and then tackling those components one at a time.

Start with a clear description of your problem and then, individually or in a group, break that problem down into its component parts. For instance, your problem might be how to make better use of space in your small garden. Some obvious components to this are the features (those that are there – fixed and changeable, those that you want), the uses (things you do and things that you want to do in the garden), time, and space.

You would then take these in turn and try to generate some solutions to your bigger problem using them. For instance, looking at the fixed features, you could consider how fixed they really are (could they be removed?), how you could extend their uses (for instance using a tree as a place to hang baskets from or to support a seat). Looking at the variable features, which do you want, which could you remove? You would obviously do more than this with each component and cover all of the components.

**Feedback** Somehow it is easier to solve a lot of small problems than one big one; this technique breaks problems down into bite-sized chunks. Used as explained, it is unlikely to give you any startlingly original solutions but it will give you solutions to problems which seemed otherwise out of reach.

**Outcome** With this technique more than most of the others you will end up with a comprehensive list of actions. Many of these, by the nature of the technique, will be readily doable.

**Variations** If you want more original ideas as well as the bite-sized approach that this technique offers then you could try breaking the problem into components and using a different technique on each of the components.

| | |
|---|---|
| Culture | ✪ |
| Techniques | ✪✪✪✪ |
| Personal development | ✪✪ |
| Mental energy | ✪✪ |
| Fun | ✪✪ |

# 15.2 Technique: Substitute

**Preparation** None.
**Running time** Ten to fifteen minutes.
**Resources** None.
**Frequency** As required.

This technique is identical to *Components* (15.1) with one fundamental difference. As with that technique, you must break the problem down into component parts but then, instead of solving these components, you insert something different as the component and then solve that, in relation to the overall problem.

Taking the example of making better use of space in a small garden we highlighted in *Components*, one key component was 'features'. We could replace 'features' with 'electricity' (that was just a component chosen at random, you could be more structured if you wanted). So the issue for this component becomes, how can we make better use of the small garden by increasing the electricity?

At first glance this doesn't make sense but as you treat this as a genuine problem some solutions start to appear. You could, for instance, improve the lighting and so have use of the garden for longer. You could heat a greenhouse or cloches and so have a longer growing season. You could support hanging baskets from the overhead power cables above the garden (or, if killing yourself is an issue, you could hang them from another form of cable support). You could have a water feature, using an electric pump.

Some of the solutions that you generate (like the overhead power cable one) are likely to be non-starters. Do not throw them out; see how you can adapt them to make them workable.

**Feedback** This technique feels very similar to *Components* when you start to use it but it quickly becomes clear that it offers more creative solutions.

**Outcome** You are still likely to generate a comprehensive set of actions from this technique but you are likely to find that they are more creative (although in some cases less workable) than with *Components*.

**Variations** This works with individuals or with teams. There is no need and no great advantage in using further creativity techniques on the component problems.

| | |
|---|---|
| Culture | ✪ |
| Techniques | ✪✪✪✪ |
| Personal development | ✪✪ |
| Mental energy | ✪✪ |
| Fun | ✪✪ |

# 15.3 Exercise: Different views

**Preparation** None.
**Running time** Five minutes.
**Resources** None.
**Frequency** Once.

Take a break from component techniques by giving your creative mental muscles a workout. Attempt an answer to all of these three short puzzles before moving on to the feedback:

- What is the result of adding 15 and 5 three times?
- A farmer was infuriated to see five rabbits eating his lettuces. He shot one rabbit – how many rabbits were left?
- Is there any way to drop an uncooked egg onto a concrete floor from 10 metres up without cracking it?

**Feedback** Don't go any further until you've attempted some sort of answer to each.

Last chance to consider your answer.

The answers are: 20 (it doesn't matter how many times you do it, you still get 20), none (the other four ran away), yes (it's actually very hard to crack a concrete floor using an uncooked egg).

Each of these puzzles comes at the question from a different direction to that you were expecting. Once you've groaned at the answers (if you hadn't already guessed them), take a minute to examine what was happening.

**Outcome** Creativity is all about seeing the world in a different way, or coming at a problem from a different direction. These puzzles work in exactly the same way. By practising this sort of puzzle, you have a much better chance of coming up with creative ideas. This is also an effective lesson for knowledge management. In each case, you knew the answer – it was the question you didn't understand. It emphasizes the need for careful questioning when you are acquiring knowledge.

**Variations** Get hold of a book of this sort of puzzle and practise the sort of thinking required. You may also find cryptic crossword puzzles give the same sort of exercise.

| | |
|---|---|
| Culture | ✪✪ |
| Techniques | ✪ |
| Personal development | ✪✪✪✪ |
| Mental energy | ✪✪ |
| Fun | ✪✪✪ |

# 15.4 Technique: Been there before

**Preparation** None.
**Running time** Ten minutes.
**Resources** Paper and pens.
**Frequency** Once with any group.

In the popular film *Groundhog Day*, the hero relives the same day over and over again. Only he is aware of this. For everyone else, each morning is the first time around. By cleverly using the time available, the hero gains new skills that he needs to change things.

Assume that you are in the same sort of time loop. You can do almost anything, because next day you will wake up back in bed, with the previous day wiped out. You can take as long as you like to develop new skills and concepts – provided it can be done one day at a time, with only your memory to preserve what has happened from day to day. How could you attack your problem? What would you do? What lessons could you learn for the real world?

**Feedback** Although in principle you could do almost anything, limit yourself to things you would be comfortable doing. Even if you knew you could get away with it, you might not rob a bank or kill someone. There's no real benefit from a solution which is in the form 'go and get lots of money and throw it at the problem', unless the repeated day comes up with a new way of making money. Instead you should look at the wider resources that could be built. If you are having trouble getting started, think through your general response to being stuck in a time loop first, before getting on to the problem.

**Outcome** This is a very mixed technique. Sometimes it will come up with nothing at all, sometimes it will produce the exact solution you were looking for. It's one to try for five minutes, and if you aren't getting anywhere, try something else.

**Variations** This one generally works best individually, but it is possible to work it with a team. If you have a team and have time, get everyone to do the exercise separately, share the results, then consider how you might change your approach if you were all sharing the experience of the repeated day simultaneously.

| | |
|---|---|
| Culture | ✪ |
| Techniques | ✪✪✪ |
| Personal development | ✪ |
| Mental energy | ✪✪✪ |
| Fun | ✪✪✪ |

# 15.5 Exercise/Technique: Long division

**Preparation** None.
**Running time** Ten minutes.
**Resources** Flip chart.
**Frequency** As required.

Try to sum up the essence of your problem or requirement in a very few words – between two and four. For each of the words, think of a small number of words that describe key attributes of the words. Attach these to the initial words with lines, in mind map fashion. Now do the same again, producing attributes of attributes. For example, with a problem of 'how to increase European sales', the key words might be European and Sales. European might have the attributes: large area, different languages, fancy food. Fancy food might have the attributes: spices, rich sauces, small portions. With all the elements filled in, pick and choose as takes your fancy. Browse over all the attributes at both levels. Make use of the sort of attribute link described in Chapter 1 (page 10) to tie back to possible solutions. Other solutions might emerge directly from the attributes. As an exercise, try out this technique on 'how to improve customer service at airline check-in'. If you are reading the recommended book for this unit, see how the different elements of charisma come in.

**Feedback** Don't worry about how silly the attributes may seem to other people. They don't have to be generally accepted or politically correct – just let them flow. It is important that you use the second level of attribute, as this often generates most positive effects.

**Outcome** It is amazing how much depth is generated by reaching down two layers. One effect of the attribute approach is that it may uncover solutions that you had rejected subconsciously for being unsuitable, which, with some modification, can be made practical.

**Variations** The number of levels and quantity of words is arbitrary, though you must have two levels of attributes to get richness, and don't want so many elements that the exercise becomes tedious. It is better if groups produce attributes individually, then share these or the linkages.

| | |
|---|---|
| Culture | ✪ |
| Techniques | ✪✪✪✪ |
| Personal development | ✪ |
| Mental energy | ✪✪ |
| Fun | ✪✪ |

# Unit 16:
# Touchy-feely – generating ideas using right-brain activities

It is very difficult to avoid slipping into left-brain thinking when trying to solve business problems. The very action of sitting around a table and saying 'let's have an ideas session' forces you into left-brain mode. You are being systematic, you are engaging a process. Ideally, to maximize the ability to create new links, you need to involve both sides of the brain. If you need to kick-start the right brain, these types of technique can be particularly effective.

Do try out the exercises as you go. Put them off until later and you probably won't ever do them. Read through the techniques. Make notes about how and when you can use them. And make sure you give them a try in the next appropriate forum.

## Unit books

The majority of people are of the opinion that they can't draw. This is reminiscent of the way most people think they aren't particularly creative – it's simply not true. Betty Edwards' classic book *Drawing on the Right Side of the Brain* explains how we tend to try to draw with the left side of the brain, but need to invoke the right – it's a direct parallel to what is occurring in creativity sessions.

You can find more information on our unit books, or buy them, from our support site: www.cul.co.uk/crashcourse.

## Web links

Links to right-brain-stimulating Web sites can be found at www.cul.co.uk/crashcourse.

# 16.1 Exercise/Technique: Set it to music

**Preparation** Get together a stack of mixed CDs.
**Running time** Ten minutes.
**Resources** A CD player and a stack of mixed CDs.
**Frequency** As required.

Start with a very eclectic set of CDs – make sure there's a good mix of classical and popular. Choose a CD at random, then a random track. Many CD players have a random function which will help with this. Spend a minute taking an overview of your problem statement and any information you have about the problem area. Then play two or three minutes of the track. As you listen to the music, have the problem area in the back of your mind. Is there anything in the words (if any) that sparks off an idea? Does the music itself make you think of anything, or remind you of anything that has happened? Make use of these associations to establish new possibilities. Try this out now on a problem you have or 'how to get more people into a specific high street store.'

**Feedback** There is an element here of using a random stimulus to generate associations, where you might find it useful to check the guidance on associations in Chapter 1 (page 10). However, using music is different to a random word or picture, as the act of listening to music – really listening, not just having music in the background – can itself provide a vehicle for moving away from your previous frame of mind.

**Outcome** This technique produces less volume than the other random stimulation techniques, but the combination of the music as stimulus and as distraction means that you will often achieve something more radical than with the alternatives.

**Variations** It is not necessary to use a piece of music you are unfamiliar with – listening to a familiar piece can generate powerful associations – but it is important not to use the same piece of music repeatedly as it becomes a rut in its own right. An interesting variant with a team is that each team member should choose a CD for another team member, consciously trying to make it as far away from their known tastes as possible. Tapes can be used, but CDs are preferable as it makes randomly selecting tracks much easier.

| | |
|---|---|
| Culture | ✪✪✪ |
| Techniques | ✪✪✪ |
| Personal development | ✪✪✪ |
| Mental energy | ✪✪✪ |
| Fun | ✪✪✪ |

# 16.2 Exercise/Technique: Da Vinci scribbles

**Preparation** None.
**Running time** Ten minutes.
**Resources** Pencil and paper or flip chart and pens.
**Frequency** As required.

This makes use of technique invented by Leonardo da Vinci – just to show that the business of creativity techniques is not exactly new. Sit down at pad with a soft pencil in your hand. Close your eyes and start to scribble. Not the scratchy scribble of a child – imagine that you are an artist, sketching in an outline of something. Only don't direct the pencil, just let it flow across the page. When you feel you've scribbled enough, open your eyes. Look at the image you have generated.

What does it make you think of? What does it remind you of? How might you use it in your problem? What characteristics of it are appropriate to a solution? What sort of new product does it imply (or could you use to deal with it)? Be imaginative – let your mind wander over just what this scribble might be. Try this technique out now on the problem 'how to make delivery grocery shopping more attractive to the customer'.

**Feedback** Leonardo used this method to come up with new inventions, which considering his track record makes it quite a promising technique. If you have problems seeing anything in your picture, think of modern art – what title might you give your artwork in a gallery? Look for suggestions in the shapes and sub-patterns. It might help to modify your scribble into something more concrete as the images emerge.

**Outcome** This technique is marginally better for coming up with new ideas than solving problems, but it is quite often a source of a solution.

**Variations** In a group you could each generate your own picture, or have a single person draw on a flip chart, then all of the group can individually think about what it implies before sharing their thoughts. Other old techniques that this is reminiscent of are seeing pictures in cloud formations and in an open fire. Given appropriate surroundings, either of these will make an effective variant.

| | |
|---|---|
| Culture | ✪ |
| Techniques | ✪✪✪✪ |
| Personal development | ✪✪✪ |
| Mental energy | ✪✪ |
| Fun | ✪✪ |

# 16.3 Technique: Touch me, feel me

**Preparation** None.
**Running time** Ten minutes.
**Resources** A wide range of textures, boxes and blindfolds.
**Frequency** As required.

We have used all sorts of ways of stimulating people to move away from their problem in order to generate original solutions. This is one that works well if you are looking for very different solutions.

Collect together a wide range of textured materials. We have used different types of fabric, sandpaper, a bowl of jelly (Jell-O), wire wool, scouring pads, rubber gloves, sea shells, toys and small models. Place these objects into boxes in such a way that no one can see them. Blindfold some or all participants and have them feel the items. They must then give a running commentary of associations and metaphors that you record onto flip charts.

These associations are then used as material to relate back to your problem and to help to generate solutions. It is important that no one sees the objects during the exercise – neither the 'feelers' nor anyone responding to the spoken associations. Once the object is clearly visible it will lose the impact of the unknown.

**Feedback** It can be difficult to persuade everybody to take part in this, which is why we have suggested the option of having a few guinea pigs. There are some who will always be keen to try this sort of a challenge.

**Outcome** This is a technique that we invented on the spur of the moment for a client who wanted to change the shape of an event as it was running. At the time we didn't have high hopes for it, but it turned out to be hugely successful at generating solutions to the problem that were radically different to other approaches. An advantage of this technique is that the resources can often be pulled together at short notice, as any working environment will have a good range of strange objects.

**Variations** You can have the whole group experiencing the textures and making associations to work on later or you can have a small subset of the group acting as guinea pigs.

| | |
|---|---|
| Culture | ✪ |
| Techniques | ✪✪✪✪ |
| Personal development | ✪ |
| Mental energy | ✪✪✪ |
| Fun | ✪✪✪ |

# 16.4 Technique: Draw it

**Preparation** Get hold of materials.
**Running time** Thirty minutes.
**Resources** Artists' materials, magazines, glue, scissors, paper, etc.
**Frequency** As required.

The brain works in strange ways. The split brain theory suggests that half of your brain handles the logical, sequential, numerical thinking while the other half handles the holistic, artistic, imagery-based thinking. Whether you can locate the physical centres of these types of thought or not, it is certainly true that it feels different to think in different modes and that it is difficult to think holistically and sequentially at the same time. This technique is aimed at tapping into different ways of thinking by forcing you to express the problem and solutions in different ways.

Take a whole selection of artists' materials and produce an image of a world where your problem is solved or where your problem just doesn't exist. Having a selection of image-rich magazines is a bonus because it means that those of us who write off our artistic ability can still produce an effective image.

Once you have produced the image, look into it for clues to the solution to your problem. What do you see in there? What associations does it have for you? List these onto a flip chart.

Now take the words that you have generated and relate them back to your problem. What links can you make that take a step towards a solution?

**Feedback** This technique is one of the most effective around at stretching thinking. In many ways it combines some of the advantages of the random stimulation techniques with a probe into the darker recesses of your mind. If you have trouble with associations, see page 10 for guidance.

**Outcome** Imagery proves useful in all sorts of circumstances for creating a new perspective and generating ideas.

**Variations** This technique can be combined with others to increase the mental distance that you have to travel. For instance, try combining it with *Random word* from Unit 12.

| | |
|---|---|
| Culture | ✪ |
| Techniques | ✪✪✪✪ |
| Personal development | ✪✪ |
| Mental energy | ✪✪✪ |
| Fun | ✪✪✪ |

# 16.5 Technique: Squirrel box

**Preparation** Produce a squirrel box.
**Running time** Ten minutes.
**Resources** Squirrel box.
**Frequency** As required.

This technique requires considerable preparation, but once prepared can be used without warning. Get hold of a shoebox, or similar container (a fancy plastic or wooden box will look more professional, but won't work any better). Put into it anything that raises the eyebrows. It can be a small object, a newspaper cutting, a photograph, part of a cereal box, as long as it is unusual and interesting or entertaining. Make maintenance of your box a background task. Whenever you see anything appropriate, squirrel it away.

When it comes to the creativity session, pick two items out at random. Look at them and/or read them through. What do they make you think of separately and together? How would some interaction between the two solve your problem or come up with a new idea?

**Feedback** The tactile nature of fishing the objects out of a box is all part of the experience – don't resort to sticking the items into a scrapbook. If possible, cycle old stuff out as you use it. The flow of new content will stop the technique from growing stale.

**Outcome** This is a particularly enjoyable association technique, which will appeal to those who like squirrelling away fascinating facts, silly stories and bizarre photographs.

**Variations** You can use the sort of book of bizarre happenings that you will sometimes find in a remaindered bookshop as a starter pack for your squirrel box, but cut out items from it, don't use the book directly. If using this technique with a group, a good warm-up is to refer to the box as a brain box. Have a second identical box with a cauliflower coated in gel in it. Ask someone to feel inside without looking. When they react say – 'whoops, wrong brain box' and substitute the real thing.

| | |
|---|---|
| Culture | ✪ |
| Techniques | ✪✪✪✪ |
| Personal development | ✪ |
| Mental energy | ✪✪✪ |
| Fun | ✪✪✪ |

# Unit 17: Natural input – using nature and science as tools to generate ideas

We can use the natural world and the scientific theories with which we try to explain how it works to generate new ways of thinking. Sometimes this can be by using our understanding of what's possible to identify some of the most fundamental assumptions we make – and to see how our ideas would develop without those assumptions. At other times we can use the beauty and complexity of nature to engage the right brain and start us thinking in new ways. We are used to looking at science for analytical solutions, but here it is being used in a totally different way – this is the artistic side of science.

Do try out the exercises as you go. Put them off until later and you probably won't ever do them. Read through the techniques. Make notes about how and when you can use them. And make sure you give them a try in the next appropriate forum.

## Unit books

Popular science books are a great way of getting a wider appreciation of all the new directions that science could take your mind. See *Light Years* by Brian Clegg, which combines a look at the individuals who have been fascinated with light through the centuries with insights into the amazing ways that light can be used. There's nothing more appropriate for creativity than light.

You can find more information on our unit books, or buy them, from our support site: www.cul.co.uk/crashcourse.

## Web links

Links to sites where you can find out more about the latest scientific developments can be found at www.cul.co.uk/crashcourse.

# 17.1 Technique: Frontiers

**Preparation** Nonc.
**Running time** Five minutes.
**Resources** None.
**Frequency** As required.

This technique is designed to bring out the frontier spirit, using (as a certain TV series put it) the final frontier as a setting. Imagine you are on a space mission on an unknown planet. Spend a minute thinking about this totally alien environment. Now what if your problem or idea requirement came up here, on this planet? What would you do? How would you solve it? Bear in mind your isolation from the rest of humanity and the sorts of science fiction technology you might be able to apply. You might need to modify the problem slightly to fit your environment, but try to fit quite closely.

**Feedback** Make sure the participants get into the spirit of this exercise. It doesn't matter if they don't like science fiction, or know nothing about it; the idiom is too strongly embedded in modern culture to be ineffective. If there is any difficulty fitting the problem into your alien planet, modify it. For example, if your problem requires customers, then have little green men, and so forth. Be prepared to use every cliché in the book.

**Outcome** *Frontiers* works best with one or more people who are really prepared to let go and let their imagination run wild. For that reason it tends to work best with those who have some experience of creativity techniques. The combination of the alien environment, lack of contact with Earth and the imagined technology can result in some spectacular ideas. They may, of course, then need bringing back to Earth, but make sure that making them practical doesn't also make them mundane.

**Variations** *Frontiers* can be worked alone, but is best as a group exercise, sparking ideas off each other. With more time available, more effort can be put into developing a scenario before going ahead with the exercise. One effective way to do this is to give each participant a copy of a science fiction short story to read the previous day. This will then be used as the scenario.

| | |
|---|---|
| Culture | ✪✪ |
| Techniques | ✪✪✪ |
| Personal development | ✪✪ |
| Mental energy | ✪✪ |
| Fun | ✪✪✪ |

# 17.2 Exercise: Leaf mould

**Preparation** None.
**Running time** Five minutes.
**Resources** A tree leaf.
**Frequency** Once.

Get hold of a reasonably broad tree leaf. Find somewhere comfortable and sit down. You are going to be asked to do a number of things with the leaf. Read the short sentence, do it, then come back and take on the next requirement. Try to focus as much as possible on one activity at a time:

- Look at the leaf in a general way: turn it over in your hand and get a feel for it.
- Look closely at the leaf. Examine the fine detail. Look at the veins, the edges of the leaf, the way it joins on to the stem and so on.
- Think into the leaf. What is under the surface? It doesn't matter if your biology is weak, just imagine what goes together to make up the leaf.
- Think from the leaf back to the tree. How would the leaf sit on the tree? What would surround it? How would the light and the air play around it?
- Finally, gently tear the leaf. Try to feel the individual parts of the leaf resisting your pressure. Look at the torn edge: how does it differ from the natural edges?

**Feedback** When we are young we look at everything with fascination, but as we grow older habit and experience dull that fascination. We all know that leaves are common and uninspiring – any garden or park is full of the things. Yet they are complex, intriguing objects.

**Outcome** Getting back a little of the naïve interest of childhood is a major step both for knowledge management and creativity. A child's creativity depends on not 'knowing' everything – taking a moment to look at leaf reveals how much we usually take for granted. Our 'knowing' is very limited indeed.

**Variations** Take the time to look at other 'everyday' things more closely. You can't do it all the time, but every now and then it's a wonderful exercise.

| | |
|---|---|
| Culture | ✪✪✪ |
| Techniques | ✪✪ |
| Personal development | ✪✪✪✪ |
| Mental energy | ✪ |
| Fun | ✪✪✪ |

# 17.3 Technique: Auntie gravity

**Preparation** None.
**Running time** Ten minutes.
**Resources** Flip chart.
**Frequency** As required.

Creativity techniques often attack the assumptions you make about the world. Many of these assumptions exist only in your head. This technique works on some of those that are real. It is particularly useful for product development.

Firstly think about a product. What capabilities does it need? What would be your absolutely ideal position? Now, take a step further. If you could overcome a fundamental law of physics, what would it be? For example, imagine that you could overcome gravity or you could develop a totally frictionless bearing. What difference could this make to your product? Imagine time ran backwards, or evolution was based on 'survival of the least fit'.

Next you need to make it real. Ideally the way to do this would be to invent a way to overcome the laws of physics, but it might be easier to look for other ways of getting the same benefits. The idea behind this technique is that once you have identified the benefits you are looking for you will start to think of ways around the limitations and develop approaches that avoid breaking any physical laws.

**Feedback** This is a technique that is harder to explain than it is to do. It really is quite easy, given a list of desired benefits, to think of all sorts of ways of making them happen. The tough part is freeing yourself up enough to get a meaningful list of benefits. The only reason for overcoming the physical laws is to allow this freedom.

**Outcome** Given a freewheeling start that allows for unlimited thinking as far as the physical laws are concerned, you will find that you generate a sizeable list of benefits attached to your ability to flout reality. This will lead to some useful ideas at the next stage where you develop those benefits within current physical reality.

**Variations** You can miss out the stage of overcoming physical laws and move straight on to trying to list benefits, but there are dangers in this. The most likely outcome is that the benefits list that you generate is merely an extension of your current customer expectations, eg the current product only smaller, faster, pinker or with more output per channel.

| | |
|---|---|
| Culture | ✪✪ |
| Techniques | ✪✪✪✪ |
| Personal development | ✪✪✪ |
| Mental energy | ✪✪ |
| Fun | ✪✪ |

# 17.4 Exercise: The thrill factor

**Preparation** None.
**Running time** Five minutes.
**Resources** None.
**Frequency** Once.

Many of the exercises and techniques in this book look at building up skills and resources you need to improve your knowledge management and creativity, but there is one fundamental element of both of these that can't really be learnt. It's the thrill factor. If your area of knowledge or the area you are trying to be creative in thrills you, you will be better able to succeed.

There's a real problem here. It may be that you will never be able to get a thrill out of your work area. In which case, the only solution may be to change what you do. Drastic, yes, but effective.

For the moment, just spend a few minutes thinking about what it is that gives you that tingle of excitement. Take in as many different areas as possible at once. Don't worry if they seem trivial – like playing with a new technical toy – get them down.

If you really want to encourage a build-up of knowledge and creativity, you will have to get more of these thrill factors into your work. Think about it.

**Feedback** This assumes that there are some things that thrill you. If you are cynical about everything, knowing that there is nothing of interest, nothing that can provide excitement, then you need to try to suspend that cynicism and find the thrill. It may not be easy, but it is possible.

**Outcome** We aren't accustomed to think about feelings in business, yet feelings can have a big impact on brain-related activities. Bringing a thrill into your work will make a very positive contribution.

**Variations** You can take a similar look at the tangential but not quite identical area of fun. What do you find fun? How can you incorporate fun elements in what you do? Fun is more strongly weighted towards creativity, where thrill balances knowledge and creativity.

| | |
|---|---|
| Culture | ✪✪✪ |
| Techniques | ✪ |
| Personal development | ✪✪✪✪ |
| Mental energy | ✪✪✪ |
| Fun | ✪✪✪ |

# 17.5 Technique: It's only natural

**Preparation** None.
**Running time** Ten to fifteen minutes.
**Resources** Flip chart.
**Frequency** As required.

We have a lot to learn from nature. Many great ideas have been adapted from nature's solutions to problems.

Think about a natural analogy to your problem. If your office is too crowded, what overcrowding issues occur in nature? If you need a new springing mechanism, what springing mechanisms occur in nature? It need not be a one-to-one match. As with any analogy, a very rough approximation is fine. The link between computer graphics and leaves may not be immediately obvious, but the development of fractals, the method of producing complex images from small mathematical 'seeds', was inspired by the way part of a leaf resembles the whole.

Having hit upon the analogy, look for ways that the natural world – geological, plant and animal – has found solutions to this problem. How can you adapt these to your problem? For instance, taking the overcrowding issue, bees swarm, some plants poison the soil around them, some animals fight to the death, some stop breeding. Any and all of these could be adapted to help generate solutions for the overcrowded office (we particularly like the fighting to the death).

**Feedback** The most important thing to remember is not to stop when you have a single example of nature doing what you need to do. Go for quantity. Jump around the whole span of nature.

**Outcome** At first glance this would appear to be a technique that is particularly suited to product development. In practice, however, it works just as well with any problem area as long as you can find a good starting analogy.

**Variations** Instead of working at finding an analogy you could force-fit one. Have a set of animals and plants and randomly assign one or two to each group as a forced analogy to this problem. Look for examples of them facing this or a similar problem and find ways that they would cope. If you are having trouble thinking of appropriate subjects, use an encyclopaedia of nature as a trigger.

| | |
|---|---|
| Culture | ✪✪ |
| Techniques | ✪✪✪ |
| Personal development | ✪✪✪ |
| Mental energy | ✪✪ |
| Fun | ✪✪ |

# Unit 18: Memories are made of this – memory techniques

Memory is at the heart of human creativity. Without memories it would be impossible to generate fresh ideas. The only creativity would be purely random exploration – which will generate new ideas, but will also waste a huge amount of time. Being able to manage your own memories effectively is a valuable aid to developing your personal creative skills. These memory techniques have a superficial value if (for instance) you wanted to remember a phone number, but a greater use from the creative viewpoint in having a better ability to generate links and chains in the mind.

Do try out the exercises as you go. Put them off until later and you probably won't ever do them. Read through the techniques. Make notes about how and when you can use them. And make sure you give them a try in the next appropriate forum.

## Unit books

Peter Russell's *The Brain Book* is an ideal introduction to the workings of the brain and of memory.

To see what can happen when the links in the brain go astray, see the fascinating account *The Man Who Mistook his Wife for a Hat* by Oliver Sacks.

You can find more information on our unit books, or buy them, from our support site: www.cul.co.uk/crashcourse.

## Web links

Links to memory-oriented Web sites can be found at www.cul.co.uk/crashcourse.

# 18.1 Exercise/Technique: Extremes

**Preparation** None.
**Running time** Five minutes.
**Resources** Quiet environment.
**Frequency** Once.

A lot of memory techniques use imagery. Whether you want to remember a set of numbers, people's names or the contents of a textbook, imagery can help fix the information in your mind. It is also an essential precursor to turning information into knowledge.

Let's say you had to remember the number 329. Using the rhyme method (see 18.4), you could portray this number as tree, shoe, line. A first try at an image might be a tree with a line of shoes leading away from it. The trouble is, this image is too mundane. The more dramatic, colourful (and yes, rude) the image is, the better it will stick. It would be better, for instance, to imagine a huge, bright red, ravenous tree rampaging through a shopping mall, ripping people's shoes off (with the feet still inside them) and lining them up down the middle of the mall. A bit unpleasant and lurid? Exactly, that's the point.

Try it yourself on these two image chains. Don't worry about the techniques, just assume you have to strengthen up these chains of images. Dog, hole, telephone, tomato. Pizza, sumo wrestler, umbrella, elephant.

**Feedback** For some reason, even when an image is confined to your mind you can be just as squeamish, prudish and reasonable as you would be when chatting to the vicar. Let rip – be dramatic, be funny, be gross – it doesn't matter as long as the image is memorable and unique.

**Outcome** This exercise isn't a specific memory technique. Instead it supports all the others. By improving the vividness of your images, you will get better retention in the other techniques.

**Variations** This exercise uses the chains of images that are commonly generated by memory techniques. Try a similar approach with a simple story – if you can't be bothered to construct a story, take the basics of a well-known fairy tale, then push it to extremes.

| | |
|---|---|
| Culture | ✪✪ |
| Techniques | ✪✪ |
| Personal development | ✪✪✪✪ |
| Mental energy | ✪✪✪ |
| Fun | ✪✪✪ |

# 18.2 Technique: Story chains

**Preparation** None.
**Running time** Five minutes.
**Resources** None.
**Frequency** Several times.

Quite often we need to remember a sequence of things, perhaps a procedure or a list. A story chain is the ideal mechanism. Build up a story involving the items in sequence. Use intense images. As you add each item, go back to the start of the story and briefly recap. So, for example, if I wanted to remember a telephone, a book and a car, I might have a story that was something like:

*A huge purple telephone with thousands of legs was wandering through the woods when it tripped over a copy of the Yellow Pages. Unfortunately a fast Jaguar XK8 (British Racing Green) was hurtling past and squashed the telephone millipede flat.*

Make it as lurid and personal as you can (I chose the Jaguar because I particularly like it). When you recap the story, don't run through a set of words, see it happening like a film unreeling in your mind.

**Feedback** You will find that you can hold a long list this way with very little effort. I've used it in one of those games where you go round saying 'I've got a bag and in it is…' and everyone adds a new item. While the other players were floundering, I had no problem remembering 30 items. Because of the chain it's slow for random access – to get to the 20th item you need to start at the beginning – but it is still very useful.

**Outcome** You will soon be effortlessly remembering long lists. It's easy to think that it's too much trouble to use a technique – so next time you have to order a round of drinks, try it.

**Variations** I've suggested recapping the list each time you add an item. With practice you can get away with an occasional recap. If you need to keep the list longer than a few hours, recap after a few hours, a couple of days and a week. Try it on different practical applications.

| | |
|---|---|
| Culture | ✪✪ |
| Techniques | ✪✪ |
| Personal development | ✪✪✪✪ |
| Mental energy | ✪✪ |
| Fun | ✪✪✪ |

# 18.3 Technique: Take a note

**Preparation** Find a short piece of classical music.
**Running time** Five minutes.
**Resources** Notepad.
**Frequency** Once.

Find a short piece of classical music – around the five-minute mark. It should be unfamiliar. Ask your friends and colleagues if you can borrow a CD or two. Find somewhere you can be undisturbed for five minutes. Sit comfortably with a notepad and listen to the music.

As you listen, let the music conjure up images. They can be obvious and direct (such as medieval church music evoking the image of a monastery) or quite unconnected with the original concept (a good example would be the way a Strauss waltz was used to accompany the shots of the rotating space station in the film *2001*). Try to bring these images into as solid a perspective as possible.

As you get the images, jot down keyword notes on the pad. It's not essential, but it would help if you are familiar with mind mapping (see Unit 1) before doing this. Don't aim for a detailed text description as this will get in the way of the visualization – just try to capture the essence of what you see in your mind's eye.

**Feedback** Cast off any concerns that this is reminiscent of the sort of music appreciation you used to do at junior school. Your aim is much more concrete, and totally grown up. This is an exercise to give muscle tone to your knowledge-building and creative skills.

**Outcome** This is a compound exercise, giving practice at forming clear images, processing fast-incoming data and working under pressure. Every area of your brain skills will benefit from this practice.

**Variations** If you have difficulty forming images, try imagining you are watching a movie with this as the background music. What sort of thing might be happening on the screen? Don't stick to a single scene, but imagine the action changes with the music.

| | |
|---|---|
| Culture | ✪✪ |
| Techniques | ✪ |
| Personal development | ✪✪✪✪ |
| Mental energy | ✪ |
| Fun | ✪✪✪ |

# 18.4 Exercise/Technique: Number rhymes

**Preparation** None.
**Running time** Ten minutes.
**Resources** Notepad.
**Frequency** Three times.

This is the classic method for remembering numbers. Each number is associated with a rhyming word. You can change the words if you can think of something better:

1 – gun
2 – shoe
3 – tree
4 – door
5 – hive
6 – sticks
7 – heaven
8 – weight
9 – line
10 (hence 0) – hen

The use is simple, but takes some practice. When you want to remember a number, make up a short story in your mind linking the nature of the number (eg the person whose phone number it is) with the objects in the number rhyme in the right order. Make the story as vivid and pictorial as you can. Go through the story a number of times to reinforce it. Pick a phone number out of a telephone directory to try out this technique.

**Feedback** Before you do some actual stories, try drawing the items on a pad with the number to reinforce the rhyme. Try it out on some actual numbers you need to remember, but haven't yet had a chance to. Remember to make the little stories as extreme, colourful, dramatic, rude as you can to fix the memory.

**Outcome** This may seem a trivial technique, but it will lock practically any number into your memory. To begin with you will use the story to recall it – later on the story will disappear, but the memory chain will remain.

**Variations** Although one try may be enough to convince you, it is best to try this out three times. Make the second time later the same day as the first. On that second attempt, do some new numbers, but also re-run the stories on the first set. Make the third try a few days later. Again, reinforce the earlier numbers. You might need to reinforce memories this way to make sure they stick.

| | |
|---|---|
| Culture | ✪✪ |
| Techniques | ✪✪✪ |
| Personal development | ✪✪✪✪ |
| Mental energy | ✪✪ |
| Fun | ✪✪ |

# 18.5 Exercise: Strengthening your ghosts

**Preparation** None.
**Running time** Ten minutes.
**Resources** Quiet environment.
**Frequency** Several times.

Sit quietly and comfortably with your eyes closed. Imagine yourself in an environment you know well. The office, a friend's house, the pub – anywhere as long as it isn't your current location. Try to build up a detailed picture of the location as you see it when you approach. The doors, the windows, the colour scheme. Walk up to the door. Imagine its detail – what is the door furniture like? Open the door – what does the handle feel like? Now go inside. Try to bring back as much as possible of your surroundings. What is the floor like? The walls?

Once you are inside, wander around. Interact with items you can remember in the environment. Don't just consider visual aspects. What do they feel like? What sounds are there? What smells?

**Feedback** Having a so-called photographic memory depends on the ability to capture and revisit images. While this can't be learnt to the extent of bringing back a whole page of a book at a time, we can all improve our imagery and ability to remember. Notice the strong dependence on the senses, a common theme when looking at memory and knowledge.

**Outcome** By undertaking this type of exercise you can enhance your ability to remember things that have just been seen more clearly. This is an ability we all have to a considerable degree, but generally it is pushed out of the way by the development of the conscious mind. Visualization also helps with your building of models and metaphors, essential for knowledge management and creativity.

**Variations** This is an exercise that benefits from several attempts. Try different locations. When the approach is working well for you, start making the imagery more creative. Imagine going somewhere you haven't been, or couldn't go (like into the core of a nuclear power station). Don't restrict yourself any more to the limitations of physics – if you want to fly, fly.

| | |
|---|---|
| Culture | ✪✪ |
| Techniques | ✪✪ |
| Personal development | ✪✪✪✪ |
| Mental energy | ✪✪✪ |
| Fun | ✪✪ |

# Unit 19: Strange translations – generating ideas from misunderstanding

Misunderstanding and mistake has been the basis for many significant inventions. The gas balloon was invented by someone who didn't realize how a hot air balloon worked. Detergents were invented when the debris of a chemical reaction proved very effective at washing out the vessel it was in. And so the catalogue of error continues. A forced misunderstanding, or even pushing ideas in an unexplainable way can be a very effective way to generate new concepts.

Do try out the exercises as you go. Put them off until later and you probably won't ever do them. Read through the techniques. Make notes about how and when you can use them. And make sure you give them a try in the next appropriate forum.

## Unit books

There are some remarkable 'weird but true' stories, often with a scientific background in Steve Silverman's book *Einstein's Refrigerator*.

You can find more information on our unit books, or buy them, from our support site: www.cul.co.uk/crashcourse.

## Web links

Web site links on misunderstanding and mistake, providing more insight into the innovative power of error, can be found at www.cul.co.uk/crashcourse.

# 19.1 Technique: It's silly

**Preparation** None.
**Running time** Ten minutes.
**Resources** Flip charts, paper and pens.
**Frequency** As required.

First spend four minutes on a conventional brainstorm. However, unlike a normal brainstorm there is one crucial difference: only silly, unworkable, impractical or obscene suggestions are allowed. Ruthlessly weed out anything practical or sensible.

Then take a step back from the output of the brainstorming. How could you modify one of the silly suggestions to make it attractive? Could you change some aspect of it? Could you remove part of it or add to it to modify it? Could you turn it round on itself? Try to do this without watering down the suggestion too much.

**Feedback** Traditional brainstorming is the weakest creativity technique, which is why it doesn't appear in this book. The problem is that it doesn't really break out of the current mode of thought and come at the problem from a totally different angle. However, by insisting that the original suggestions are outrageous, it is possible to ensure that conventional viewpoints are ignored. Don't allow excessive argument over what is or isn't silly. If there's any doubt, don't allow it.

**Outcome** The ideas generated by this technique may have little connection with the actual problem, but the second stage will pull some around to a more realistic approach. This is, in effect, a variant of all the problem distortion techniques, where it is the solution that is being distorted rather than the problem.

**Variations** It is possible to work this one alone, but it is much better with a team of four to seven people. One variant is to split a group in two. The separated groups spend a few minutes generating impossible solutions, then swap solutions and try to make each others' solutions feasible. The initial 'crazy idea' session can also be done with individuals thinking up ideas alone, which are shared later (potentially anonymously on paper or electronically). This way there will be less inclination to be embarrassed by silly ideas. You can liven up the event by giving everyone water pistols with which to squirt anyone who writes up a sensible idea.

| | |
|---|---|
| Culture | ✪✪✪ |
| Techniques | ✪✪✪ |
| Personal development | ✪✪ |
| Mental energy | ✪✪✪ |
| Fun | ✪✪✪ |

# 19.2 Exercise: Cloak and dagger

**Preparation** None.
**Running time** Five minutes.
**Resources** Notepad.
**Frequency** Once.

Imagine you had a small amount of text – a page of A4. You are in a small room which contains only a PC, a desk with three drawers, and a bookcase. The bookcase has half a dozen thick reference books on it, and a couple of filing boxes. How would you hide the text in such a way that it was retrievable by you, and on plain view, but not retrievable by someone else? You can use whatever tools you like to turn the text into a readily concealed form, provided the tools can be hidden away too.

**Feedback** If you haven't spent a couple of minutes thinking of ways of achieving this goal, go back and do it before reading on. Try to be as creative as possible.

I once needed a creative solution to this problem for a novel, and asked a hotshot computer programmer. He suggested using a picture on the PC. Pictures are stored in files which specify the colour of each dot (pixel) that makes up the picture. By using the least important bit of data for each dot, you can store a lot of information without making an obvious difference to the picture. Of course, you would need appropriate software to accomplish this, but that's just a tool. Interestingly, since then, a software company has started selling such a piece of software. This isn't the only solution, nor the most creative – it's just one example.

**Outcome** It might seem that thinking out the answer to such an unlikely problem won't help everyday creativity, but the processes involved are perfect for strengthening the creative ability.

**Variations** The advantage of this type of exercise is that you can think up your own with very little effort. Just put together a near-impossible requirement (anything from a 'locked room' murder mystery to an automatic shoelace tier) and spend a couple of minutes working on solutions.

| | |
|---|---|
| Culture | ✪✪ |
| Techniques | ✪ |
| Personal development | ✪✪✪✪ |
| Mental energy | ✪✪ |
| Fun | ✪✪✪ |

# 19.3 Technique: Lost in translation

**Preparation** None.
**Running time** Ten minutes.
**Resources** World Wide Web access.
**Frequency** As required.

There are now facilities available on the World Wide Web which automatically translate from English to other languages and back again. At the time of writing, the best known of these is available from the Alta Vista site, www.altavista.com – but others are available. First write up a paragraph about your problem. It should include your 'how to' statement and a little about why you need to solve this problem and what it means to the company. Now pass this paragraph through a translator from English to another language. Re-translate back from the other language to English.

Read through the paragraph. The translation process will have introduced various misunderstandings and confusions into the text. Often the result is hilarious. Think of solving this newly stated problem. Think how aspects of the new statement could provide solutions for the original statement. As an exercise, try this out on a problem you face at the moment.

**Feedback** Most techniques work by moving your viewpoint – this one moves the problem and sees what the outcome is. Translation is infamous for causing strife by changing meanings – here the worse the translation, the better.

**Outcome** This technique is marginally better at problem solving than idea generation, but is quite capable of moving an existing idea in a totally unexpected direction provided the translation is bad enough.

**Variations** You may like to try passing the paragraph back and forth between languages several times to see how it progresses. If the translation facility can handle translations between two other languages (eg German to Portuguese), try a three-way translation, via two other languages then back to English. There are also PC-based products with a similar functionality. One of the better known examples is Power Translator Professional. These can be used as an alternative if there is no Web access. However, they tend to be more effective, and will often only work between English and another language, making them less effective for managed confusion.

| | |
|---|---|
| Culture | ✪ |
| Techniques | ✪✪✪✪ |
| Personal development | ✪✪ |
| Mental energy | ✪✪✪ |
| Fun | ✪✪✪ |

# 19.4 Technique: They're winning

**Preparation** Scenario.
**Running time** Ten minutes.
**Resources** None.
**Frequency** Once with any group.

This technique relies on deception, so can only be used with discretion. It depends on the fact that, given the knowledge that someone else has achieved a solution to a problem, most inventive people will come up with something, even if they had no idea previously. There have been famous (unintentional) examples of this in history, such as Charles with the gas balloon, and Bell with the telephone.

It does need a little preparation. Think of a likely scenario that would spur on the group. In the early days of the space race, the USA was kicked into action by the knowledge that the Russians had already got a satellite into orbit. You need a fictional equivalent of the Russians. It can be a competitor company, scientists in another country, whatever – but we 'know' that they have achieved a solution. Make up a few facts which are vague enough to avoid steering those participating, but add an element of truth. For instance, the man who thought it up is reported to be a heavy drinker, or the original prototype was much too heavy. Now sit back and let the group speculate. The results can be remarkable.

**Feedback** If you want to use this technique more frequently, you can't keep up the deception, but you can get the participants to pretend that it's true. It works well with the pretence, but it works better with certainty – though you must let the participants down gently. This isn't a technique that works well as an individual – it is very dependent on the interplay of ideas. Note that this technique is also quite useful for justifying a creative solution that someone won't accept. 'Rumour has it, the competition is already doing this very successfully.'

**Outcome** This isn't a technique for generating totally new ideas, but is excellent for cracking stubborn problems.

**Variations** This technique is effectively reverse-engineering a non-existent solution. A variant is to reverse-engineer a real solution to a rather different problem and use this as input to the process.

| | |
|---|---|
| Culture | ✪✪ |
| Techniques | ✪✪✪✪ |
| Personal development | ✪✪ |
| Mental energy | ✪✪ |
| Fun | ✪✪ |

# 19.5 Exercise: Spinning knowledge

**Preparation** Familiarize yourself with the basics of finding things on the Web.
**Running time** Ten minutes.
**Resources** Access to the World Wide Web.
**Frequency** Once.

Choose a subject that you know very little about. It should be something quite specific without requiring heavy technical knowledge – like rose pruning or the basics of how a compact disc works. Using the World Wide Web, see how much you can find out about the subject in ten minutes. You don't need to absorb everything, but try to make sure that you know where to get back to information that is particularly relevant. If you don't know much about the Web, enter your topic in the Google search engine (http://www.google.com).

**Feedback** The volume of information you can amass this way is quite frightening – in fact part of the skill of using the Web is being able to filter down from a huge number of possible sources to the information you want. It's also worth bearing in mind that the Web isn't always the best source of information. If you want, for example, something you might find in a dictionary or an encyclopaedia you might be better with a book or a CD ROM – but for most topics, the Web is superb.

**Outcome** Knowledge is dependent on being able to get hold of the right information quickly when you need it. Increasingly the World Wide Web is the easiest way to do this. If you aren't particularly hot at finding information on the Web, see Unit 26 for information on the book *The Professional's Guide to Mining the Internet*. Using the Internet well is a non-optional skill for those who wish to build their creative knowledge base.

**Variations** It is easy to lose track of time when using the Web. Consider using a kitchen timer to give you a warning when ten minutes is up.

| | |
|---|---|
| Culture | ✪✪✪ |
| Techniques | ✪✪ |
| Personal development | ✪✪✪✪ |
| Mental energy | ✪ |
| Fun | ✪✪✪ |

# Unit 20: Creative comms – stimulating new approaches by forcing different modes of communications

Communication is an essential part of group creativity. Unless we can toss ideas around a group and get effective input from all the members the group is not working efficiently. It is for this reason that it's probably best not to have a group engaged in creativity larger than around seven or eight people, as the number of channels of communication between each individual becomes unmanageable. The techniques in this unit get those involved to think about communication differently – forcing them both to think about communication and to bring more creativity into the process.

None of these techniques can be done individually as an exercise, but do read through the techniques. Make notes about how and when you can use them. And make sure you give them a try in the next appropriate forum. For the moment, this an ideal opportunity to catch up on your unit books.

## Unit books

Two books which emphasize the importance of communication in international business: *Riding the Waves of Culture* by Fons Trompenaars is the bible for those engaged in cross-cultural business, while *Blunders in International Business* by David Ricks highlights the case studies where things have gone wrong.

You can find more information on our unit books, or buy them, from our support site: www.cul.co.uk/crashcourse.

## Web links

Links to Web sites that explore human communication can be found at www.cul.co.uk/crashcourse.

# 20.1 Technique: In the dark

**Preparation** Obtain blindfolds, arrange coffee or tea break.
**Running time** Fifteen minutes to two hours.
**Resources** Half as many blindfolds as participants; space for movement.
**Frequency** Once with any group.

Needs an even number of people. Half the group are blindfolded, the other half are left without. Each blindfolded person is given another person as their minder. This exercise should take place across a coffee or tea break. The blindfolded person has to go through the usual activities they might undertake in such a break – getting a drink and a biscuit, going to the toilet, chatting with others, but under the guidance of the sighted person.

**Feedback** At the end of the break take five minutes to get feedback from the participants. How did the blindfolded people find these simple activities? Were the helpers helpful or a hindrance? What was unexpectedly difficult? How did the helpers feel?

**Outcome** By piggybacking on a natural break, this exercise can afford to take a little more time than is usual in this book. The exercise has a strong element of teambuilding and ice-breaking. There is a mutual bond from the shared experience, and a forced interaction between blindfolded person and helper which will help break the ice. It also will generally inject energy and fun into a part of a meeting or training session that can be quite dangerous. Although breaks are essential, they can provide a negative distraction with participants tempted to phone the office or sink into a near-somnolent state – this exercise makes sure this doesn't happen.

**Variations** You can stretch this exercise to fit the available opportunities. If you are involved in a residential session, it can be extended considerably. We have been involved in sessions where a whole evening was spent in blindfold/helper pairs, including time spent in the bar and a full evening meal. Whether this takes place in an open environment like a hotel or a closed conference centre, it can have a huge impact on the participants.

| | |
|---|---|
| Culture | ✪✪✪✪ |
| Techniques | ✪ |
| Personal development | ✪✪✪✪ |
| Mental energy | ✪✪✪ |
| Fun | ✪✪✪ |

# 20.2 Technique: Out for the count

**Preparation** None.
**Running time** Two minutes.
**Resources** Enough open space for all participants to stand up, ideally in a circle.
**Frequency** Once with any group.

Get everyone standing up, in a circle if space permits. Start everyone clapping in rhythm. This should be reasonably quick, around two claps per second. Once the clapping is well established, get everyone to count loudly together. Each number should coincide with the clap. Get them to run from one to ten, then back down ten to one. Do this twice. You will need to talk between runs to organize them – give them a bit of warning along the lines of 'okay, here we go, from one to ten then back down ten to one, and... (two claps) one, two, etc.' Once they are feeling confident get them to do the same in French (again, have two goes).

**Feedback** Groups will get along reasonably well until it comes to counting backwards in French. As most people learn foreign numbers in sequence, counting backwards is much harder, resulting in chaos. This is a great way to get a group re-energized after lunch without giving them indigestion. Point out the way that this attempt to shift language changes the nature of the problem, and how it illustrates the way we chain concepts and memories together in our minds.

**Outcome** The exercise gets them out of their seats and active. When everything goes wrong on the French, there is usually considerable laughter. A big plus for this one is it's very quick, there is no preparation and it can use any room configuration.

**Variations** To make the exercise a little longer (and generate more hilarity), after running the exercise, tell them this is an old choirmaster's technique. In Anglican chant, psalms are sung in two groups of ten notes, so choirs often learn the chant by singing one to ten, then ten to one. As they were so good the first time (it doesn't matter whether they were or not) you are going to repeat it, but sing the numbers. Do it exactly as before but sing up a scale as the numbers go up, and down as the numbers come down. Give them the starting note as you finish the introduction – make sure this is low enough to be able to sing nine higher notes after it.

| | |
|---|---|
| Culture | ✪ |
| Techniques | ✪ |
| Personal development | ✪✪ |
| Mental energy | ✪✪✪ |
| Fun | ✪✪✪✪ |

# 20.3 Technique: Buy me

**Preparation** None.
**Running time** Ten minutes.
**Resources** None.
**Frequency** Once with any group.

Send out the group as individuals to find an object somewhere in the location other than the meeting/event room. They have to bring something back within two minutes. It should be something interesting, which they aren't going to get into too much trouble for moving. When everyone is back, each person has 30 seconds to sell their object: to describe why the organizer should spend his or her money on it. The person who sells their item best wins a prize. Ideally no more than seven or eight people should be involved, as it gets boring if too many objects are covered. Allow a minute at the end for returning objects.

**Feedback** React to enthusiasm and humour in the sales technique. Keep the process tight.

**Outcome** The process of going out and getting the objects is a good energy generator. It is possible to lose energy during the selling stage, as at any one time most of the team are not active, hence the need to keep process tight. It helps to have each salesperson stand up, and to encourage the audience to comment. However, the prime benefit of this exercise is as a change of direction. Encourage the participants to bear their object and their sales talk in mind when they return to the subject of the session – it might lead to some very original thinking.

**Variations** If conditions don't permit it, you can get people to sell objects they have about their person, though this removes the considerable advantages of getting them moving out of the room. A variant which can be very effective is to get each team member to sell a piece of their clothing, which they must remove before sale. Ideally give them the opportunity to leave the room to remove it – you may get some more daring items that way, and the more daring, the more effective as a stimulus.

| | |
|---|---|
| Culture | ✪ |
| Techniques | ✪ |
| Personal development | ✪✪✪✪ |
| Mental energy | ✪✪✪ |
| Fun | ✪✪✪ |

# 20.4 Technique: Blindfold birthday

**Preparation** Obtain blindfolds (not essential – see variations).
**Running time** Five to ten minutes.
**Resources** Blindfolds; enough space for teams to line up and mill around a little.
**Frequency** Once with any group.

Split the group into teams, ideally with at least five people per team. Their task is to get into a line in order of their birthdays. The problem is, they have to do it blindfolded, without speaking. Give the teams two minutes to discuss tactics (with the promise not to mention their birthdays). At this point the blindfolds go on. Mix the order of the individuals within each team, in case of collusion. Now there is silence for three minutes while they attempt to get in the right order. If they feel they are in the right order, they should indicate it by all holding their hands in the air. Note the possible winner, but don't stop the rest until the time is up.

**Feedback** Remember to check the birthdays – they may not have it right. Spend a minute getting a feel for the tactics used – see if the approach varies from team to team.

**Outcome** There is a good combination of creative thinking and energy in this exercise. Being blindfolded makes the participants more aware of other senses, and can result in some interesting interaction, giving a degree of ice-breaking too.

**Variations** If there is time, a good way of making this an even more effective timeout is to have an initial five-minute session when each team makes blindfolds for another. This also means that the exercise can be performed without preparation, apart from having the materials available. We have found that items typical to a meeting room – a sheet of flip chart paper, sticky tape and whiteboard pens – can produce some very creative blindfolds. The exercise has been attempted without the initial tactics talk, but it can be very frustrating for those taking part – not recommended.

| | |
|---|---|
| Culture | ✪✪ |
| Techniques | ✪ |
| Personal development | ✪✪ |
| Mental energy | ✪✪✪✪ |
| Fun | ✪✪✪✪ |

# 20.5 Technique: Lego™ construction

**Preparation** Obtain resources.
**Running time** Ten to fifteen minutes.
**Resources** A large supply of Lego™ bricks; a simple Lego™ construction to copy; blindfolds; at least two rooms.
**Frequency** Once with any group.

The object of the warm-up is to copy a simple Lego™ structure. Divide the group into teams:

- One is the eyes.
- One is the mouth.
- Two are the hands, arms and legs.

The eyes can see what is being copied but can't speak and can't see what is being built. The mouth can speak and can see what is being built, but can't see what is being copied. The hands, arms and legs can't see (they wear blindfolds).

In one room the eyes look at the original structure, then pass instructions to the mouth. The mouth directs the hands, arms and legs through the building process using these instructions. The mouth can't touch the Lego™ bricks or his or her fellow team members.

The first team to complete the construction accurately wins. Unless you have extra time, ignore the colour of the bricks.

**Feedback** In this warm-up, as in work teams, you are dependent upon your fellow team members. It is frustrating when there is a bottleneck. It is easy to blame the slowest point in the team for the frustrations of the team as a whole. It often seems that you could do the job better on your own. Some roles cause members of the team to feel excluded and it is easy to leave them this way. When you are under pressure it is easy to focus on task and tough to think of the team members.

**Outcome** With a discussion session afterwards, this warm-up provides important teamworking lessons.

**Variations** The division of the team is arbitrary, as is its size. You could run it with teams of three (one constructor) or introduce additional roles into the process. If you wanted to build in lessons about communication, you should forbid note taking and could introduce additional steps between the eyes and the mouth.

| | |
|---|---|
| Culture | ✪✪ |
| Techniques | ✪ |
| Personal development | ✪✪✪✪ |
| Mental energy | ✪✪✪ |
| Fun | ✪✪✪ |

# Unit 21: Going green – environmental techniques to enhance creativity

The environment in which we try to be creative can have a huge effect on the outcome. Getting away from sources of stress and introducing unusual external stimuli can make a huge amount of difference. All too often we try to be creative sitting at a desk (just like we do every day), or sitting round a meeting table. Look for opportunities to approach creative thinking in a different environment. Schedule a meeting in a Jacuzzi, or visit the pub. When working on your own, just going for a walk in the country or taking a bath can be a great help. We are used to making do with environment in business – it's time to take charge.

Do try out the exercises as you go. Put them off until later and you probably won't ever do them. Read through the techniques. Make notes about how and when you can use them. And make sure you give them a try in the next appropriate forum.

## Unit books

Two recommendations that combine the impact of the environment with some very creative views on life are Bill Bryson's excellent insider/outside tour of the British Isles, *Notes from a Small Island*, and Pete McCarthy's beautiful evocation of the best and worst of Ireland in *McCarthy's Bar*.

You can find more information on our unit books, or buy them, from our support site: www.cul.co.uk/crashcourse.

## Web links

Web links to alternative ways of getting an environmental stimulus, or having a different style of meeting can be found at www.cul.co.uk/crashcourse.

# 21.1 Exercise/Technique: Something completely different

**Preparation** A problem or idea required.
**Running time** Ten minutes.
**Resources** None.
**Frequency** Once.

This is an approach to enhancing your creativity that is best tried when you have a problem in mind or an idea you are working on. The activity is simple – do something completely different, unconnected with your problem, for ten minutes. This should involve an activity with lots of input, not simply sitting still, having a drink or chatting. While you are doing this different thing – it might be reading a book on a totally different subject, going for a walk, watching the TV – keep your problem in mind, even though you are really concentrating on what it is you are doing. Look for things in what you are doing that will provide inspiration with your problem. This might mean looking at what you are doing in a quite different way. At the end of the ten minutes, return to your problem.

**Feedback** Note that this is very different approach to *Unconscious creativity* (21.2), looking for positive inspiration in an unconnected field. This is one of the reasons this book emphasizes the value of reading – and reading a wide range of subjects – because the opportunities for sparking an idea are very significant. As a side benefit, you will come back to your thoughts refreshed by the change, but that isn't the main aim.

**Outcome** Many of the great ideas of the past have come from looking at something very different and drawing parallels. The mind is always using models and metaphors to hang ideas on: here we are fertilizing this process.

**Variations** Don't always use the same distraction, though some will deliver again and again.

| | |
|---|---|
| Culture | ✪✪✪✪ |
| Techniques | ✪✪ |
| Personal development | ✪✪✪ |
| Mental energy | ✪✪✪ |
| Fun | ✪✪✪ |

# 21.2 Technique: Unconscious creativity

**Preparation** A problem or idea required.
**Running time** Ten minutes.
**Resources** None.
**Frequency** Once.

For this exercise you need a problem or an idea that you are working on. It needs to be fresh, rather than something you've been working on for days. If there isn't anything appropriate, use an artificial problem like 'how to develop a new type of children's snack' or 'how to cut down waiting time in accident and emergency departments'.

Spend five minutes thinking through the problem area. Positively avoid solutions. Just think about what the problem is, who is involved in it, what happens at the moment and so on. Now put the problem to one side. Revisit it briefly (just the problem, not solutions) just before you go to sleep.

Come back to the problem after three to four days. Spend a minute thinking about it, then sit down with a piece of paper and write down what you could do. Don't analyse, just let whatever comes to mind flow out. If nothing comes after a few seconds, start to write anything at all without 'steering' the thoughts, then pull yourself gently back to the problem.

**Feedback** Sometimes this technique won't deliver, but surprisingly often, partly formed ideas will emerge. As Guy Claxton points out in *Hare Brain, Tortoise Mind* (see Unit 9 unit books), we are capable of much more unconscious effort than we normally admit. Many creativity techniques involve taking the unconscious by surprise. This approach lets the unconscious take its own pace. It's not necessarily better, but makes a valuable alternative.

**Outcome** If you find that this approach delivers, consider using it as an explicit technique, but the important thing is to allow time for unconscious connections to be made.

**Variations** You need to be able to let go of the problem consciously to let the unconscious deal with it – yet any important problem will nag at you. If you can use an electronic diary or task list to alert you in a few days' time, your conscious mind will be more comfortable letting go.

| | |
|---|---|
| Culture | ✪✪✪✪ |
| Techniques | ✪✪ |
| Personal development | ✪✪✪✪ |
| Mental energy | ✪✪ |
| Fun | ✪✪ |

# 21.3 Exercise/Technique: Go gallery

**Preparation** Find an art gallery displaying modern art.
**Running time** 30 minutes.
**Resources** None.
**Frequency** Once.

This is a very simple exercise. Find an art gallery displaying modern art. Go and visit. Spend half an hour wandering round looking at the exhibits. That's it.

Well, almost. When you are looking around, take a rather different approach to the usual gallery visitor. Look at each painting or sculpture or installation in turn. Don't spend a long time – perhaps 30 seconds or a minute for each. In that time do one thing only. Consider what the artwork makes you think of. Don't worry if the piece is a load of rubbish that you wouldn't give house-room to – that's not the point. Just let the inspirations flow.

**Feedback** If you are the sort of person who hasn't time for modern art (or art in general), don't give this one a miss – it is particularly suitable for you. You have to be able to suspend your normal irritation that 'so-called art' that could have been done by a chimpanzee commands huge prices. All you are doing is using the art as a launchpad for your own thoughts and ideas.

**Outcome** There's a double benefit from this one. Just getting out of your normal habitat can help enhance your creativity, but using the works of art as provocation for different ways of thinking can be very valuable.

**Variations** If you haven't got easy access to a gallery, get hold of one of the excellent CD ROMs of art or find something appropriate on the World Wide Web (see the support Web site for suggestions). As an alternative, a scrap yard or any site of urban or industrial decay can be equally effective. In fact, come to think of it, they're probably more artistic too.

| | |
|---|---|
| Culture | ✪✪✪ |
| Techniques | ✪✪ |
| Personal development | ✪✪✪✪ |
| Mental energy | ✪✪ |
| Fun | ✪✪ |

# 21.4 Technique: Game theory

**Preparation** Obtain a computer adventure game.
**Running time** Thirty minutes.
**Resources** Computer.
**Frequency** Several times.

Get hold of a computer-based adventure game. If you aren't sure what this is, talk to a teenager or ask at your local computer games shop. Glance through the instructions, but don't worry too much about them. Launch into the game and spend around half an hour exploring it. Don't spend much longer, unless you want to for entertainment. But come back to the game a number of times.

**Feedback** It may seem strange to recommend as a practical exercise what many would regard as an adolescent pastime, but an adventure game contains two prime challenges. To succeed in such a game, you need to build knowledge of your environment and solve puzzles. Because the environment is artificial, the knowledge is 'pure' – it isn't something you can already have gathered elsewhere, so the practical experience is guaranteed to be valuable. Similarly, the puzzles are specifically designed to require creative solutions.

Elsewhere we have recommended adventure games as a way of changing the viewpoint. In that case, we suggested using 'walkthroughs' to guide you through the puzzles, as the aim was to get you into a different frame of mind. Here, the aim is to improve your knowledge development and creativity, so you should try to solve the puzzles and find your way around without help.

**Outcome** Few activities combine more effective practice at two of the prime aspects of brainpower.

**Variations** This is definitely one to use outside your conventional working environment, as even the most enlightened management is liable to raise an eyebrow if this is described as knowledge management and creativity training.

| | |
|---|---|
| Culture | ✪✪✪ |
| Techniques | ✪✪ |
| Personal development | ✪✪✪✪ |
| Mental energy | ✪✪ |
| Fun | ✪✪✪✪ |

# 21.5 Technique: Snapshots

**Preparation** Half an hour preparation time around the site; obtain resources.
**Running time** Ten minutes.
**Resources** Rough maps of the site for each team; instant camera, or digital camera plus PC, or video camera and TV.
**Frequency** Once with any group.

Before the exercise, take five shots around the location of the session using one of the technologies suggested in the preparation section. The pictures should be of something that is clearly identified, but not easily spotted. The places that are pictured should be outside the meeting room, but within a very short walking distance. The teams are given a rough map of the area and are shown the five images. Their task is to mark on the map where the five images are located.

**Feedback** If a team gets all five images before time allowed is up, you could have a bonus image up your sleeve to keep them occupied. The team that gets all five first, or comes closest, wins a prize.

**Outcome** Snapshots is a great multi-purpose activity, getting people moving, out of the meeting room and searching in a creative manner.

**Variations** A number of variants are possible here. You can show all five images up front, or have one image on show for the first two minutes, one for the next two minutes and so on (this means the teams have to manage time better). If the images are shown up front, you could repeat them throughout, or you could have two or three viewing sessions through the event. An inversion of this exercise requiring considerably more equipment and quite a bit more time is possible. Note down on a sheet a number of interesting items or views around the meeting room. Each team is sent out with some form of instant camera, and has to return with shots of as many of the required targets as possible. This variant is particularly challenging because you can include mobile targets like people.

| | |
|---|---|
| Culture | ✪✪ |
| Techniques | ✪✪ |
| Personal development | ✪✪ |
| Mental energy | ✪✪✪✪ |
| Fun | ✪✪✪✪ |

# Unit 22: Spatial thinking – right-brain group sessions

When you are trying to get a group functioning more creatively it is important to engage them in activities that bring in the right side of the brain to ensure all-round creativity. The techniques in this unit are largely concerned with spatial thinking, one form of activity that ensures that the right brain is active. Puzzles and problems involving spatial thinking can be a great way to kick-start creative thought.

Do try out the exercises as you go. Put them off until later and you probably won't ever do them. Read through the techniques. Make notes about how and when you can use them. And make sure you give them a try in the next appropriate forum.

## Unit books

Elsewhere we recommend de Bono's *Serious Thinking* book – but when engaged in spatial thinking a better de Bono product is his *Super Mind Pack*, which is much more a workout for the brain.

Taking a very different approach, don't be put off by the title of Martin Gardner's superb *Colossal Book of Mathematics*. This is no dull textbook, but rather a tour of all that is entertaining and mind-boggling in recreational maths, with plenty of puzzles and spatial thinking. It's a fantastic creative workout.

You can find more information on our unit books, or buy them, from our support site: www.cul.co.uk/crashcourse.

## Web links

Links to sites with puzzles and activities that use this approach to engage the right-hand side of the brain can be found at www.cul.co.uk/crashcourse.

# 22.1 Exercise/Technique: The magic tunnel

**Preparation** Obtain paper.
**Running time** Five minutes.
**Resources** A sheet of A4 (or Letter) paper per team; enough space for the teams to be well separated, or in breakout rooms.
**Frequency** Once with any group.

Split the group into teams of no more than five or six. Each team is given a sheet of paper. Their task is to pass the entire team through a hole in the sheet of paper. The whole must be surrounded by unbroken paper, and no other items are to be used. The first team to achieve this is the winner. As an exercise, try this out yourself before reading on.

**Feedback** Point out the apparent impossibility on first approaching it. If no one completes the exercise in five minutes, demonstrate the solution; if a team does, get them to show the rest what they did. Emphasize the spatial thinking involved – what's needed is to produce a long strip of paper, then make a hole down the middle of it. Often teams will generate an intermediate solution by 'cheating' – say by passing the team's names through a hole in the paper. Applaud this, but then add in the requirement to pass the actual people through bodily.

Solution. Fold the paper in two. Make a series of four tears, from the folded edge towards the other edge, leaving a clear centimetre of untorn paper in each case.

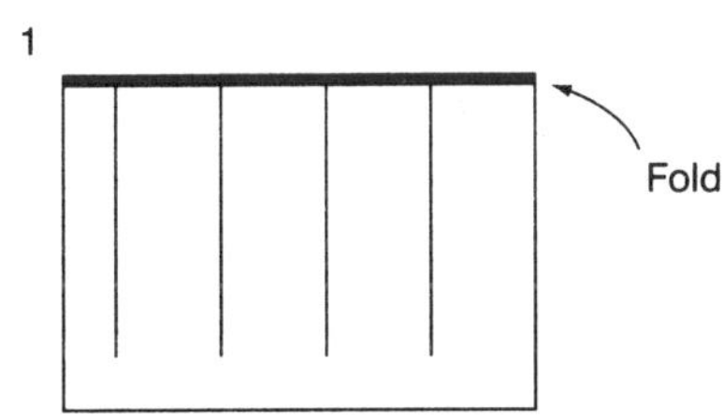


Make three tears in the opposite direction, between the original tears. Again, leave a clear centimetre at the end.

2

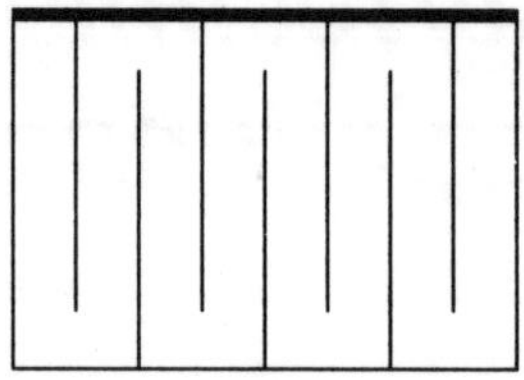

Tear along the crease of the three central creased end points. Open out the sheet of paper. It will make a paper ring, plenty big enough to pass a person through. Practice this before the event.

3

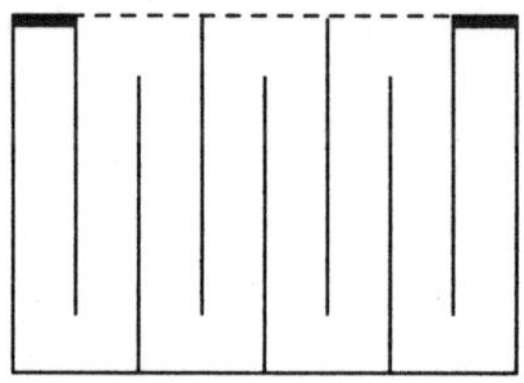

**Outcome** An excellent exercise in spatial thinking.

**Variations** None.

| | |
|---|---|
| Culture | ✪✪ |
| Techniques | ✪✪ |
| Personal development | ✪✪✪✪ |
| Mental energy | ✪✪ |
| Fun | ✪✪✪ |

# 22.2 Technique: Handcuffs

**Preparation** Make handcuffs.
**Running time** Five minutes.
**Resources** A string handcuff or a length of string per participant; enough space to work in.
**Frequency** Once with any group.

String handcuffs consist of a length of string (at least one metre, preferably longer) with a loop tied at each end. The loop should be large enough to slip a hand in and out of easily. If you haven't prepared the loops in advance, this can be the first stage.

Get the group into pairs with one handcuff per person – with an odd number you will have to take part. Ask one of each pair to slip both hands through the loops in their handcuffs. Ask the other member to slip a hand into one loop, then take the other end and pass it over their partner's handcuffs (between the handcuff and the body), finally slipping their remaining hand through. They are now linked. Their objective is to separate themselves without taking their hands out of their loops, or untying or cutting the string.

We have seen many ingenious solutions (cheating outrageously) but the 'correct' answer is to take the centre of your string through your partner's wrist loop and over the back of their hand. Voilà! You are free. You may find that you have actually tied a tighter knot at this stage. If so, reverse the process and then do it again in the opposite direction.

**Feedback** Very few people have come across this exercise but those that have must be asked to keep the solution to themselves. Be sure to demonstrate that the solution is possible at the end.

**Outcome** Touching and close contact are extremely effective at breaking down barriers, while the exercise itself requires good, right-brain-stimulating, spatial thinking. The outcome depends upon the participants' approach. Some treat it as a cerebral exercise and will stand thinking through the problem. Most leap straight in.

**Variations**

If using this as an early, ice-breaking exercise add an additional challenge. For instance, while separating yourselves, find out two things about your partner that will surprise everyone else.

| | |
|---|---|
| Culture | ✪✪ |
| Techniques | ✪ |
| Personal development | ✪✪✪✪ |
| Mental energy | ✪✪✪ |
| Fun | ✪✪✪ |

# 22.3 Exercise: Quick on the draw

**Preparation** None.
**Running time** Ten minutes.
**Resources** Notepad.
**Frequency** Once.

Most of us are convinced that we are bad at drawing. But try this exercise before you dismiss your own abilities.

Without anything to look at, draw a picture of a house with a person and a car outside it. Don't spend more than a couple of minutes over it. Put that picture aside. Now take a toy or a cartoon-style picture (rather than a photograph) and draw a copy of it. Don't use a clever technique like squaring off the paper, and try to draw fluidly rather than in minute detail. If things start going horribly wrong, throw the picture away and start again.

**Feedback** You will probably find you were much better at copying than at producing the first drawing. Most adults' drawings of the car, the house and the child don't differ much from a five-year-old's. How is it possible that your drawing skills improved so much between the two pictures? After all, there's nothing too challenging about a car or a house. In fact, we are mostly much better at drawing than we allow – but we are limited by our ability to visualize and by the certainty that we 'can't draw'. A number of other exercises in this book help with visualization. Here, we are just aiming for an understanding of a classic limitation of creativity.

**Outcome** This exercise isn't designed to turn you into an artist, though you may well find you can draw a lot better than you thought. Instead it should put across the importance of visualization, and give a potential boost to your creativity.

**Variations** Given your new-found abilities, try copying a photograph of a person. The result is usually much more like a real person than your visualized person, but still varies hugely from the original. Why is that? What could you do differently?

| | |
|---|---|
| Culture | ✪✪ |
| Techniques | ✪✪ |
| Personal development | ✪✪✪✪ |
| Mental energy | ✪ |
| Fun | ✪✪ |

# 22.4 Technique: Towering

**Preparation** Obtain resources.
**Running time** Five minutes.
**Resources** Roll of brown paper or newspaper, and roll of sticky tape per team; enough space to work in.
**Frequency** Once with any group.

The group is split into teams of three to four people. This exercise will only work with two or more teams. The teams are given the challenge to build the tallest free-standing tower they can, using only the paper and tape you give them. At the end of the time period, the towers must be totally unsupported.

**Feedback** There may not be an outright winner, as the ceiling could limit height, but be prepared to choose a winner on a combination of height and artistic appeal – or several winners. If any of the towers look particularly flimsy, try blowing them to see if they fall over – this will amuse the other teams – but still count them as successful. The exercise benefits from a silly prize, e.g. small bag of sweets.

**Outcome** The tower-building exercise gets the team working together, but the primary aim is to get the individuals involved doing something completely different from the task in hand to increase creativity.

**Variations** You should allow teams with the insight to do so to move to a different part of the room or into the corridor if this gives a greater ceiling height. Taking this exercise outside can be interesting (especially with light winds). Given longer, the exercise can be specifically to build the most attractive tower at least two (or three) metres in height. This would allow for some artistic input with whiteboard pens, and more consideration of the form of the tower, rather than its height. Various alternative materials can be used. Try wallpaper lining paper or photocopier paper. Can be run with no means of joining the paper, or only paperclips, but allow the teams a little longer in this case.

| | |
|---|---|
| Culture | ✪✪ |
| Techniques | ✪ |
| Personal development | ✪✪✪ |
| Mental energy | ✪✪✪ |
| Fun | ✪✪✪✪ |

# 22.5 Technique: Plane sailing

**Preparation** Obtain paper.
**Running time** Five minutes.
**Resources** An A4 (or Letter) sheet per participant; normal meeting or training room.
**Frequency** Once with any group.

Split the group into teams. Each team is given a sheet of paper for each team member. They then have three minutes in which each member of the team makes a paper plane. During the three minutes, they also have to decide which plane is to represent their team, without trying the planes out. At the end of the three minutes, the elected team members line up and send off their paper planes. The winner (with the plane that flies farthest) gets a small prize. Something appropriate like a cheap toy plane goes down well.

**Feedback** It is quite possible that each team has several planes that might be winners. One of the lessons of this exercise is that there isn't a single right answer to a problem – but you have to become comfortable with choosing an option and getting on with it, rather than continuing to dither over the possible outcomes.

**Outcome** This isn't a particularly high energy timeout, but it is an excellent one for getting the participants away from their current train of thought and putting them onto new directions. Choosing a plane to represent the team without seeing it fly is an important part of the exercise, both to emphasize the possibility of more than one right answer and to point out the risk inherent in many decisions.

**Variations** Don't be tempted to let them try out the planes before the shoot-out, for the reasons given above. It can be fun to have a second test where all planes are used, but still try the selective approach first. To increase the energy boosting in good weather conditions, consider taking the participants outside to do this exercise. If there is a handy bridge, gallery or balcony from which the planes can be launched, so much the better. This technique can also be used at the end of session as a way of making feedback less boring – get them to make their feedback forms into paper planes.

| | |
|---|---|
| Culture | ✪✪ |
| Techniques | ✪ |
| Personal development | ✪✪✪ |
| Mental energy | ✪✪✪ |
| Fun | ✪✪✪ |

# Unit 23: Selection techniques – which idea is best?

Often it's not the actual generation of ideas that presents the biggest problem. Once the ideas have been produced, it is still necessary to select appropriate ideas, to refine them and to prepare for selling and implementation if they are not to remain just ideas but to be put into practice. Using appropriate techniques at these later stages is just as important as getting the ideas in the first place.

Do try out the exercises as you go. Put them off until later and you probably won't ever do them. Read through the techniques. Make notes about how and when you can use them. And make sure you give them a try in the next appropriate forum.

## Unit books

This unit's book reflects on the way choices and decisions have influenced the growth of some of the greatest businesses of the late 20th century. Robert X. Cringeley's *Accidental Empires* is subtitled *how the boys of Silicon Valley make their millions, battle foreign competition and still can't get a date*, which is a good indicator that this is anything but yet another dull business book.

You can find more information on our unit books, or buy them, from our support site: www.cul.co.uk/crashcourse.

## Web links

An Excel spreadsheet shows a simple approach to quantifying the evaluation of different ideas and Web links are provided to sites with information on decision support at www.cul.co.uk/crashcourse.

# 23.1 Technique: The £100 bid

**Preparation** None.
**Running time** Five minutes.
**Resources** None.
**Frequency** As required.

When you have had a particularly successful session you will have walls covered with raw ideas and you will have developed some of those into more complete solutions that are suitable for implementation. How do you select from this mess? The simplest way is simply to say 'Choose' and then see what happens. A more democratic way of choosing is using a £100 (or $100) bid.

Give everyone in the group a notional £100 and instruct them that they can spread this over the ideas in any way they choose. They can put all £100 onto one idea, they can split it over two or they could even put £1 onto 100 different ideas.

Once everybody has had an opportunity to bid, sum the money attached to each idea and the idea with the highest amount is taken forward.

**Feedback** This is a relatively fast and painless way of selecting from a list. It has an advantage over the slightly easier process of putting stickers next to your favourites because it allows more precise weighting. If you feel very strongly about an idea you can make that feeling have an effect. If you are really not too worried then this will also be reflected in your votes.

**Outcome** Having used this technique, groups are almost always satisfied with the decision. Sometimes there is a plea to allow one more idea past the hurdle and, depending upon the next stage, this is rarely a problem. Obviously if you have too many pleas for additional ideas to sneak through then you are diluting the effect of having made a selection.

**Variations** The amount given for distribution is somewhat arbitrary. We have found that £100 allows for enough variations to avoid limiting people but is faster than, say, £1,000. Alternatively give each participant five coloured stickers as their 'cash'.

| | |
|---|---|
| Culture | ✪✪ |
| Techniques | ✪✪✪✪ |
| Personal development | ✪✪ |
| Mental energy | ✪✪ |
| Fun | ✪ |

# 23.2 Technique: SWOT

**Preparation** None.
**Running time** Fifteen minutes (or significantly more depending upon approach).
**Resources** None.
**Frequency** As required.

This technique is another one for selection, ideally where there is a relatively small range of options to choose between. Most people will have come across it in other circumstances but not usually as a way of selecting ideas.

For those who have not used the technique, SWOT stands for Strengths, Weaknesses, Opportunities and Threats. The results are normally expressed as a quadrant on one sheet of paper for easy viewing.

Take each idea in turn and analyse the Strengths, Weaknesses, Opportunities and Threats attached to each of those that you might take forward. Use the results to select those that offer you the best combination of maximizing the positives and minimizing the negatives. In some circumstances you might be trying to develop a really safe idea. This would mean minimizing negatives. In some circumstances you might be trying to push your organization further, in which case you would look to maximize the positives.

Naturally, the degree of analysis that you go into will depend upon the importance of this selection. This does not involve judging the importance of the final idea but the importance of being absolutely right in the selection at this stage.

**Feedback** The advantage of this technique is that most people in a group have used it before and settle quite comfortably into using it for idea selection. It can, however, be very time consuming, particularly if you develop the analysis to a very detailed level.

**Outcome** It may take time but you will have a selection that everyone feels is detailed and complete.

**Variations** If you are working with a group that is large enough to split into teams then you can divide the ideas amongst them for the initial SWOT analysis and they can feed back their results.

| | |
|---|---|
| Culture | ✪✪ |
| Techniques | ✪✪✪✪ |
| Personal development | ✪✪ |
| Mental energy | ✪✪ |
| Fun | ✪ |

# 23.3 Exercise: Material gains

**Preparation** None.
**Running time** Five minutes.
**Resources** Notepad.
**Frequency** Once.

This isn't particularly related to evaluation, but helps give the creative mental muscles a workout. Think of a broad area of manufacturing, where the materials used are fairly constant. For example, it might be cars (steel), planes (lightweight metals), office buildings (glass and concrete) or crockery (clay). Note down the manufacturing area at the top of the page of your notepad. Below it put four circles. In the first put the material(s) you are familiar with. In each of the others, put a totally different material. For example, for cars the materials might be water, carpet and rubber.

In the remainder of the time, let your eyes skim over the materials and slot in below any thoughts you have on the positive implications of making this product from the material. Don't try to be systematic and work through one of each, just let the ideas flow. Don't link implications to practicalities. For instance, a positive implication of making cars out of water is that they'd be easy to park – it doesn't matter how it would work.

**Feedback** You might find it difficult to start with to stay positive. After all, a car made from water is ludicrous. Yet all creative ideas sound crazy to start with. You often need a change of viewpoint and a refinement of the idea before it becomes useful. The trouble is, we tend to squash them too early. This enforced positiveness will help restrain your natural tendencies.

**Outcome** This is also very good practice for thinking differently about very solid, very everyday things, an essential for creativity.

**Variations** Here we are using this approach to broaden your creative thinking; however, this technique could be used as a practical creativity technique for specific purposes. Thinking of the implications of building a car out of water, carpet and rubber – and what you would have to do to make them work – would be an excellent way to develop a new car (out of conventional materials) that had some genuinely new features.

| | |
|---|---|
| Culture | ✪✪ |
| Techniques | ✪✪ |
| Personal development | ✪✪✪✪ |
| Mental energy | ✪ |
| Fun | ✪✪✪ |

# 23.4 Exercise/Technique: Basic option evaluation

**Preparation** Nonc.
**Running time** Fifteen minutes.
**Resources** Notepad, pen.
**Frequency** As required.

Where you have a number of options to choose between, a simple option evaluation can make it much more practical to go for the right choice. Try out this exercise on a real-life evaluation, like choosing a new car or DVD player:

List the options on a piece of paper. If there are more than three or four, try to eliminate some immediately as totally unacceptable.

Now list the criteria by which you will decide between options. What will you use to distinguish them? Again, keep to a handful of the most important criteria.

Finally, score each option against each criterion. Use either a 1 to 10 scale or a High/Medium/Low scale. Combine the results.

This should give you a ranking of the options according to these logical criteria. However, it shouldn't be used as a fixed decision, but rather a guide to put alongside your intuition. If your gut feel differs from the logical assessment, try to see why. Are there criteria you are ignoring? Are some much more important than others?

**Feedback** Options can arise at several stages in a negotiation. You could be choosing between different bids, between different suppliers and products, between different combinations of variables. The only requirement is that you have a known set of options to choose between. This process helps you understand your decision better and come to a more effective choice.

**Outcome** By taking a systematic approach you can ensure that you have considered all the options, and that you are picking one with a conscious awareness of the criteria by which you will make the choice – the outcome is a more rational, thought-through decision.

**Variations** If you are finding wide variation between criteria, try *Sophisticated option evaluation* (23.5).

| | |
|---|---|
| Culture | ✪✪ |
| Techniques | ✪✪✪✪ |
| Personal development | ✪✪ |
| Mental energy | ✪✪ |
| Fun | ✪ |

# 23.5 Exercise/Technique: Sophisticated option evaluation

**Preparation** None.
**Running time** Twenty minutes.
**Resources** Notepad, pen.
**Frequency** As required.

Sometimes criteria aren't enough to decide between options. You need to be able to give different weightings to say that, for example, price is twice as important as delivery times. The process used is much the same as in *Simple option evaluation* (23.4), but will take a little longer. As before, use the selection of a new car, or something similar, for the exercise.

List the options on a piece of paper. Even more so than with a simple evaluation, it is important that you restrict the list to perhaps three or four. Then list the criteria by which you will decide between options. What will you use to distinguish them? Again, keep to a handful of the most important criteria. Before going any further, weight the criteria. Give one criterion the value 1 and give each other criterion a value that reflects its relative importance compared with that key criterion – for example, if it's half as important, give it a value 0.5. If it's twice as important, make it 2.

Finally, score each option against each criterion using a 1 to 10 scale. When you have done this, multiply each score by the criterion weightings before adding up the results.

This should give you a ranking of the options according to these logical criteria. However, it should only be a guide to put alongside intuition. If your gut feel differs from the logical assessment, try to see why. Are there criteria you are ignoring?

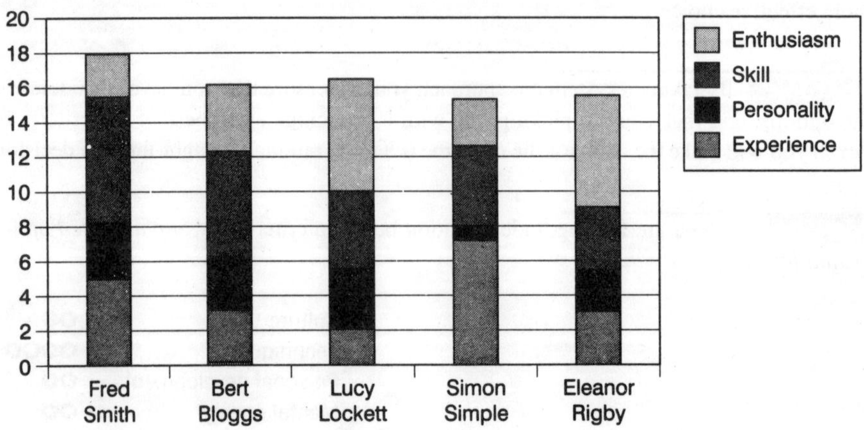

**Feedback** Options arise at several stages in a negotiation. You could be choosing between bids, between different suppliers and products, between different combinations of variables. Adding weighting to the process makes the evaluation more finely tuned.

**Outcome** By taking a systematic approach you can ensure that you have considered all the options, and that you are picking one with a conscious awareness of the criteria by which you will make the choice – the outcome is a more rational, thought-through decision.

**Variations** If the numbers are getting a bit of a strain, you may find it helpful to use a spreadsheet instead of paper. See the support site for an example.

| | |
|---|---|
| Culture | ✪✪ |
| Techniques | ✪✪✪✪ |
| Personal development | ✪✪ |
| Mental energy | ✪✪ |
| Fun | ✪ |

# Unit 24: Changing group dynamics – more energy and fun

It's impossible to over-stress the importance of getting energy and a sense of fun into a group if it's going to be creative. There is nothing more likely to stop your thinking from taking off than having a low energy, miserable group.

The techniques here are mostly group oriented, but you can try out the first as an exercise, and still make sure to read through the techniques. Make notes about how and when you can use them. And make sure you give them a try in the next appropriate forum.

## Unit books

We've already seen fun in business – in this recommendation we combine fun and that most mind-challenging of genre, science fiction. Try practically anything by Terry Pratchett, the remarkable *Hitchhiker's Guide to the Galaxy* books by Douglas Adams, or a superb novel that combines humour, science fiction and business – Frederik Pohl and Cyril Kornbluth's *The Space Merchants*.

You can find more information on our unit books, or buy them, from our support site: www.cul.co.uk/crashcourse.

## Web links

Links on changing group dynamics can be found at www.cul.co.uk/crashcourse.

# 24.1 Exercise/Technique: You're an animal

**Preparation** Obtain resources
**Running time** Two minutes plus thirty seconds per participant.
**Resources** Timer or large clock and a noise-maker are useful; enough open space for all participants to sit round.
**Frequency** Once with any group.

Give the participants two minutes to think of the animal that they think best represents them. They have to be able to say why, what special characteristics this implies, which other animal(s) they will get on with particularly well and which animals will be enemies. Then go round the group, giving each member a maximum of 30 seconds to put this across to the others. As an exercise, try this on yourself.

**Feedback** This is largely a self-running exercise, but you will need to monitor the time strictly and be prepared to cut off an individual if they over-run. Probably the most effective way to do this is to have a loud noise-maker and sound it when the 30 seconds is up. You must also ensure that you get complete answers. Make it clear the time is still running if they don't give all the required information.

**Outcome** An effective ice-breaker which tells a little about the individuals involved, and how they see themselves, in a different and fun way.

**Variations** If group members can all be issued with water pistols (and the room can take it – consider operating outside in good weather; fresh air is a natural energy booster), get them to soak anyone who overruns their 30 seconds. An interesting variation if you have the time is to have a third stage where the individuals get up from their seats and rearrange themselves so that they are near at least two other animals they are friendly with, and a minimum distance (say two metres) from all animals that they don't get on with. This both injects extra energy and ensures some listening during the descriptions rather than mentally practising their own information.

| | |
|---|---|
| Culture | ✪✪✪ |
| Techniques | ✪ |
| Personal development | ✪✪✪ |
| Mental energy | ✪✪✪ |
| Fun | ✪✪✪ |

# 24.2 Technique: Bursting with energy

**Preparation** Obtain balloons.
**Running time** Three minutes.
**Resources** Lots of uninflated balloons (at least three per participant); enough space for each team to stand together on open floor.
**Frequency** Once with any group.

Split the group into teams. Each team should be given a set of (uninflated) balloons. There should be at least three balloons per person and preferably more. The task is simple. Without using any tools, the teams are to inflate their balloons and burst them. As each balloon bursts, the team shouts out the number of balloons burst so far by their team. The team with the most burst balloons in the time (or using up all their balloons first) wins.

**Feedback** Note that a team that decides not to inflate its balloons fully to save time may have found it harder to burst them. Find out how the teams went about organizing the tasks – did everyone blow and pop, or were tasks allocated? Find out any observations from this.

**Outcome** A huge energy booster, this one. There's lots of movement and physical activity, while most people find the act of popping a balloon slightly stressing, so there's extra nervous energy generated. Can be very noisy and exuberant – probably not a good idea to run this one in a quiet area.

**Variations** The choice between operating with two teams and several can make this exercise work quite differently in large groups. Each has benefits, but the usual advantages of keeping a group down to six or seven apply. An effective variation is to split the time available into blowing time and popping time. This means that everyone tries both activities, and balloons have to be tied off, which adds to the confusion. The split-time variation can be run two ways. Either you have a specific time for the changeover (say two minutes for blowing, one for popping), or, more interestingly, let the team decide when to switch, but once they have gone from blowing to popping, they can't go back.

| | |
|---|---|
| Culture | ✪✪ |
| Techniques | ✪ |
| Personal development | ✪ |
| Mental energy | ✪✪✪✪ |
| Fun | ✪✪✪ |

# 24.3 Technique: On the square

**Preparation** Obtain paper.
**Running time** Two minutes.
**Environment** One or two sheets of A4 (or Letter) paper per team; enough space for all the participants to be standing up in teams.
**Frequency** Once with any group.

Split the group into teams. Try for as few teams as possible, with up to about 30 people per team. Put the sheets of paper on the ground in front of the teams. For teams of up to five in size, use half an A4 (or Letter) sheet for each team. Between five and ten use a full sheet, and above ten put appropriate numbers of sheets together. The object of the exercise is to get all of the team standing on their sheet(s) of paper. No parts of the body can touch the ground or any other means of support other than the paper or other team members.

**Feedback** If the exercise proves too simple, get the team to halve the sheet size and try again. In fact, it is worth doing this anyway to make sure that there is a more dramatic challenge. *On the square* is a very quick exercise, so repeating it is not a problem.

**Outcome** Like all the best warm-ups, *On the square* gets people out of their seats, involved in physical interaction with one another and laughing. If the sheet is very small it can also prove an interesting challenge to work out how to get everyone on board.

**Variations** Generally this is best run as an exercise where everyone attempts to achieve the goal, but with even-sized teams, it can be run as a first-to-complete exercise. As it can, in theory, be done with any sized group, it might be worth having a final extra session where everyone in the group, however large, attempts the exercise together.

| | |
|---|---|
| Culture | ✪✪ |
| Techniques | ✪ |
| Personal development | ✪ |
| Mental energy | ✪✪✪✪ |
| Fun | ✪✪✪✪ |

# 24.4 Technique: Magic carpet

**Preparation** Obtain rug.
**Running time** Ten minutes.
**Resources** A rug or strong length of fabric for each team (large enough for the whole team to stand on); open space on a polished floor.
**Frequency** Once with any group.

The object of this activity is for teams to race, on carpets, across a room. There need to be clear start and end points. Divide the group into teams and give each team a rug (make it a very cheap one because it may well be destroyed). Teams larger than six people will find this activity very hard, so keep them small.

The teams must stay on their rug and move the rug across the room. They can do this in any way that works for them but no part of their bodies may touch the ground off the rug.

**Feedback** It is unlikely that you will run this warm-up without a rug being torn or one of the team members falling from the rug. You must establish in advance whether there is a sanction for this (such as returning to the start) other than the delay caused by reorganizing the team. No prizes are necessary in an exercise like this. The most effective way we have seen is to have one or more team members at the front holding the leading edge of the rug and for all team members to jump simultaneously. Those at the front pull the rug forward as they all jump. It is also possible to move the rug by sliding it rather than jumping.

**Outcome** This is a very physical exercise which is great for raising energy levels. It can forge small teams but, like any team activity, can also create minor conflicts when mistakes occur.

**Variations** If you only have one rug, you can time each team across the room. This is less effective than a straight race as later teams are able to watch the technique of earlier ones and also because the need to stand around waiting lowers energy.

| | |
|---|---|
| Culture | ✪✪ |
| Techniques | ✪ |
| Personal development | ✪ |
| Mental energy | ✪✪✪✪ |
| Fun | ✪✪✪✪ |

## 24.5 Technique: Peer groups

**Preparation** None.
**Running time** Five minutes.
**Resources** Enough room for all group members to mingle.
**Frequency** Once with any group.

Get the entire group standing up. Tell them you would like them to get together in teams whose surnames start with the same letter (with a smaller group, make this surnames A to C, etc. as appropriate – you will need to prepare this ahead of time). If they haven't achieved this after two minutes, stop them anyway. Now you want them teamed up with people who drive the same make of car. After a minute or so, stop them again. Now you want them together with people with the same colour of underwear. After a minute or so, return them to their seats.

**Feedback** Allow more time for the first session, because with practice it becomes easier to get together with similar people. To start with there will be some tentative asking others, until someone takes the initiative and stands on a table (or equivalent), shouting their selection at the top of their voice. An excellent aspect of this particular exercise is that the bigger the numbers are, the better. We have used it with several hundred people to great effect.

**Outcome** Almost pure energizer, this is an excellent one to pull out of the bag at a moment's notice to revive a flagging group or to get them into the frame of mind for concentration. We have used it very effectively with a group that has spent most of the afternoon being lectured, when we wanted some positive contribution from them.

**Variations** You can use almost anything to group people, though ideally it should have a relatively small number of options (age, for instance, is too broad). Colour of underwear is a great finisher, because it has a slight frisson of naughtiness, leaving the participants on an energetic high. Don't be tempted to replace it with something more tame, whatever the audience. If you want an alternative finisher, make sure it has a similar connotation (e.g. what you wear in bed).

| | |
|---|---|
| Culture | ✪✪ |
| Techniques | ✪ |
| Personal development | ✪ |
| Mental energy | ✪✪✪✪ |
| Fun | ✪✪✪✪ |

# Unit 25: Refinement techniques – polishing up your ideas

Every new idea, without exception, is capable of being destroyed. However great the idea turns out to be, in the early stages it is fragile. It's rather like little green shoots, easily trampled on. Later, when they have had time to grow, the shoots can resist and survive. Similarly, it's only after refinement that we can sensibly shoot down an idea. The refinement techniques in this unit will help bring an idea to its best, an essential before it can be implemented.

Do try out the exercises as you go. Put them off until later and you probably won't ever do them. Read through the techniques. Make notes about how and when you can use them. And make sure you give them a try in the next appropriate forum.

## Unit books

A fascinating book that looks at the refinement of products to make them more usable, which is well worth reading whatever your line of business, is Donald Norman's *The Design of Everyday Things*. A must.

You can find more information on our unit books, or buy them, from our support site: www.cul.co.uk/crashcourse.

## Web links

Links to find out more on stakeholders and the development and refinement of products can be found at www.cul.co.uk/crashcourse.

# 25.1 Technique: Signposts

**Preparation** None.
**Running time** Five minutes.
**Resources** None.
**Frequency** As required.

*Signposts* can be used either to make it clearer which idea of a list to choose, or to enhance an idea that has already been selected.

For selection, the technique itself is mind-bogglingly simple. You merely list all of the things about the idea that are positive. Yes, that's it. The next question is, why would you bother?

Most people take evaluation to mean critique, and critique means to criticize negatively. When you ask for an open evaluation of ideas you tend to get a whole list of negatives. Then you find that proponents of particular ideas start defending them against attack and rational thought flies out of the window.

Structuring the evaluation into listing positives and listing negatives separately makes the whole process less emotive, less confrontational and more effective. It is generally also a good idea to list positives before listing the negatives because then there is less defensiveness about the negatives.

If you are using *Signposts* to refine rather than select, once you have stated the positives, go on to say how can you make these good points even better. You will then want to use the *Hazard markers* technique (25.2) to complete the refinement process.

**Feedback** This takes very little time and is a necessary stage of the process. Don't drop it.

**Outcome** *Signposts* followed by *Hazard markers* gives a much clearer picture of where the ideas stand and can actually lead to further development.

**Variations** When evaluating a collection of ideas you can either take each idea and list positives and negatives or take all of the ideas through *Signposts* first and then go through *Hazard markers* with them all. Usually with two or three ideas we find that the second approach works; with more than this it makes sense to stick to an idea at a time and go through both halves. Evaluation can be done in the whole group or in smaller teams with feedback.

| | |
|---|---|
| Culture | ✪✪ |
| Techniques | ✪✪✪✪ |
| Personal development | ✪✪ |
| Mental energy | ✪✪ |
| Fun | ✪✪ |

# 25.2 Technique: Hazard markers

**Preparation** None.
**Running time** Five minutes.
**Resources** None.
**Frequency** As required.

*Hazard markers* has already been introduced in *Signposts* (25.1). This is the negative stage where the previous one was positive. In other words, for this technique you list all of the negatives associated with the idea.

Having done this you have a decision to make. What are you going to do about it? Decide how complete and how positive you need the developed ideas to be and then you can either accept the negatives you have listed or do something about them.

If you are going to do something about them you can either attack them directly or, given time and an idea that warrants it, you could go back to problem-solving techniques using this negative as the problem.

This starts to sound like an infinite loop. You will always be able to find negatives for any idea and if you then go back to problem solving you will continue around and around and around. That is why the decision about the completeness of the answer is important. This helps you to decide where to stop the loop.

**Feedback** Like *Signposts*, this takes very little time and is a necessary stage of the process. Don't drop it. It's important that you undertake *Signposts* first, and keep the results in front of you as you undertake this technique. The reason is that it's easy to lose the good aspects of an idea while fixing the bad. Make sure that the *Signposts* benefits stay in the idea while you work out the negatives.

**Outcome** *Hazard markers* lets you understand what further development is still needed to make your idea work.

**Variations** When evaluating a collection of ideas you can either take each idea and list positives and negatives or take all of the ideas through *Signposts* first and then go through *Hazard markers* with them all. Usually with two or three ideas we find that the second approach works, with more than this it makes sense to stick to an idea at a time and go through both halves. Evaluation can be done in the whole group or in smaller teams with feedback.

| | |
|---|---|
| Culture | ✪✪ |
| Techniques | ✪✪✪✪ |
| Personal development | ✪✪ |
| Mental energy | ✪✪ |
| Fun | ✪✪ |

# 25.3 Exercise: Horse whispers

**Preparation** None.
**Running time** Five minutes.
**Resources** None.
**Frequency** Once.

Here's an exercise to refine your creative thinking skills. A man stands in the centre of a large field. There are four horses in the field, one at each corner – a bay horse, a chestnut horse, a white horse and a black horse. For reasons we needn't go into, the man has to kill his horses. If he must remain at the centre of the field, the horses stay at the four corners and he is a perfect shot, how can he make sure that none of his horses remain alive using only three bullets?

**Feedback** Don't go any further until you've attempted an answer. If you get one quickly, there are at least three solutions – try for another.

Last chance to consider your answer.

One solution is that only three of the four horses are his, so he only needs to shoot three to make sure that none of his horses remain alive. A second is that one of his horses was already dead of the terrible disease that was about to claim the others – hence his need to shoot them. A third is that the white horse was a chalk carving and had never been alive. There are more possibilities too.

**Outcome** Apart from the creative exercise in coming up with a solution, there is an interesting lesson here. We are conditioned from an early age to expect a single right answer to a problem. Often in reality there are many potential right answers, something that those who depend on creativity and knowledge management forget at their peril.

**Variations** Can you devise any more solutions to the problem?

| | |
|---|---|
| Culture | ✪ |
| Techniques | ✪ |
| Personal development | ✪✪✪✪ |
| Mental energy | ✪✪ |
| Fun | ✪✪✪ |

# 25.4 Technique: Second-best solution

**Preparation** None.
**Running time** Five minutes.
**Resources** None.
**Frequency** As required.

Sometimes one idea stands out above all others. This could be because it is a truly novel idea that has surprised and impressed those who have generated it. It could also be that it is a comfortable idea that will not shake things up too much and everyone knows they can live with. If you suspect that the second of these is the case then you might consider using *Second-best solution.*

For this technique you merely send the participants back to the voting stage and ask them to select a second-best solution that they can then work on further. If the best solution was one that they were comfortable with, you might want to give additional instructions about choosing an idea that has an element of discomfort but that has appeal nonetheless.

It is important not just to take the second idea that was voted for. With the best idea out of the way, views may change about the second best. Also, all of those people who voted for the best solution will feel cheated if you don't give them any say in what is second best.

The final stage of this technique is to go through a short brainstorming session about what it would take to make this idea better than the one that has been voted for as best. By all means use one of the idea-generating techniques for this.

**Feedback** With instructions about choosing an uncomfortable idea this technique is a great way of injecting novelty into the solution chosen. There is no reason at all why the 'second best' solution should not prove better than that first chosen.

**Outcome** You can decide to take forward just one of the two ideas selected (best and second best) or you can take them both forward for further development.

**Variations** You can build this technique into the selection process by asking people to evaluate the best solution and also the solution that is appealing but could never work or makes the group uncomfortable or needs significant changes before taking it forward.

| | |
|---|---|
| Culture | ✪✪ |
| Techniques | ✪✪✪✪ |
| Personal development | ✪✪ |
| Mental energy | ✪✪ |
| Fun | ✪ |

# 25.5 Exercise/Technique: Stakeholders

**Preparation** None.
**Running time** Fifteen minutes.
**Resources** None.
**Frequency** As required.

When selecting and refining ideas it is easy to base your actions on a single viewpoint – your own. However, there are very few creative actions that will have no effect on anyone else. If you have an idea that hasn't been fully thought through, use that in this exercise. Otherwise try a fictional idea like 'let's shut down two of our three factories and concentrate all the effort at one location'.

Spend a minute identifying who the stakeholders are. Who will be affected by your idea? Who might want to have an input into your idea? Who can influence whether or not your idea is success?

Then, for each stakeholder or group of stakeholders try to put yourself in their position. How would they see your idea? What would putting it into practice do to them? How might they react? If they would see your idea negatively, could you modify the idea (or the way it's implemented) to still achieve what it's designed to achieve but with greater stakeholder satisfaction?

**Feedback** When thinking about your idea from the stakeholders' viewpoints try as much as possible to get a genuine flavour of how they would see your idea.

**Outcome** If you achieve an effective stakeholder analysis you will know whom you might need to take action to influence if your idea is to succeed, and also will minimize the risk of disaffected stakeholders shooting down your idea.

**Variations** It may be possible to canvass stakeholders direct. This is a good thing to do, but can be time consuming. Bear in mind also that they may say something rather different from their actual thoughts.

| | |
|---|---|
| Culture | ✪✪✪ |
| Techniques | ✪✪✪✪ |
| Personal development | ✪✪ |
| Mental energy | ✪✪ |
| Fun | ✪✪ |

# Unit 26: Knowledge expansion – more techniques to help personal knowledge management

As we have already seen, the degree to which you can expand and manage your personal knowledge base will have a direct impact on your personal creativity. These exercises and techniques are designed to help with personal knowledge management.

Do try out the exercises as you go. Put them off until later and you probably won't ever do them. Read through the techniques. Make notes about how and when you can use them. And make sure you give them a try in the next appropriate forum.

## Unit books

In the 21st century we have available a facility that is capable of totally transforming personal knowledge management – the Internet. Unfortunately, all too often, those who hope to use the Internet in this way are frustrated by this unstructured, baffling mess of information. This unit's recommendation is *The Professional's Guide to Mining the Internet* by Brian Clegg, not a guide to the Internet itself, a form of book that is out of date as soon as it is published, but rather a guide to the skills and techniques necessary to get the most out of the Internet.

You can find more information on our unit books, or buy them, from our support site: www.cul.co.uk/crashcourse.

## Web links

Links to help with your use of the Internet to support your personal knowledge base can be found at www.cul.co.uk/crashcourse.

# 26.1 Exercise: On the box

**Preparation** Check TV schedules.
**Running time** Thirty minutes.
**Resources** TV, notepad.
**Frequency** Once.

Look through the TV schedules and find a number of different types of programme where interviewing (in the broadest sense) is liable to take place. Watch several separate chunks of interviewing in action – perhaps five minutes at a time. Concentrate on what the interviewer is doing. Make notes of how he or she tries to extract information from the interviewee. Look for open or closed questions (can they be answered with a single word, or do they require detailed description?). Look for questions that elicit facts, and questions that elicit feelings. How does the interviewer handle an interviewee who is trying to avoid the question?

**Feedback** Try to distil down the most effective aspects of the interviewer's technique as a set of personal pointers. Even if your role doesn't involve explicit interviewing, these techniques will be useful. Whenever you are talking to someone else to increase your knowledge level you are, in fact, interviewing. Most of us could improve our skills here significantly.

A key aspect of doing this well, which the professionals on TV have off to a fine art, is to minimize the obtrusiveness of the techniques they are using. It is the answers people are interested in, rather than the questions. Because of this, you will have to concentrate with unusual care on just what the interviewer is doing.

**Outcome** By incorporating a few of the tricks of professional interviewer into your repertoire you can increase the effectiveness of your knowledge gathering significantly.

**Variations** If you get the chance, also try this out with speech radio, particularly in a heavyweight political or news show. Consider taping the interviews (speech or TV) so you can play them back a few times to pick up the fine detail.

| | |
|---|---|
| Culture | ✪✪ |
| Techniques | ✪✪ |
| Personal development | ✪✪✪✪ |
| Mental energy | ✪✪ |
| Fun | ✪✪ |

# 26.2 Exercise/Technique: Category magic

**Preparation** A set of information you need to structure or understand.
**Running time** Ten minutes.
**Resources** Notepad.
**Frequency** Once.

Although the brain probably doesn't use categories to store information, it's a good way to break down concepts and facts to make them easier to understand. Sometimes categories are obvious. They may be 'good' or 'bad', or simple context categories like 'make of car' or 'type of Web site'. In other cases, the categories don't spring to mind. This technique will help in such circumstances.

Spend a minute or two jotting down bullet points from the information. Note key aspects of the information, specific items of information that can stand alone. Now take three of these items at random. You could use a spreadsheet or write your items on cards to do this. See if you can find a feature that two items share, but the third doesn't. Note down this feature as a category.

Select three at random again and repeat the process several times. There is no right or wrong number – do it until you seem to be running out of new categories or you've got at least ten categories.

Look through the categories list, seeing if any sensibly combine. Then try to allocate the items of information to the different categories. You may need to revisit category generation if you don't have a good set, but it's surprising how often you will have.

**Feedback** This approach won't generate every possible category – but you are just trying to find a structure that works. If you are comfortable with the outcome, the categories are fine.

**Outcome** With a little practice the categories often come together without needing this technique, but it's valuable if you have trouble generating categories. It can be used for everything from structuring information to generating an outline report.

**Variations** If you don't have a set of information you need to structure right now, spend a minute writing down at least ten reasons why you like your favourite thing, and use those instead to get the practice.

| | |
|---|---|
| Culture | ✪✪ |
| Techniques | ✪✪✪ |
| Personal development | ✪✪✪✪ |
| Mental energy | ✪ |
| Fun | ✪ |

# 26.3 Exercise: Doing and knowing

**Preparation** None.
**Running time** Five minutes.
**Resources** Notepad.
**Frequency** Once.

Think back over the last week and pick out between half a dozen and ten activities you undertook. Make them quite different, anything from reading a newspaper to performing brain surgery. List the activities, and rate each out of ten for your doing ability – your skill level, and your knowing ability – your knowledge level.

Next, note activities where there is a significant difference between the two scores. What does this imply to you about the activity and your approach to it? Remember, in this context, 'knowing' is about the activity itself, so in our example of reading a newspaper, it would involve your knowledge of the mechanics of reading, not your knowledge of current affairs.

Finally, where you have high knowledge scores, think how you might be able to use that knowledge in totally different circumstances. Where you have low scores, think how you might be able to apply some other source of knowledge if you had need of it. What if you had to explain one of these topics to a group of children, or needed to find a viable alternative – what knowledge would you call on?

**Feedback** Often we have to transfer knowledge from one area to another, or combine bits of knowledge to make a new whole. It is interesting to see how much our own knowledge correlates with our skills. It is quite possible, for instance, to be a great computer programmer without having the faintest idea how computers work, or to be an excellent wood carver with no knowledge of the chemical makeup of wood.

**Outcome** The aim of this exercise is to improve your understanding of what knowledge is, and to be more aware of how you deal with gaps in your knowledge, an essential process in good knowledge management.

**Variations** Think about valuations. Do we think more of highly skilled people in a particular field or of highly knowledgeable people? Do these valuations vary from field to field?

| | |
|---|---|
| Culture | ✪✪ |
| Techniques | ✪ |
| Personal development | ✪✪✪✪ |
| Mental energy | ✪ |
| Fun | ✪✪ |

# 26.4 Exercise: Fact quest

**Preparation** None.
**Running time** Ten minutes.
**Resources** Whatever reference facilities you normally use.
**Frequency** Once.

There are many sources of information which can expand your knowledge and excite your creativity. This exercise focuses on the knowledge library at your fingertips. Think for a moment of your surroundings at work. What sources of information are there to hand – books, CDs, intranet and Internet, company databases, magazines and newspapers? Jot them down. Think of your environment at home too. Jot down what is available there. Try your normal reference facilities to come up with answers to these questions (allow no more than ten minutes):

- Napoleon Bonaparte's birthday
- The atomic weight of caesium
- What are the actual words of that well-known quote about 'for whom the bell tolls' – and who wrote it?
- A definition of prelibation
- Yesterday's share price for British Airways
- The name of the chief executive of Ford UK
- The type of laser used in a laser printer

**Feedback** Don't worry if you wouldn't normally want to know half these things, just find them out. If your resources include the Internet, that's great, but be a little careful about using the World Wide Web for getting hold of specific facts. Not only will you sometimes come to a wrong answer, it often isn't the best way to come to a pure fact. See *The Professional's Guide to Mining the Internet*, this unit's recommended book, for more on using the Internet safely for research.

**Outcome** Good knowledge skills include the ability to get hold of facts – and you never know just what those facts are going to be. This exercise tests your resources.

**Variations** Feel free to try out different types of fact beyond the categories I've listed here. You might like to get someone else in your own area of speciality to put together a fact list. But don't miss this more general exercise – you never know just what facts you might need.

| | |
|---|---|
| Culture | ✪✪✪ |
| Techniques | ✪✪✪ |
| Personal development | ✪✪✪✪ |
| Mental energy | ✪ |
| Fun | ✪✪ |

# 26.5 Exercise: Binning paper

**Preparation** None.
**Running time** Ten minutes.
**Resources** Your files, notepad.
**Frequency** Once.

Look through your personal files and documents. Many of us keep copies of a huge range of information sources for future reference. We are not looking at books here, but magazines, journals, newspapers, cuttings, memos, papers and so forth.

Make a note of the principal sources. Now see if there are ways you can dispose of these mountains of paper and move to a more accessible source of the same information. Is the journal, magazine or newspaper available on CD ROM? If so, you will be able to find the information you need when you need it much quicker, without being surrounded by junk piles. Is the information you need available online? Are the memos or e-mails you have printed archived in an electronic form? As long as there is a secure, searchable repository you can dispose of your paper and find things more easily.

**Feedback** It can be quite a wrench to lose those piles of paper, but make sure you are hanging onto them for the right reason. Information can only contribute to knowledge if it is readily available and can be integrated with other sources. A five-foot stack of magazines has very limited chances of doing this effectively. Occasionally there is a good reason for sticking to paper – for example, CD ROM versions of magazines often don't include the advertising, and it may be that you need the advertising for some reason, but often you can compromise by combining the CD ROM with the latest version of the magazine.

**Outcome** Getting rid of paper sounds a mundane, time management sort of activity, but the reason you stored this paper was to make it an active part of your knowledge base, and it can't do that if the information contained in it isn't readily accessible. Indexed electronic forms make this much more practical.

**Variations** Sometimes it is worth scanning documents to include them in an electronic knowledge base, but beware the magpie inclination – make sure the information is being collected for a reason.

| | |
|---|---|
| Culture | ✪✪✪ |
| Techniques | ✪✪✪ |
| Personal development | ✪✪✪✪ |
| Mental energy | ✪✪ |
| Fun | ✪✪ |

# Unit 27: Spock rules – logic exercises to challenge the brain

These are not so much personal exercises as techniques that can be used to get a whole group thinking in a logical way – even so, there is an opportunity to have a go yourself in one case, and with friends in another. Although a creative leap may seem the opposite of logical solution, both involve making new connections, and though we have stressed the need to engage the right brain, as most of us are more left brain oriented, this doesn't mean that left-brain, logical activities should be ignored. Cryptic crosswords form another good exercise along these lines.

Do try out the exercises as you go. Put them off until later and you probably won't ever do them. Read through the techniques. Make notes about how and when you can use them. And make sure you give them a try in the next appropriate forum.

## Unit books

A cheap and cheerful book to give you a whole collection of exercises is *Brain Teasers* from the Pocket Puzzlers range.

A very different type of mental exercise can be had by reading a book like *Psychoshop* by Roger Zelazny and Alfred Bester, or almost anything by Gene Wolfe, where simply working out what is going on is itself an enjoyable mental challenge. Equally, try a classic whodunit murder mystery, where the challenge is to solve the murder before the author gives it away.

You can find more information on our unit books, or buy them, from our support site: www.cul.co.uk/crashcourse.

## Web links

Links to find further opportunities to be challenged can be found at www.cul.co.uk/crashcourse.

# 27.1 Technique: One spare square

**Preparation** Create playing boards (see below).
**Running time** Ten minutes.
**Resources** A playing board per team; room for teams to stand in a well-spaced line.
**Frequency** Once with any group.

This exercise needs teams of an even number of four or more, but six or eight works best. If you have an odd number of participants, join in yourself or use a waste paper basket as the final team member. Each team needs a playing board. This is a line of squares, one for each team member to stand in and one spare. The playing board could be carpet tiles, sheets of flip chart paper or something created in advance.

The exercise starts with half the team at each end of the board (one per square). The two halves face each other, with the spare square in between them. The two halves take turns to move and they can only move into the spare square by stepping into it, if it is directly in front of them, or by 'jumping' someone facing them. They cannot jump more than one person. The objective of the game is to swap the two halves of the team.

**Feedback** Once a team has failed a few times, the exercise may appear impossible. Reassure them that it can be done. Try it a few times beforehand with small objects to get comfortable. You can give hints as the exercise progresses. A useful one is that you should never face someone's rear unless you are stacked at an edge – ie in the start or end position. Another is, never move into an empty space unless you already have someone facing your way directly behind you, or the edge of the board. Don't give clues too soon.

**Outcome** This exercise has an unusually strong combination of physical movement and thinking. There might be some messages about communication come out of it, since team members will have different views of the solution.

**Variations** As an additional challenge, try combining two teams and solving it with twice as many people. The principle is the same, but the chance for error increases. To add energy, leapfrog the 'jumps', rather than going round each other.

| | |
|---|---|
| Culture | ✪✪ |
| Techniques | ✪ |
| Personal development | ✪✪✪ |
| Mental energy | ✪✪✪✪ |
| Fun | ✪✪✪✪ |

# 27.2 *Technique: Contract fishing*

**Preparation** Prepare contracts and rods.
**Running time** Five minutes.
**Resources** A large number of sheets of paper with paperclips taped to them (at least ten sheets per team). If the papers can be in the form of spoof contracts, so much the better. For each team, a stick with a longish piece of string attached (2–3 metres) and a magnet fixed to the end of the string. Any room format where a small section of the room can have a row of tables placed across it.
**Frequency** Once with any group.

Make a barrier with tables, and place all the sheets of paper on the floor on the far side of the barrier. Give each team a fishing pole. Describe the scenario: the company has decided to allow all groups in the company to tender for any work required. Rather than go through the time-consuming business of requests to tender, all contracts are placed in a pool. Whichever team fishes out a contract gets to undertake it. An individual in the team will be fishing: at regular intervals you will ask them to hand over the rod, until everyone has had a go. During the process notify them at the intervals necessitated by the team size when to hand over the pole. Get the rest of the team to encourage the fisher.

**Feedback** Count up the contracts each team has and award the winner some sort of prize. Point out that, while this is probably a good way to allocate contracts, to make it effective, they would have to have the option of throwing a contract back if they didn't want it.

**Outcome** This can generate a lot of energy, especially when more than one person goes for the same contract.

**Variations** For a longer, more thought-provoking version, each contract should be labelled with a duration and a value. The team can only hold contracts with (say) 100 duration points. Their aim is to maximize value, and they can throw contracts back into the pool.

| | |
|---|---|
| Culture | ✪✪✪ |
| Techniques | ✪ |
| Personal development | ✪✪ |
| Mental energy | ✪✪✪✪ |
| Fun | ✪✪✪✪ |

# 27.3 Exercise/Technique: Ands

**Preparation** None.
**Running time** Three minutes.
**Resources** No special requirements.
**Frequency** Once with any group.

Split the group into small teams (two or three). The challenge is to be the first team to be able to tell a (very) short story in which the word 'and' appears five times in a row, yet the story still makes sense. As soon as a team has a possible solution, they should alert the organizer. The other teams should be put on hold while the story is told. Try this yourself as an exercise before reading any further.

**Feedback** Early attempts may well stretch the rules considerably. Be positive about them, but allow the other teams to continue, finding alternative solutions. If none of the teams has a result in five minutes, award the best attempt with a prize. Make sure you are able to provide a valid solution if one has not been reached. A simple example is as follows: 'Smith and Jones, the butchers, want a new shop sign. It comes back from the sign writers with the words poorly spaced. Smith calls the sign writer and says, "This is no good. I want the spaces between 'Smith' and 'and' and 'and' and Jones to be the same."'

**Outcome** This is not an exercise that will inject a huge amount of energy, so it is best applied when the group already has plenty of enthusiasm, but you need a change of direction. The requirement to think laterally is a good preparation for creative work. You can artificially add a small energizer by requiring the teams to stand in different parts of the room while they work on their solutions, rather than sitting round a table.

**Variations** If the solution is reached too quickly (or you want to show off to the group), set the challenge of increasing the 'and' count to seven. This requires a slightly broader interpretation of the rules. Now the sign writer is producing a sign for a charity walk. Again the spacing is faulty. 'I want the spaces between Northumberland and "and" and "and" and Andover to be the same.'

| | |
|---|---|
| Culture | ✪✪ |
| Techniques | ✪ |
| Personal development | ✪✪✪✪ |
| Mental energy | ✪✪✪ |
| Fun | ✪✪✪ |

# 27.4 Technique: Rules rule

**Preparation** Obtain cards.
**Running time** Five minutes.
**Resources** An over-sized pack of cards or a PC with projector and a program to throw up random cards; any arrangement of room, provided all participants can see the cards.
**Frequency** As required.

Turn a card up and put it to one side. Then 'play' the remaining cards. Each one is turned up alongside the original card. You then state whether the card is valid or not, and discard it. The card is valid if it fits the rules of the game, but the group does not know the rules. Their task is to deduce the rules. As soon as someone feels they know what is happening, stop the process and listen to their theory. If it is true, the exercise is finished. If not, continue until someone can describe the rules.

Rules are up to you, but must be applied consistently. Examples might be 'the card must follow a card of a different suit', or 'a card must be bigger in value than the previous card'. If this proves too easy, join rules; for example, 'a red must follow a black unless it is a face card, in which case it can follow anything'.

**Feedback** Have a number of rules in reserve. If the rule is deduced quickly, say that was a practice round and run again with a more complex rule. If someone guesses wrong, point out the dangers of making assumptions with incomplete evidence – but a timely guess may win the game.

**Outcome** This is an effective way of warming up the creative juices, but warn the participants that an analytical approach is not ideal in the early stages of creativity, when it is best to ignore rules, logic and practicality.

**Variations** The same principle can be applied to anything where a rule can be deduced. Numerous physical puzzles can be used, for example a box with holes in, where a marble is dropped in one hole and emerges from another and the participants have to deduce the internal structure of the box. Such hands-on variants are best done with a number of artefacts, working in small teams.

| | |
|---|---|
| Culture | ✪✪ |
| Techniques | ✪✪ |
| Personal development | ✪✪✪✪ |
| Mental energy | ✪✪✪ |
| Fun | ✪✪✪ |

# 27.5 *Exercise/Technique: Racing demon*

**Preparation** Obtain cards.
**Running time** Ten minutes.
**Resources** A pack of playing cards per person; one or more tables.
**Frequency** As required.

This once-popular game works well as a warm-up. Each team member has a pack of cards. Each shuffles their pack and places 13 cards face down on the table. When they are ready, a nominated person says 'go'. The players turn up the top card of the 13. The aim is to be the first to dispose of these 13 cards (the demon). They are removed by building piles of cards of the same suit from Ace to King in the centre of the playing area. All piles are shared – anyone can put a card on any pile (but an Ace must be used to start it). To make this action more practical, the player can also play from the remainder of the pack in traditional patience (solitaire) fashion – by turning over three cards at a time, and if the card uncovered will fit on a pile it can be played. Make sure that participants understand that there are no turns – you play as fast as you can. To use this as an exercise you will need to get some friends involved.

**Feedback** A quick demonstration may be useful. As soon as one player in the team has disposed of the 13 cards, play stops.

**Outcome** It might seem that a card game is unlikely to raise energy, but the need to watch many different spots for the opportunity to play makes this a very intense game. Make the players stand for extra energy.

**Variations** In the full game, play stops when the first demon is disposed of, but the winner is decided by counting up the number of cards each person has played. Everyone but the player without a demon subtracts twice the number of cards left in their demon from their total. This makes the game more tactical, but involves a longer finish, reducing the impact as warm-up. It also requires that each pack has a different back pattern so that cards can be counted.

| | |
|---|---|
| Culture | ✪✪ |
| Techniques | ✪✪ |
| Personal development | ✪✪✪ |
| Mental energy | ✪✪✪ |
| Fun | ✪✪✪✪ |

# Unit 28:
# Making it happen – techniques to expedite implementation

As discussed in Chapter 1, the creative process is more than just a matter of idea generation. Once you have developed your idea and refined it, there is a need to put in a little time getting ready for selling the idea and for implementing it – otherwise it is liable never to get off the drawing board. We tend to skip over this part of the creative process, in part because it seems less interesting than idea generation – but it is no less necessary.

Do try out the exercises as you go. Put them off until later and you probably won't ever do them. Read through the techniques. Make notes about how and when you can use them. And make sure you give them a try in the next appropriate forum.

## Unit books

This unit's recommendation is a classic business book examining one of the biggest problems to beset implementation. *The Mythical Man Month* by Frederick P. Brooks is about the management of computing projects, but its lessons around the limitations of assuming that throwing more and more people at a problem will result in a faster solution are valuable for anyone.

You can find more information on our unit books, or buy them, from our support site: www.cul.co.uk/crashcourse.

## Web links

Links on planning and implementation can be found at www.cul.co.uk/crashcourse.

# 28.1 Technique: Planning for selling

**Preparation** None.
**Running time** Thirty minutes.
**Resources** Notepad.
**Frequency** Once.

There is a real danger of getting fired up with a great idea and rushing out to tell everyone about it without being sure how you will sell it (see the feedback section for an example of this being got wrong, then corrected).

Before telling the world, think briefly about selling. Draw up the key selling points of your idea. Why should it appeal to the people who are going to make the decision on whether or not it is carried out? How can you influence them to be swayed in your favour? Try this out on a real idea you might have, or if there's nothing pending try it on a fictional idea like 'let's make a new product to the opposite end of the market from the one we normally concentrate on' – eg to luxury/high end market if you are generally focused on mass market, to mass market if you normally focus on the other end – or use another dimension in this fashion.

**Feedback** When two members of 3M's staff, Fry and Silver, devised the Post-it Note they rushed out tell the 3M management about their great idea without thinking about how to sell it. Bits of paper that don't stick very well? The idea was immediately rejected.

But Fry and Silver then applied creativity to selling the idea into the company. They made up a set of prototype Post-it Note blocks and gave them to the secretaries and PAs of 3M's senior executives. When supplies ran out there was a huge demand for replacements. The secretaries and PAs were told they would get more when 3M made the product. Suddenly the idea seemed a great one.

**Outcome** In an ideal world your great idea should be accepted for what it is immediately. In the real world, though, it's necessary to sell the concept, whether it's into an organization, to your family or to whoever is going to make the decision on implementation. A little time spent working on selling points and methods can avoid wasting a lot of effort in developing the idea.

**Variations** Like Fry and Silver, you could look for a different, creative way to sell your ideas. The possibilities are endless.

| | |
|---|---|
| Culture | ✪✪✪✪ |
| Techniques | ✪✪✪✪ |
| Personal development | ✪✪✪ |
| Mental energy | ✪ |
| Fun | ✪✪ |

# 28.2 Technique: Planning for implementation

**Preparation** None.
**Running time** Thirty minutes.
**Resources** Notepad.
**Frequency** Once.

Like planning for selling, it is also worthwhile putting some basic effort into planning for implementation. This can both help sell the idea and make it much easier when it comes to putting it into place.

This planning does not have to be a detailed exercise with a project management package, but rather should be quick and simple thinking through of the important points of implementation. Specifically consider:

- What are the key milestones along the way? Pick two to seven clear stages in the implementation where you can check on progress and ensure that remedial action isn't necessary.
- What resources will be required? Don't work in huge detail, but do use estimated quantities – eg 'two software engineers for one day each' rather than 'people'.
- Who will you call on if things go wrong?
- How will you call on them?

**Feedback** Try this simple planning process on anything you are going to implement some time in the fairly near future – and bear it in mind as other ideas come along.

**Outcome** Planning tends to be overlooked because we're fired up with an idea and just want to go out and do something – but taking the time to get some basic elements of planning in place can make all the difference between implementation and failure.

**Variations** If you are familiar with and comfortable with project management software you could use it to undertake such planning, but still keep a broad-brush approach.

| | |
|---|---|
| Culture | ✪✪✪✪ |
| Techniques | ✪✪✪✪ |
| Personal development | ✪✪✪ |
| Mental energy | ✪ |
| Fun | ✪ |

# 28.3 Exercise: Story time

**Preparation** Find a book of short stories.
**Running time** Thirty minutes.
**Resources** Short story.
**Frequency** Once.

The planning stage is one where you particularly need to do something different on a regular basis to stay fresh. Reading a short story can be more than just entertainment – done the right way it can enhance your creativity. Find a short short story (no more than five or six pages). It should be challenging, whether it's science fiction or just about an extreme circumstance – it shouldn't be everyday. Read the story through.

Now spend a few minutes thinking about the story. What did the author do and say that was unexpected, or that you don't normally encounter in real life? What sort of point(s) of view does the story use? Try to get below the surface of the story into the mind of the writer.

**Feedback** In putting together a story the writer suspends reality and looks at life differently. This is essential for creativity. If you are having difficulty finding an appropriate story, use one from *Imagination Engineering* (see Unit 1 unit books). How else would you describe a story written from the point of view of a nasturtium, or a story that describes itself being written backwards from the last word to the first?

It's important to stress the need for unusual fiction. Great literature often portrays very ordinary circumstances. Feel free to read that as well, but this exercise needs something more – that glimpse of a different world that will inspire a new viewpoint in the reader.

**Outcome** Familiarizing yourself with the way a writer suspends reality and devises a fictional world with an alternative viewpoint is excellent preparation for being more creative.

**Variations** Although this is labelled a one-off exercise, you can get plenty more value by keeping up your fiction reading. If you see reading as part of your lifetime learning, rather than just entertainment, perhaps you can give it a higher priority. A regular diet of unusual fiction will keep your creativity on the bubble.

| | |
|---|---|
| Culture | ✪✪✪ |
| Techniques | ✪✪ |
| Personal development | ✪✪✪✪ |
| Mental energy | ✪✪ |
| Fun | ✪✪✪ |

# 28.4 Exercise/Technique: The top ten list

**Preparation** None.
**Running time** Five minutes.
**Resources** None.
**Frequency** Weekly.

Note your top ten concerns for the coming week. Put the list somewhere very visible. If you have staff, e-mail them a copy.

Whenever you start a task, glance at the top ten list. Does the task influence your top ten? If it doesn't, you may still do it, but bear in mind its relative unimportance. If you are asked to do something that doesn't fit with your list and you are short of time, say 'no'. Next week, when you draw up your list, make sure there are changes. There may be ongoing priorities, but if everything stays the same from week to week you are stagnating.

**Feedback** This is a good exercise to perform right now, but should also be performed on a weekly basis to ensure that you have the time to get your important ideas to implementation.

**Outcome** The top ten list cuts through your potential activities to the essentials. It's great both for work and at home. I was introduced to the idea of sharing your list with staff by Nick Spooner, MD of Internet commerce company Entranet. Nick used his top ten list to communicate priorities to his staff – before long they all had their own lists in public view. This has significantly improved the company's effectiveness. A side effect of the top ten list is to reduce irrelevant interruptions. A meaningful look at the list as someone comes close can cause them to reassess their priorities.

**Variations** It may be necessary to have several lists. For example, top ten customers and top ten milestones. The actual subjects need to be matched to your line of business, but don't be tempted to have more than two or three – you need to be able to take in the lists at a glance.

| | |
|---|---|
| Culture | ✪✪✪✪ |
| Techniques | ✪✪✪ |
| Personal development | ✪✪✪✪ |
| Mental energy | ✪ |
| Fun | ✪✪ |

# 28.5 Exercise: Scribbling

**Preparation** None.
**Running time** Thirty minutes.
**Resources** Notepad or word processor.
**Frequency** Once.

This exercise is simple to describe, harder to do. Write a short story. Try to cover an unusual topic – you might try science fiction or the sort of 'twist in the tale' story that Roald Dahl was so good at. Don't say 'I can't write' or 'it won't be any good'. You aren't entering the Booker Prize, this is an exercise in creativity.

The suggested time is 30 minutes – try to keep to this. You should be able to get an undisturbed 30 minutes somewhere in your schedule. Your output needn't be long. *Imagination Engineering* features a short story by American writer Gene Wolfe that only runs to around 400 words – but it's no less effective because of that.

**Feedback** This exercise follows on from *Story time* (28.3) so that you have a reminder of how stories are put together. If a topic doesn't come to mind, take a couple of totally unrelated items – perhaps something you can see around you and something mentioned on the news – and bring them together in a strange situation. Why has it happened? What do the people involved feel? What will they do? Don't wait for inspiration – force yourself to start writing, however terrible you feel the output is.

**Outcome** Creative writing can be quite an unpleasant exercise, but there is no doubt that it stimulates your creative responses and will help you to tone up your creativity. It provides good practice at thinking of new and creative ways of selling ideas.

**Variations** If you've time to do the exercise twice, do it a second time in slightly different circumstances. Come up with a topic by putting a person from a work of fiction you enjoy into a dangerous situation in a favourite film. Spend a couple of minutes jotting down initial thoughts. Then leave it three or four days before you write it. The unconscious is a powerful tool for creativity – if you've got the time, it's worth adding it to your weaponry.

| | |
|---|---|
| Culture | ✪✪ |
| Techniques | ✪✪ |
| Personal development | ✪✪✪✪ |
| Mental energy | ✪ |
| Fun | ✪✪ |

# Unit 29: Right-brain teamwork – more exercises to encourage groups to engage the right brain

We are near the end of the course now, and the final two units concentrate on exercises to enhance group and individual creativity. Creativity is not something you can be taught, but it is something that you can develop through practice. The sort of right-brain exercises and techniques in this unit help develop a creative frame of mind.

Do try out the exercises as you go. Put them off until later and you probably won't ever do them. Read through the techniques. Make notes about how and when you can use them. And make sure you give them a try in the next appropriate forum.

## Unit books

Time off in this unit to catch up on the reading you haven't quite finished from the previous units.

## Web links

More links to suitably right-brain Web sites can be found at www.cul.co.uk/crashcourse.

# 29.1 Technique: The wrong drawing

**Preparation** Produce drawings.
**Running time** Five to ten minutes.
**Resources** A number of pre-drawn objects on cards or flip charts; tables that partners sit either side of. If using a flip chart, have desks arranged so that half the group has their back to it.
**Frequency** Once with any group.

Divide the group into pairs and have one of each pair nominated the describer and one the artist. The describer has to describe an object on the card or the flip chart, but can only use geometric shapes, their orientation and position on the page in doing so. There must be no general comments about the overall subject or style. The artist then draws it, based on this description. The ideal situation is that the describer cannot see the drawing being produced.

For instance, a house might be drawn as a large square with a flattened triangle on top arranged in such a way that the long side of the triangle rests on and slightly overlaps the top edge of the square. It has four smaller squares inside the larger one… and so on. You can also see how difficult it would be to produce a drawing that has much more than the faintest resemblance to the original template.

**Feedback** The winners are the pair with a set of drawings most like the templates. Make sure that everyone has the opportunity to laugh at the efforts of all of their competitors.

**Outcome** This timeout is relatively low energy and is useful more as a way of switching away from the matter in hand than for building energy levels.

**Variations** This technique can be run with no preparation if you write up a subject to be drawn rather than draw a template picture. Templates can be taken from young children's colouring books to avoid unnecessary effort and artistic stress. If the numbers are relatively small, or space is limited, an alternative is to have a single describer with everyone else attempting to reproduce the same template. If you don't want to run the exercise in pairs, have one individual describe to everyone else.

| | |
|---|---|
| Culture | ✪ |
| Techniques | ✪ |
| Personal development | ✪✪✪ |
| Mental energy | ✪✪✪ |
| Fun | ✪✪✪ |

# 29.2 Technique: Abstract drawing

**Preparation** None.
**Running time** Five to ten minutes.
**Resources** Paper and pens; tables that partners sit either side of.
**Frequency** Once with any group.

Divide the group into pairs and have one of each pair nominated the describer and one the artist. The describer has to draw an object using at least one circle and at most ten further lines. These lines need not be straight. The describer then relays verbally to the artist what he or she has drawn, using only geometric shapes and their orientation and position on the page. The artist attempts to reproduce the picture. The ideal situation is that the describer cannot see the drawing being produced. It is clear that the artist must not be able to see the original drawing.

**Feedback** This timeout works in exactly the same way as *The wrong drawing* (29.1) but has a slight twist in that the describer can influence the complexity of the task. It has the advantage of requiring no preparation, but is more variable in result than *The wrong drawing*.

**Outcome** The winners are the pair with a set of drawings most like each other. Make sure that everyone has the opportunity to laugh at the efforts of all of their competitors.

**Variations** It is clear that the circle and ten lines are arbitrary. It is a simple matter to vary this. You could even make it specific to a particular subject by including a relevant shape in the list of requirements. An interesting variant is one where the set of objects used to construct the picture are specified beforehand (for example one circle, one triangle, two straight lines, two dots and one wiggly line). Both participants independently produce a picture using these objects, then compare results. If using this approach, let one person draw the picture first, attempt to 'project' the picture mentally to the other, then have the second draw their picture. It is probably best to combine one attempt using this independent approach with another using the describer/artist approach. As before, one individual could describe to the whole group.

| | |
|---|---|
| Culture | ✪ |
| Techniques | ✪ |
| Personal development | ✪✪✪ |
| Mental energy | ✪✪✪ |
| Fun | ✪✪✪ |

# 29.3 Exercise/Technique: PR from Hell

**Preparation** Think up one target per team.
**Running time** Five minutes.
**Resources** Table per team.
**Frequency** Once with any group.

Each team is given a target for which to produce a slogan. They have four minutes to devise an effective slogan, then each team tries out their slogan on the rest of the group. The winning slogan is rewarded. The catch here is that the target should be something that is particularly hard to sell. Try to make the targets as outrageous as possible, while bearing in mind your audience. Examples might be:

- Vlad the Impaler is running for mayor
- Selling cheap electronics to the Far East
- An anti-flatulence tablet
- Selling paper warships to the navy

**Feedback** If there's time, get the teams to describe how they reached their slogan. Often initial hilarity will lead to a dry patch. How did they get their result? Was it democratic or autocratic? Was it a team effort or individual within the team? There is no right answer here, we're just helping them understand how they work together. In one presentation using this technique, the third suggestion came out as an 'anti-flatulence table' – try this as an alternative.

**Outcome** The sillier you can make the targets, the more energy you are liable to induce (in the examples above, flatulence tablets will do more for a team than trade with the Far East, for example). This is a good timeout to revitalize creative thought, as the feedback pushes the participants into thinking about how they work together.

**Variations** The exercise works slightly better with different targets for each team, but can be used on a single subject. To keep it short we've limited the output to producing a snappy slogan, but there are a number of variations here. With more time, your teams could produce an advertising jingle, a full-scale advertisement (optionally on video), a press release or a newspaper advert. It is worth emphasizing if acting is involved that they are best sticking to 'straight' acting. Intentional comedy is extremely hard for amateurs to make work, and whatever they do will be unintentionally funny anyway.

| | |
|---|---|
| Culture | ✪ |
| Techniques | ✪ |
| Personal development | ✪✪✪ |
| Mental energy | ✪✪ |
| Fun | ✪✪✪✪ |

# 29.4 Technique: Passing the buck

**Preparation** Obtain ball.
**Running time** Three minutes.
**Resources** One tennis ball sized ball.
**Frequency** Once with any group.

Give the ball to one member of the group. Do not make any suggestion that they move away from seats, tables, etc. Their task is to get the ball around the whole team in such a way that it does not get passed to the person sitting next to them. Time the activity. Tell them how long it took, and ask them to halve it. When they've had another go, ask them to get it down to three seconds.

**Feedback** If someone doesn't spot it, give them a hint after a while that they needn't stay seated or in the same positions. Most of the ways of speeding up the exercise involve changing from throwing the ball (and dropping it) to quick means of passing it – for instance, a slightly sloping row of hands down which the ball is rolled. The quickest means is for them all to get round the ball and touch it at roughly (though inevitably not exactly) the same time.

**Outcome** The principal aim here (and it's one that is worth explicitly pointing out) is to spot that the restrictions that stop us from achieving something are often self-imposed. No one said that they had to stay in position, but almost always the first attempt or two will involve doing so. It is also interesting (and again worth pointing out) that moving the goal posts a bit (halving the time) often doesn't generate a creative solution, while moving them a long way does. By standing up they immediately remove one restriction – there is no one sitting next to them. For good measure, it also shows that what is initially assumed is impossible often isn't. Despite all this learning, it does inject a small amount of energy too.

**Variations** There aren't many obvious variations, though obviously the object passed could be almost anything, though it should be small and none-delicate enough to encourage an original inclination to throw it (a frisbee, for instance).

| | |
|---|---|
| Culture | ✪✪✪ |
| Techniques | ✪ |
| Personal development | ✪✪✪ |
| Mental energy | ✪✪✪ |
| Fun | ✪✪✪ |

# 29.5 Technique: Fontastic

**Preparation** None.
**Running time** Ten minutes.
**Resources** Digital camera plus PC, or video camera and TV per team; enough room for each team to have at least two metres square of clear floor area – ideally in separate rooms.
**Frequency** Once with any group.

Each team is to produce a body font and capture it on digital camera or video. To do this, the team members spell out as many capital letters of the alphabet as they can, using only their bodies. One member of the team captures each letter using the camera (if using video, just a couple of seconds on each letter, not a video of the whole process). The role of camera operator must rotate every time to make sure everyone takes part.

**Feedback** The winning team is the one with the most legible letters – if there's a draw, decide on the quality of the font.

**Outcome** This can be a riotously noisy activity, so make sure the environment is conducive to it. There's lots of energy and ice-breaking (difficult not to when you've been in such contortions together).

**Variations** It is possible to use this activity without the cameras as a true instant exercise, in which case it could appear in any of the three categories. However, it works much better with the cameras, as otherwise the participants don't get to see their own letters, nor the activities of the other teams, and this is a major part of the value. Other variants are to get the teams to produce numbers or pictures using their bodies. This last option is valuable if you haven't enough resources to have small teams – making letters with a big team is less challenging, but making a picture of a house is more stretching. The exercise is more intimate if the participants have to lie on the floor, rather than attempt the letters standing up – you may wish to make this a requirement.

| | |
|---|---|
| Culture | ✪✪✪ |
| Techniques | ✪ |
| Personal development | ✪✪ |
| Mental energy | ✪✪✪✪ |
| Fun | ✪✪✪✪ |

# Unit 30: Mental workout – personal creativity exercises

As the course comes to an end there's a chance to give yourself a final mental workout.

## Unit books

Two last books to help stretch your mind. From the popular science genre, *Longitude* by Dava Sobel is a fascinating study of one man's attempts to overcome a seemingly impossible challenge. As a fictional challenge, try Joge Luis Borges' mind-twisting *Labyrinths*, stories replete with mind-bending originality that enables the reader to see the world in a whole new way.

You can find more information on our unit books, or buy them, from our support site: www.cul.co.uk/crashcourse.

## Web links

Further sites to enhance personal creativity can be found at www.cul.co.uk/crashcourse.

# 30.1 Exercise: Metaphorically speaking

**Preparation** None.
**Running time** Five minutes.
**Resources** Newspaper or Web news site, notepad.
**Frequency** Several times.

Use a newspaper (or a Web news site) to generate a list of five items. They could be people, places, events, objects – anything, as long as the five are quite different. Now spend no more than a minute on each item, jotting down a series of metaphors, with short reasons attached. For example, one of the items in today's news is about London's Docklands. I might think Docklands is like:

- A forest – because there are lots of tall buildings
- A graveyard – all the monuments
- A beehive – activity in an alien environment

Etc.

**Feedback** Don't think too much about your metaphors, just let them flow. If you have real problems getting started, think of the key attributes of whatever you are trying to create a metaphor for, then think of other things with similar attributes. But you should aim to make metaphor formation natural, as it will produce attributes you weren't consciously aware of. Getting better at metaphor formation supports creativity in several ways. Knowledge and memory both depend on metaphor and imagery, to cope with new but similar cases and to store information in the image-oriented brain. A metaphor can often be used to solve a problem or generate an idea. By saying that a problem is like something, we can find new approaches. Finally, metaphor is valuable in improving your personal creativity when writing – it's powerful stuff.

**Outcome** Metaphor is a cornerstone of brain skills; this exercise enhances your brain's ability to deal with difficult problems and to remember important issues.

**Variations** Five minutes is enough for one session, but this is an exercise you could repeat regularly for a while. Perhaps weekly for a month, then reinforce every few months, keeping the metaphorical (in more than one sense) mental muscles in trim.

One of the great things about using metaphor as a way to exercise the mind is that it can be done at any time, wherever you are. Next time you are in your car listening to the radio, construct a metaphor for something you hear. Or, if you are sitting bored in a concert, look around for a subject to make a metaphor for. It's quick, easy and effective.

| | |
|---|---|
| Culture | ✪✪ |
| Techniques | ✪✪ |
| Personal development | ✪✪✪✪ |
| Mental energy | ✪✪ |
| Fun | ✪✪✪ |

# 30.2 Exercise: Holistic awareness

**Preparation** None.
**Running time** Ten minutes.
**Resources** Quiet, comfortable location.
**Frequency** Once.

Don't panic if this sounds too 'knit your own yoghurt' – suspend your disbelief and try it before judging. It's difficult to phrase an exercise like this without occasionally using waffly terms, but the aim is not at all vague.

Find somewhere you can sit or lie comfortably without outside interference. Breathe slowly and regularly. Close your eyes (as long as you can do this without falling asleep). Visualize your body. Start at your head – think inside your head, then let your imagination work outwards, as if you were moving slowly outwards. Pause at the skin, thinking about the interface between your body and the world. Then work gradually down your body to your feet. Finally expand outwards, taking in all of the room.

**Feedback** It is important not to get analytical during this exercise. Your aim is not to think *about* what you visualize, merely to visualize it. Experience it with your virtual senses, but don't judge it or try to put what you experience into some sort of pigeonhole. Looking at yourself and your surroundings with such detachment can be very difficult to start with. You may need a few attempts to pull it off.

**Outcome** This exercise brings out two things – a feeling for abstract visualization, and practice at focusing on a very specific subject in an overall way, rather than trying to break it down into detail or fit it into categories. This is a valuable underlying skill for dealing with knowledge, and can also help improve your recall from memory.

**Variations** An extension to the exercise if you've time (or try it on a repeat session) is to continue after taking in the room. Return your awareness to your body. Start to move one limb very gently, then another. Try to keep your awareness working in the same holistic way as the motion occurs, experiencing the movement and the interface between your body and the world.

| | |
|---|---|
| Culture | ✪✪ |
| Techniques | ✪✪ |
| Personal development | ✪✪✪✪ |
| Mental energy | ✪ |
| Fun | ✪✪ |

# 30.3 Exercise: On the edge

**Preparation** None.
**Running time** Ten minutes.
**Resources** Notepad.
**Frequency** Regularly.

Choose an area of personal knowledge – a field in which you consider yourself something of an expert. The aim of this exercise is to test the limits of your knowledge, feeling out the gaps. Spend a couple of minutes drawing out a keyword map of what you know (see Unit 1 for a reminder on such maps).

Now highlight some aspects of your map. Is there knowledge you know is quite old in a fast-changing area? Highlight it. Where are the edges of your knowledge? What parts of it are fuzzy, or border into a different discipline you don't know about, or go into more technical detail than you can handle?

Pull out the highlighted areas onto a separate sheet of paper.

**Feedback** The detail of widening your knowledge isn't an instant activity, but this exercise has produced an action list for further investigation. At the very least you should check that your ageing knowledge isn't past its sell-by date – in some areas knowledge has a very short shelf life. You may also like to push the boundaries – to expand into some of those fringe areas. The aim isn't to make you a know-it-all, but to be sure of the solidity of your essential knowledge, which often requires a grounding in surrounding areas even if you haven't deep expertise.

**Outcome** You should get an internally driven plan for sharpening up your knowledge in a key area. There will, of course, be external sources of need too, which are covered in other exercises.

**Variations** Most of us have several areas of knowledge, but keep the exercise focused on a single subject, and have another go another time for a different area. Consider making this a regular process – the frequency depends on how quickly your knowledge area changes.

| | |
|---|---|
| Culture | ✪✪ |
| Techniques | ✪✪ |
| Personal development | ✪✪✪✪ |
| Mental energy | ✪ |
| Fun | ✪✪ |

# 30.4 Exercise: Muddled model

**Preparation** None.
**Running time** Five minutes.
**Resources** None.
**Frequency** Once.

We understand the world by using models – it's impossible to grasp the whole, so we think of something simpler to get the picture. Sometimes we don't even know that our models are inaccurate or just plain wrong. For hundreds of years the model of the world as a flat disc was accepted. Even now, many people don't realize that the model of the atom as a set of electrons rotating round like planets round a central nucleus is a convenient fiction.

Sometimes inaccurate models are more appealing than the truth. An old legend says that the tide is caused by an immense crab coming out of its hole to hunt for food. The water rushes into the hole, causing the tide. This is both wrong and illogical, but who cares? It's a lovely picture. Take a pair of complex natural phenomena, like a rainbow or why the sky is blue. It doesn't matter whether or not you know the real reason, but for each phenomenon invent three totally different and probably incorrect models of what's happening. Go for appeal, not likeliness.

**Feedback** It sometimes takes a while to realize that most of what we 'know' is based on models, but then, unless the entire workings are visible and comprehensible, what else can we base our understanding on?

**Outcome** Incorrect models are a great source of creativity. Much fiction depends on the premise 'what if' – what if an accepted model wasn't true. Science fiction does this boldly – what if people lived on a totally different planet, what if the French revolution had never happened. Conventional fiction has more subtle what ifs – what if a person behaved this way, or a relationship developed like this – but it is still modelling.

**Variations** This exercise increases your general creativity, but you could also apply the approach to a specific problem. Dream up totally fictional reasons why the problem could be occurring and solve them – then see what the solutions would do in the real world.

| | |
|---|---|
| Culture | ✪✪ |
| Techniques | ✪✪ |
| Personal development | ✪✪✪✪ |
| Mental energy | ✪✪ |
| Fun | ✪✪✪ |

## 30.5 Exercise: Rapt concentration

**Preparation** None.
**Running time** Five minutes.
**Resources** A quiet place.
**Frequency** Several times.

Concentration is a great gift – but it is something we are all bad at. This extremely simple exercise will help boost your powers of concentration.

Find yourself a quiet place where you can have five minutes without distraction. Sit quietly and take a few slow breaths. Now begin to count up from one in your head. Continue to do so as long as you can concentrate purely on the numbers without anything else – anything – creeping into your thoughts.

It won't take long the first time. Repeat a number of times, trying to increase your concentration span.

**Feedback** In fact it's hardly ever possible to get past ten at a first go. Some thought, however small, will usually manage to creep in. It won't stop you counting – you will continue on automatic pilot, but the numbers will have lost your concentration. You may find you need to repeat this exercise on a number of occasions to get any significant improvement.

**Outcome** Often we don't need to give total concentration to what we are doing, and some great ideas can come out of thoughts that take place in the background. However, there are occasions when total focus is intensely useful to carry out a critical action. What's more, simple awareness of the impracticality of pure concentration will be of value – for instance, next time you have to give a presentation.

**Variations** Counting is the simplest way of performing this exercise, but you can also perform it by listening to music, and trying to concentrate solely on the notes being played, or by looking at a simple set of abstract shapes and only thinking about the shapes themselves.

| | |
|---|---|
| Culture | ✪✪ |
| Techniques | ✪✪✪ |
| Personal development | ✪✪✪✪ |
| Mental energy | ✪ |
| Fun | ✪✪✪ |

# 4 Review

## PULLING IT TOGETHER

In the 30 units of the course you will have tried out a wide range of exercises and added a whole collection of techniques to your toolbag. Where now?

Begin by re-reading Chapter 1. Get the basics well established. Make sure you are familiar with the five paths of creativity. Get the four-stage creative process firmly fixed in mind, so that when faced with a problem you can pull in the appropriate techniques. In the appendices at the back of the book you will find listings that will enable you to pick out a technique that's particularly appropriate for one of the paths, or particularly relevant to one of the four stages.

Next, try to establish a regular creativity slot in your diary. This should be a ring-fenced portion of time when you can really think about problems, give a technique a try, generate new ideas. It's a time for forward-looking, rather than desperately trying to catch up. If you think your diary is already overloaded, don't worry. If you haven't time to get everything done anyway, it shouldn't matter if you lop off a little more.

As a minimum we'd suggest setting aside 20 minutes a week – anyone should be able to do this. Some organizations allocate half a day per week to these personal or ground-breaking projects. If you can manage that, it's ideal.

Next, be prepared to use your techniques. Remember that creativity can only be practised, not taught. When you have a problem, when you need an idea, when you are starting on a project or a new piece of work, dip into your creativity toolkit. There is a temptation not to do this. Almost inevitably you will be under time pressure to get on with the job. But failing to take a moment to think, to use a technique if necessary, is a false economy. It's like trying to take a car's wheel nut off with your bare hands because you haven't got the time to go and get a wrench.

Above all, find opportunities to use what you've learnt. Without use your creative ability will atrophy.

One final thought – read. Reading is one of the easiest and most pleasurable ways to fuel the knowledge store that underlies your creativity. Read voraciously and as widely as possible. If you didn't have time to read all the unit books, continue picking them off. But make sure you read.

# COLLECTED READING LIST

## An overview of the unit books from the course

[Pocket Puzzlers] (2000) *Brain Teasers*, Sterling

Abraham, J (2000) *Getting Everything You Can Out Of All You've Got*, Piatkus, London

Adams, D (1988) *The Hitchhiker's Guide to the Galaxy*, Pan, London

Adams, S (2000) *The Dilbert Principle*, Boxtree,

Belbin, M (1995) *Team Roles at Work*, Butterworth Heinemann,

Borges, J L (2000) *Labyrinths*, Penguin,

Brooks, F P (1995) *The Mythical Man Month*, Addison-Wesley

Bryson, B (1996) *Notes from a Small Island*, Black Swan

Buzan, T and Buzan, B (2000) *The Mind Map Book*, BBC, London

Claxton, G (1998) *Hare Brain, Tortoise Mind*, Fourth Estate, London

Clegg, B (1999) *Creativity and Innovation for Managers*, Butterworth Heinemann, London

Clegg, B (2001) *Capturing Customers' Hearts*, FT/Prentice Hall, London

Clegg, B (2001) *Light Years*, Piatkus, London

Clegg, B (2001) *The Professional's Guide to Mining the Internet*, Kogan Page, London

Clegg, B and Birch, P (2000) *Imagination Engineering*, FT/Prentice Hall, London

Cringeley, R X (1996) *Accidental Empires*, Penguin, Harmondsworth

de Bono, E (1993) *Serious Creativity*, HarperCollins, London

de Bono, E (1998) *Super Mind Pack*, Dorling Kindersley

Edwards, B (1993) *Drawing on the Right Side of the Brain*, HarperCollins, London
Feynman, R (1992) *Surely You're Joking, Mr Feynman?*, Vintage, London
Gardner, M (2001) *The Colossal Book of Mathematics*, Norton
Gleick, J (1997) *Chaos*, Minerva
Keyes, D (2000) *Flowers for Algernon*, Gollancz
Klein, N (2001) *No Logo*, Flamingo, London
McCarthy, P (2001) *McCarthy's Bar*, Hodder & Stoughton, London
Norman, D (1998) *The Design of Everyday Things*, MIT Press
Peters, T (1997) *The Circle of Innovation*, Hodder & Stoughton, London
Pohl, F and Kornbluth, C (1984) *The Space Merchants*, John Goodchild
Ricks, D (1999) *Blunders in International Business*, Blackwell
Russell, P (1980) *The Brain Book*, Routledge
Sacks, O (1986) *The Man who Mistook his Wife for a Hat*, Picador
Semler, R (2001) *Maverick!*, Random House, London
Silverman, S (2001) *Einstein's Refrigerator*, Andrews McMeel
Sobel, D (1998) *Longitude*. Fourth Estate, London
Trompenaars, F (1997) *Riding the Waves of Culture*, Nicholas Brealey
von Oech, R (1986) *A Kick in the Seat of the Pants*, HarperCollins, London
Wells, H G (2000) *The Complete Short Stories*, Phoenix
Wolfe, G (1992) *Castleview*, Hodder & Stoughton, London
Yerkes, L (2001) *Fun Works*, Berrett-Koehler
Zelazny, R and Bester, A (1998) *Psychoshop*, Vintage
Zelazny, R and Linskold, J (1998) *Donnerjack*, Avon

# Appendix

## RANDOM WORDS

Feel free to invent your own words, but this list will give you a prompt if you need some in a hurry. Don't try to select a word to fit the problem, pick one at random. The list is 60 long to facilitate the method popularized by Edward de Bono of choosing an item by checking the second hand of a watch.

1. Cat
2. Gold bar
3. Desk
4. Stopwatch
5. Fire
6. Forest glade
7. City
8. Autumn
9. Doll's house
10. Dragon
11. Magic carpet
12. War
13. Peace
14. Scales
15. Cigar
16. Hat
17. Chewing gum

18. Spittoon
19. Rainbow
20. Dolphin
21. Fence
22. Pain
23. Button
24. Mirror
25. Compact disc
26. Air freshener
27. Happiness
28. Flower
29. Christmas
30. Swan
31. Teeth
32. Breakfast
33. Map
34. Glue
35. Bark
36. Bikini
37. Scar
38. Bed
39. Box
40. Music
41. Wallpaper
42. Missing
43. Photograph
44. Wind chimes
45. Hole
46. Share
47. Telephone
48. Cartoon
49. Baby
50. Sunset
51. Telescope
52. Silence
53. School
54. T shirt
55. Freedom
56. Road
57. Sea
58. Sweat
59. Monk
60. Shelf

# PEOPLE FOR 'SOMEONE ELSE'S VIEW'

Feel free to invent your own persona, but this list will give you a prompt if you need some in a hurry. Don't try to select a person to fit the problem, pick one at random. The list is 60 long to facilitate the method popularized by Edward de Bono of choosing an item by checking the second hand of a watch.

1. Hercule Poirot
2. Sherlock Holmes
3. A Rabbi
4. A Roman Catholic priest
5. A poet
6. A trapeze artist
7. A circus clown
8. A surgeon
9. A nasturtium
10. George Washington
11. Groucho Marx
12. Karl Marx
13. Beethoven
14. A computer programmer
15. Robin Hood
16. A mass murderer
17. A pet rabbit
18. The President of the United States
19. Marilyn Monroe
20. A plumber
21. A Roman centurion
22. William Shakespeare
23. Attila the Hun
24. A prostitute in Paris
25. Queen Elizabeth the First
26. A beggar in Bombay
27. Superman
28. The Pope
29. A New York cab driver
30. Donald Duck
31. A blind person
32. Paul McCartney

33. A court jester
34. An ant
35. Billy the Kid
36. Count Dracula
37. Winston Churchill
38. A Martian
39. A *Star Trek* character
40. Queen Victoria
41. Jane Austen
42. Oscar Wilde
43. An *X-Files* character
44. A World War 2 fighter pilot
45. A nurse
46. Winnie the Pooh
47. Alice (in Wonderland)
48. Bart Simpson
49. Charlie Chaplin
50. A bee keeper
51. Bill Gates
52. Margaret Thatcher
53. The Phantom of the Opera
54. Hercules
55. James Bond
56. A stage magician
57. A druid
58. Cyrano de Bergerac
59. A mermaid
60. Joan of Arc

## TECHNIQUES WITH HIGH CULTURE RATINGS

| *Ref.* | *Title* |
|---|---|
| 3.5 | Chunks and breaks |
| 4.5 | Questioning everything |
| 6.3 | Versatile coat hangers |
| 8.1 | Challenging assumptions |
| 10.3 | The little black book |
| 11.5 | No time to read |
| 12.5 | An excellent mistake |
| 13.1 | It's a steal |
| 20.1 | In the dark |
| 21.1 | Something completely different |
| 21.2 | Unconscious creativity |
| 28.1 | Planning for selling |
| 28.2 | Planning for implementation |
| 28.4 | The top ten list |

## TECHNIQUES WITH HIGH TECHNIQUES RATINGS

| *Ref.* | *Title* |
|---|---|
| 1.1 | Surveying your mind |
| 1.3 | Random picture |
| 7.1 | The level chain |
| 7.3 | Attributes |
| 7.5 | Technical creativity |
| 8.1 | Challenging assumptions |
| 8.2 | Distortion |
| 8.4 | Reversal |
| 8.5 | Size matters |
| 11.1 | Fantasy |
| 11.2 | Someone else's view |
| 11.4 | Metaphor |
| 12.1 | Random word |
| 12.2 | Cool site |

| | |
|---|---|
| 12.4 | Quotations |
| 13.2 | Inside view |
| 13.3 | Evil genius |
| 13.5 | Morphology |
| 15.1 | Components |
| 15.2 | Substitute |
| 15.5 | Long division |
| 16.2 | Da Vinci scribbles |
| 16.3 | Touch me, feel me |
| 16.4 | Draw it |
| 16.5 | Squirrel box |
| 17.3 | Auntie gravity |
| 19.3 | Lost in translation |
| 19.4 | They're winning |
| 23.1 | The £100 bid |
| 23.2 | SWOT |
| 23.4 | Basic option evaluation |
| 23.5 | Sophisticated option evaluation |
| 25.1 | Signposts |
| 25.2 | Hazard markers |
| 25.4 | Second-best solution |
| 25.5 | Stakeholders |
| 28.1 | Planning for selling |
| 28.2 | Planning for implementation |

## TECHNIQUES WITH HIGH PERSONAL DEVELOPMENT RATINGS

| *Ref.* | *Title* |
|---|---|
| 1.1 | Surveying your mind |
| 1.4 | Life saver |
| 2.3 | Twisters |
| 3.3 | Water into wine |
| 3.5 | Chunks and breaks |
| 4.3 | Round the world |
| 4.5 | Questioning everything |
| 5.1 | Altered states |
| 5.4 | Pub quiz |

6.3 Versatile coat hangers
6.5 Going down
7.2 Cars and goats
8.3 Birthday bonanza
9.3 Get another life
10.2 Sense and sensibility
10.3 The little black book
10.4 All that glisters
10.5 Programmed thought
11.3 Get a laugh
11.5 No time to read
12.5 An excellent mistake
15.3 Different views
17.2 Leaf mould
17.4 The thrill factor
18.1 Extremes
18.2 Story chains
18.3 Take a note
18.4 Number rhymes
18.5 Strengthening your ghosts
19.2 Cloak and dagger
19.5 Spinning knowledge
20.1 In the dark
20.3 Buy me
20.5 Lego™ construction
21.2 Unconscious creativity
21.3 Go gallery
21.4 Game theory
22.1 The magic tunnel
22.2 Handcuffs
22.3 Quick on the draw
23.3 Material gains
25.3 Horse whispers
26.1 On the box
26.2 Category magic
26.3 Doing and knowing
26.4 Fact quest
26.5 Binning paper
27.3 Ands
27.4 Rules rule
28.3 Story time

| | |
|---|---|
| 28.4 | The top ten list |
| 28.5 | Scribbling |
| 30.1 | Metaphorically speaking |
| 30.2 | Holistic awareness |
| 30.3 | On the edge |
| 30.4 | Muddled model |
| 30.5 | Rapt concentration |

## TECHNIQUES WITH HIGH MENTAL ENERGY RATINGS

| *Ref.* | *Title* |
|---|---|
| 1.2 | Knots |
| 1.5 | Ideas to get you fired |
| 5.2 | Yes! |
| 5.3 | Circle of energy |
| 5.5 | Beam me up |
| 9.1 | Spoon and string |
| 9.2 | Piggyback plus |
| 9.4 | Sit on my lap |
| 9.5 | The paperclip race |
| 12.3 | Found objects |
| 14.2 | I am and I know |
| 14.4 | Steeplechase |
| 14.5 | Giants, witches and dwarves |
| 20.4 | Blindfold birthday |
| 21.5 | Snapshots |
| 24.2 | Bursting with energy |
| 24.3 | On the square |
| 24.4 | Magic carpet |
| 24.5 | Peer groups |
| 27.1 | One spare square |
| 27.2 | Contract fishing |
| 29.5 | Fontastic |

# TECHNIQUES WITH HIGH FUN RATINGS

| *Ref.* | *Title* |
|---|---|
| 1.2 | Knots |
| 1.5 | Ideas to get you fired |
| 2.1 | This is my friend |
| 2.2 | Tower of Babel |
| 2.3 | Twisters |
| 2.4 | Follow my leader |
| 9.1 | Spoon and string |
| 9.2 | Piggyback plus |
| 9.3 | Get another life |
| 9.4 | Sit on my lap |
| 11.3 | Get a laugh |
| 11.5 | No time to read |
| 12.3 | Found objects |
| 13.2 | Inside view |
| 14.3 | Makeover |
| 14.4 | Steeplechase |
| 14.5 | Giants, witches and dwarves |
| 20.2 | Out for the count |
| 20.4 | Blindfold birthday |
| 21.4 | Game theory |
| 21.5 | Snapshots |
| 22.4 | Towering |
| 24.3 | On the square |
| 24.4 | Magic carpet |
| 24.5 | Peer groups |
| 27.1 | One spare square |
| 27.2 | Contract fishing |
| 27.5 | Racing demon |
| 29.3 | PR from Hell |
| 29.5 | Fontastic |

# TECHNIQUES SUITED TO STAGE 1 – UNDERSTANDING THE PROBLEM

| *Ref.* | *Title* |
|---|---|
| 1.1 | Surveying your mind |
| 3.1 | Compass |
| 3.2 | Obstacle map |
| 3.4 | Destination |
| 4.1 | Do nothing |
| 4.2 | Up and down |
| 4.4 | Time slices |
| 4.5 | Questioning everything |
| 6.1 | Excellence |
| 6.2 | Restatement |
| 6.4 | Mud slinging |
| 7.1 | The level chain |

# TECHNIQUES SUITED TO STAGE 2 – GENERATING IDEAS

| *Ref.* | *Title* |
|---|---|
| 1.3 | Random picture |
| 1.4 | Ideas to get you fired |
| 7.1 | The level chain |
| 7.3 | Attributes |
| 7.4 | Found story |
| 7.5 | Technical creativity |
| 8.1 | Challenging assumptions |
| 8.2 | Distortion |
| 8.4 | Reversal |
| 8.5 | Size matters |
| 11.1 | Fantasy |
| 11.2 | Someone else's view |
| 11.4 | Metaphor |
| 12.1 | Random word |
| 12.2 | Cool site |

| | |
|---|---|
| 12.3 | Found objects |
| 12.4 | Quotations |
| 13.1 | It's a steal |
| 13.2 | Inside view |
| 13.3 | Evil genius |
| 13.5 | Morphology |
| 15.1 | Components |
| 15.2 | Substitute |
| 15.4 | Been there before |
| 15.5 | Long division |
| 16.1 | Set it to music |
| 16.2 | Da Vinci scribbles |
| 16.3 | Touch me, feel me |
| 16.4 | Draw it |
| 16.5 | Squirrel box |
| 17.1 | Frontiers |
| 17.3 | Auntie gravity |
| 17.5 | It's only natural |
| 19.1 | It's silly |
| 19.3 | Lost in translation |
| 19.4 | They're winning |
| 21.5 | Snapshots |

# TECHNIQUES SUITED TO STAGE 3 – SELECTION AND REFINEMENT

| *Ref.* | *Title* |
|---|---|
| 1.1 | Surveying your mind |
| 23.1 | The £100 bid |
| 23.2 | SWOT |
| 23.4 | Basic option evaluation |
| 23.5 | Sophisticated option evaluation |
| 25.1 | Signposts |
| 25.2 | Hazard markers |
| 25.4 | Second-best solution |
| 25.5 | Stakeholders |

# TECHNIQUES SUITED TO STAGE 4 – PLANNING FOR SELLING AND IMPLEMENTATION

| *Ref.* | *Title* |
|---|---|
| 28.1 | Planning for selling |
| 28.2 | Planning for implementation |
| 28.4 | The top ten list |